Language Policy Processes and Consequences

BILINGUAL EDUCATION & BILINGUALISM

Series Editors: Nancy H. Hornberger *(University of Pennsylvania, USA)* and Colin Baker *(Bangor University, Wales, UK)*

Bilingual Education and Bilingualism is an international, multidisciplinary series publishing research on the philosophy, politics, policy, provision and practice of language planning, global English, indigenous and minority language education, multilingualism, multiculturalism, biliteracy, bilingualism and bilingual education. The series aims to mirror current debates and discussions.

Full details of all the books in this series and of all our other publications can be found on http://www.multilingual-matters.com, or by writing to Multilingual Matters, St Nicholas House, 31–34 High Street, Bristol BS1 2AW, UK.

BILINGUAL EDUCATION & BILINGUALISM: 98

Language Policy Processes and Consequences

Arizona Case Studies

Edited by
Sarah Catherine K. Moore

MULTILINGUAL MATTERS
Bristol • Buffalo • Toronto

Library of Congress Cataloging in Publication Data
Language Policy Processes and Consequences: Arizona Case Studies/Edited by Sarah Catherine K. Moore.
Bilingual Education and Bilingualism: 98.
Includes bibliographical references and index.
1. Language policy—Arizona—Case studies. 2. Education, Bilingual—Arizona—Case studies. 3. English language—Study and teaching—Immersion method—Case studies. 4. English language—Study and teaching—Arizona—Foreign speakers—Case studies. I. Moore, Sarah Catherine K., 1977- editor of compilation.
P119.32.A75L36 2014
306.44'9791–dc23 2014003589

British Library Cataloguing in Publication Data
A catalogue entry for this book is available from the British Library.

ISBN-13: 978-1-78309-194-2 (hbk)
ISBN-13: 978-1-78309-193-5 (pbk)

Multilingual Matters
UK: St Nicholas House, 31–34 High Street, Bristol BS1 2AW, UK.
USA: UTP, 2250 Military Road, Tonawanda, NY 14150, USA.
Canada: UTP, 5201 Dufferin Street, North York, Ontario M3H 5T8, Canada.

Website: www.multilingual-matters.com
Twitter: Multi_Ling_Mat
Facebook: https://www.facebook.com/multilingualmatters
Blog: www.channelviewpublications.wordpress.com

The policy of Multilingual Matters/Channel View Publications is to use papers that are natural, renewable and recyclable products, made from wood grown in sustainable forests. In the manufacturing process of our books, and to further support our policy, preference is given to printers that have FSC and PEFC Chain of Custody certification. The FSC and/or PEFC logos will appear on those books where full certification has been granted to the printer concerned.

Typeset by Techset Composition India (P) Ltd, Bangalore and Chennai, India.
Printed and bound in Great Britain by the CPI Group (UK Ltd), Croydon, CR0 4YY.

Contents

List of Contributors

Beatriz Arias, Center for Applied Linguistics and Arizona State University

Giovanna Grijalva, Arizona State University

Tim Hogan, Arizona Center for Law and the Public Interest

Margarita Jimenez-Silva, Arizona State University

Karen E. Lillie, State University of New York at Fredonia

Amy Markos, Arizona State University

Sarah Catherine K. Moore, Center for Applied Linguistics

Terrence G. Wiley, Center for Applied Linguistics and Arizona State University

Wayne E. Wright, Purdue University

1 SEI in Arizona: Bastion for States' Rights

Karen E. Lillie and Sarah Catherine K. Moore

Those involved in making and enforcing public school policy
should ensure that their actions are lawful.
La Morte, 2008: 1

Recent discussions on educational language policy, particularly in contexts involving restriction, compulsory or repression-oriented policies (e.g. Wiley, 2007, 2010, 2013), have discussed the power of state governments over school law and federal policy. Federal laws have played an important role in monitoring K–12 educational settings despite the fact that public education is not specifically mentioned in the US Constitution (La Morte, 2008). Federal regulation is due, in part, to funding and oversight under the Elementary and Secondary Education Act (ESEA). State governments, however, particularly through state statutes and school board rules, tend to have a heavier hand in educational policy matters, more so than at the local government level. As La Morte (2008) discusses, there is a 'myth of local control' in education policy – while many believe that local districts have control over schools, the power truly often lies within state governments, since they are responsible for dispersing funds to schools and districts. A problematic issue within the structure of school funding is that all three levels of government have a say in what happens in schools, and it is rare that all three agree. Situated within the complexity of contextual issues, such as the politics, economy and ideologies inherent around language and schooling, the effects of language policies on educational settings can be potentially devastating in their execution. Such is the case in Arizona.

English-Only in the US: A Brief History

The United States is multilingual in its nature, a nation founded by immigrants. A largely held myth is that English is its official language.

English may be the de facto language, but by no means is English the sole language through which all persons conduct themselves. Throughout US history, language has been taken for granted and often contested during eras when politics, financial considerations and national defense issues emerged as contentious, and during which opposition to the perceived influx of immigrants 'taking over' increased. Widespread desires for declaring English as the national language of the United States, which would further weaken the status of minority languages, emerged early in this nation's history (Cashman, 2006; Crawford, 2000a, 2000b, 2004; Wiley, 2004, 2013; Wiley & Wright, 2004; Wright, 2011).

The US Constitution does not identify one language *de jure*; in fact, when its authors debated the question of language, such codification was deemed unnecessary due to the dominance of English (Kloss, 1998 [1977]; Wiley, 2004, 2010). Benjamin Franklin was one of the earliest to publicly argue against any type of bilingualism and push for an official English status. This occurred with the Pennsylvania Germans (Cashman, 2006; Crawford, 2000a, 2000b; Wiley, 2004). Once Franklin realized that the votes he needed were from those for whom English was not their dominant language, Franklin changed his mind and began withholding his English-only sentiments in an effort to embrace his desired political allies.

Pockets of English-only ideologies swept through other areas of the US territories as time passed and land was conquered. Meanwhile, Louisiana maintained bilingualism rigorously, despite once struggling against an imposed English-only governor in the mid-1800s. Native Americans were aggressively stripped of land and their languages to the point where language loss is significant and troubling even today (Del Valle, 2003; McCarty, 2004; Weinberg, 1995). The 'civilize the savage' notion was born, in part, out of nationalist-oriented sentiment, and the language policies surrounding actions against the Native population were highly repressive in nature and ideologically driven (see, especially, McCarty, 2013, on language policies affecting Native Americans; also Wiley, 2007, 2010). The Spanish-speaking population in California was also denied land, as *greaser laws* came into effect (Crawford, 2000a, 2000b; see also Del Valle, 2003). Under the California Land Act of 1851, English was used as a means of dominance, requiring *Californios* to demonstrate land ownership via English-only courts. In Hawai'ian schools, children were routinely assigned to certain schools based on their English proficiency (Lippi-Green, 2012; Wiley, 2010; Wilson, 2014). Hawai'ians succeeded to some extent, however, in maintaining their language while also adding English as a language of wider communication. Beginning with the First World War of the 20th century, xenophobic sentiments spread the idea that to be a 'Good American' one must have 'Good English' (Crawford, 2000a, 2000b). Thus, those who were seen as non-English-speaking were persecuted (e.g. Germans, Japanese) and in some cases even placed in internment camps on American soil.

Sociohistorical trends over the past couple hundred years demonstrate tendencies toward repression- and restrictive-oriented language policies throughout US history, as evidenced by some language policy scholars who have attempted to make sure policy lessons are learned from history (Wiley, 2007, 2013; also Crawford, 2000a, 2000b; Gándara *et al.*, 2010), particularly in regard to discussions on the history of bilingual education in the States (e.g. Wright, 2011; also García, 2009). The adage of history repeating itself when unknown is exemplified by the most recent 30 years of language policy and bilingual education in the United States. This recent wave of English-only sentiment began in a traditionally liberal state (California), and has touched one of the country's first states which had previously championed bilingualism (Massachusetts). This more current surge of attempts at bolstering the position and use of English in the US has been primarily aimed at education, and is known as the *English-Only Movement* (Crawford, 2000a, 2004).

The English-Only Movement

The English-Only Movement was largely initiated, funded and propagandized by the group known as US English in the early 1980s (Cashman, 2006; Crawford, 2000a, 2004; Del Valle, 2003). Spearheaded by the late Senator S.I. Hayakawa and Dr J. Tanton,[1] the main focus of this organization was to make English the official language of the United States. In 1981, Hayakawa proposed the English Language Amendment, which was intended to be added to the Constitution and thus meet that goal (Crawford, 2004). This did not succeed. Two years later, US English was established.

Many of the arguments made by this group and other English-only proponents stem from false ideological beliefs about immigration and revolve around politics, economics, power and fear of the 'other'. In fact, some major ideological falsehoods presented during the English-Only Movement were that: (a) English has always been the social glue holding Americans together; (b) immigrants refuse to learn English like those immigrants of 'yesteryear'; (c) immersion is the best way to learn a language; and (d) language diversity will lead to language conflict, ethnic hostility and political separatism (Cashman, 2006; Crawford, 2000a, 2000b; Crawford & Krashen, 2007; Tollefson, 1991; Wiley & Wright, 2004). Eventually, an English-only bill called the Bill Emerson English Language Empowerment Act was passed by the House of Representatives in 1996, but not by the Senate (Del Valle, 2003; H.R. 123, 1996). Although the passage of a constitutional amendment has not been successful, individual states have taken up where the English-Only Movement failed. At the time of this publication, 31 states[2] have passed some type of English-only bill aimed at general language restriction in the areas of courts, social services and other venues, but not necessarily in education.

The Attack on Bilingual Education

The 1990s introduced another campaign initiative, similar in sentiment to US English (i.e. English-only), but focused neither on immigration policy or official English: *English for the Children*. This new attack on language was more directly focused on destroying any vestiges of bilingual education, which were so hard won in previous cases and federal legislation (Del Valle, 2003). While prior legal findings, such as *Meyer v. Nebraska* (1923), *Farrington v. Tokushige* (1927), *Lau v. Nichols* (1974), Title VII of the ESEA (otherwise known as the Bilingual Education Act, 1968), and *Castañeda v. Pickard* (1981), did not stipulate bilingual education as the program model for instruction of English learners (ELs), these all helped ensure linguistic minority rights were upheld and that children were able to receive an equal education.[3] The entire premise of *Lau*, for example, was that regardless of the degree of equality in the curriculum and materials provided to students, ELs' education was unequal by virtue of the fact that they could not comprehend the lesson being delivered if they were not taught in a language they could understand.

Courts have dealt with language minority rights (especially, for example, in terms of violations of the Equal Education Opportunity Act or the 14th Amendment[4] of the Constitution), but courts are reluctant to make decisions regarding the type of education program that should be in place for ELs (Wiley, 2013). This is also true at the federal level. The federal government has an influence over states via legislation and laws, especially through funding to local education agencies (e.g. school districts). However, the federal government defers to states in the matter of how best to educate ELs (Del Valle, 2003; Johnson, 2009; Wiley, 2013; Wright, 2011).

In 2002, after multiple reauthorizations of the BEA, Title VII was eliminated by the *No Child Left Behind* Act (NCLB, 2001), and the new Title III[5] replaced Title VII in addressing EL concerns. Title III not only shifted its focus from multilingualism to an emphasis on English acquisition, but it also reinforced states' capacity for selection of the language program to be used with ELs (Wright, 2011). The one stipulation that is required is that the program must be 'research based'.

Because states have this jurisdiction, certain groups have had a more solid footing on which to promote and perpetuate English-only sentiment by attacking bilingual education in schools. Three states have implemented restrictions on program models involving non-English media of instruction, each resulting from voter-based initiatives. English for the Children, a campaign spearheaded by a multi-millionaire software entrepreneur named Ron Unz, has worked toward the elimination of bilingual education through various state-based movements (Combs, 2012; Crawford, 2000a, 2000b, 2004; Wright, 2011). These 'Unz initiatives' have been possible because some states' laws allow for voter initiatives, or propositions, to be voted upon if a certain number of registered voters petition for its inclusion on a ballot (Combs, 2012; Wiley, 2004).

Using media-friendly terms and catchphrases, Unz sought to foster voter support to shift a landscape which included bilingual education to one now largely occupied by monolingual English programs. Unz began his campaign in California in the 1990s, claiming that the initiative was to help children and immigrants in 'their right to learn English' (Wiley & Wright, 2004: 150). Five major assumptions were the foundation of the English for the Children initiative (e.g. Wiley, 2004; Wiley & Wright, 2004):

(1)   the English language is a 'language of opportunity';
(2)   that immigrant parents are 'eager to have their children learn English';
(3)   that schools have a 'moral obligation' to teach English;
(4)   high dropout rates in California signaled that this was because the state was doing a poor job in 'educating immigrant children'; and
(5)   that 'young, immigrant children acquire second languages easily'.

The message to the voters had common sense appeal since English needed to be taught to students and the message ideologically appealed to voters. The inherent assumptions were that with concentrated time-on-task, children would be able to learn English 'quickly and rapidly', which would help ensure that their futures would be brighter politically, economically and socially. Unfortunately, 'most people thought they were voting for English' (Crawford & Krashen, 2007: 51), as the wording of the ballots was misleading and seemed to offer the choice of either bilingual education or English (see also Crawford, 2007).

California: Proposition 227

In 1998, 61% of California voters passed the English for the Children initiative as *Proposition 227*. This meant that children were to be involved in 'sheltered English instruction' (SEI) for one year of school (aka, 180 days, conflicting with research regarding the typical 5–8 years necessary to achieve full second language proficiency; see, for example, August & Hakuta, 1997). Bilingual education was now essentially outlawed, unless students obtained a state waiver. These waivers were notoriously difficult to obtain.[6] Parents were also able to sue teachers if they felt that the teacher was not complying with the law regarding no use of the native language (Gándara *et al.*, 2010). In short, Prop. 227 made promises that by eliminating bilingual education and focusing heavily on English-only instruction, students would learn English more quickly and therefore perform better in school and have stronger academic outcomes.

In the years since its passage, Prop. 227 has not successfully promoted consistency across its programs nor kept its promise that ELs' academic achievement would improve. A five-year longitudinal study conducted by

Parrish *et al.* (2006) found tremendous variation in the types of programs that were in place, even in Year 2 after the passage of Prop. 227. Wentworth *et al.* (2010) looked at data from the California Standards Test during 2003–2007 to investigate the achievement gap post Prop. 227. Wentworth *et al.* determined that:

> it is clear that current and former English learners are not achieving the same levels of academic success as their peers who enter school already knowing English … [and that there was] not a clear association between the implementation of Prop 227 and consistent achievement gains for English learners relative to English-only students. (Wentworth *et al.*, 2010: 48)

Arizona: Proposition 203

Two years after California's Prop. 227, Arizona passed *Proposition 203*. Arizona's version of Unz's anti-bilingual initiative defined English as 'the language of economic opportunity' (Cashman, 2006: 50), and also allowed parents to sue any school personnel who used a language other than English. Waivers were allowed but rarely known about (Cashman, 2006; Wiley & Wright, 2004; Wright, 2005). As in California, this proposition effectively dismantled bilingual education but it took several years for Prop. 203 to be enacted. As a result, almost a decade of confusion regarding the program models allowable under Prop. 203 ensued (Davenport, 2008, 2011).

Initial passage of Proposition 203

Prop. 203 was approved in November of 2000 with 63% of the vote in its favor. Prop. 203 is legally a part of the Arizona Revised Statutes (A.R.S.) §15-751 through §15-757 (A.R.S., 2000). State statutes are highly significant: these usually further define education policy with regard to specifics, such as issues like student:teacher ratios and subjects that must be taught (La Morte, 2008). Prop. 203's text dictates that:

> The People of Arizona find and declare … the English language is the national public language of the United States of America and of the state of Arizona. … Immigrant parents are eager to have their children acquire a good knowledge of English, thereby allowing them to fully participate in the American Dream of economic and social advancement. (Arizona Voter Initiative, 2000: Section 1)

It goes on to read much like Prop. 227, in that schools and the government are morally responsible for making sure children know English so that they may become 'productive members of society', that previously, schools had done an 'inadequate job of educating immigrant children', and that 'young immigrant children can easily acquire full fluency in a new language, such as English, if they are heavily exposed to that language in the classroom at an early age' (Arizona Voter Initiative, 2000: Section 1). This continues Prop. 227's idea that languages can be learned quickly and in settings where English is the medium of instruction.

The waiver question

Initially in Arizona, bilingual education was allowed if a waiver was obtained by a parent. To do so, parents were required to apply in person every year, and schools were to provide alternative choices for program types and materials that would then be available to the students (A.R.S. §15-753; see also Wright, 2005). If a waiver was successful, students were to be placed in an environment where bilingual education 'techniques' were used or 'other generally recognized educational methodologies permitted by law' (A.R.S. §15-753; Wright, 2005). If 20 or more parents of students *in the same grade level* apply for a waiver, then the school must provide these types of environments. The likelihood of this occurring, however, is slim.

For a student to have been granted a waiver, they had to prove one of three things: (1) that they are older than 10 years; (2) that they have special needs which must then be proved to be beyond the limited English skills possessed by the child (and thus approved by the principal); or (3) they already know English. Specifically, to clarify the latter, the law states:

> the child already possesses good English language skills, as measured by oral evaluation or standardized tests of English vocabulary comprehension, reading, and writing, in which the child scores approximately at or above the state average for his grade level or at or above the 5th grade average, whichever is lower. (A.R.S. §15-753: B.1)

These 'language skills' were determined by the language proficiency tests in place; now, however, there is only one test which determines the proficiency of a student and it is known as the Arizona English Language Learner Assessment (AZELLA). The criteria set in order to be approved for a waiver made it unlikely that parents would be successful in their endeavors even if they tried to obtain (or knew about) one for their child. As Wright (2005) rightly pointed out:

> the irony is that ELLs under 10 cannot be in a bilingual program unless they are designated as fluent English proficient (FEP), meaning they are no longer ELL students. And if they are not ELL students, there is no need to obtain a waiver, as waivers are only for ELLs. (Wright, 2005: 14)

Massachusetts: Question 2

While Arizona's leadership struggled with the implementation of Prop. 203, English for the Children moved to the East Coast: specifically,

Massachusetts. There, the initiative passed in November of 2002, with 68% of the voters determining that Question 2 was the way forward for educating ELs. Like the propositions before it, Question 2 almost completely eliminated bilingual education in a state which had been one of the first to initiate and sign a bilingual education law in 1971 (Smith *et al.*, 2008; Uriarte *et al.*, 2010). Massachusetts had a long history of offering transitional bilingual education (TBE), but Question 2 was successful largely because some policymakers and educational leaders were concerned that ELs were taking too long to achieve academically in that model. Smith *et al.* (2008) also noted that EL parents were worried that their children were not integrating fully in school, and that their English was not up to par for their perceptions of desired future job prospects and higher education.

Question 2 was fully implemented in the fall of 2003,[7] shifting EL instruction to Massachusetts's version of SEI. This version of SEI is broken into two components: 'sheltered content instruction' and 'English as a second language (ESL) instruction'. The Massachusetts Department of Education requires that ELs get 1–2.5 hours of ESL instruction a day, depending on their proficiency level (Smith *et al.*, 2008). The wording found in Question 2 is very similar to Propositions 227 and 203, and follows the phrase wherein it is believed that the ELs should be in SEI for 'a temporary transition period not normally intended to exceed one school year' (Smith *et al.*, 2008: 295; see also Gándara *et al.*, 2010; Uriarte *et al.*, 2010). The law is also comparable regarding use of the native language. Question 2 does indicate that use of the native language is allowed for clarification purposes as long as the assessment and materials are in English. Uriarte *et al.*, however, noted that 'in order to minimize the use of native languages, the law encourages schools to place children of different languages but of similar English fluency together' (Uriarte *et al.*, 2010: 69). Also, like the other Unz initiatives, Question 2 did not delineate clearly the pedagogy or practice for what this SEI should look like in classrooms. Massachusetts was different from California and Arizona in one small way: they did not eliminate all bilingual education opportunities (Smith *et al.*, 2008). In addition to the possible waivers for bilingual education for 20 or more desirous students of the same native language group (whose parents must all get waiver requests), Question 2 'did not do away with two-way bilingual programs' (Smith *et al.*, 2008: 296). Further, students could transfer to a school which had a bilingual setting.

Waivers for Question 2's SEI are also similar to those in California and Arizona, including the stipulation that waiver requests must be made in person, by the parent (Uriarte *et al.*, 2010). Ironically, like Arizona, the waiver is also automatically allowed if the student *already knows English*. For those students under than 10 years of age and designated as ELs, they were to be enrolled in Massachusetts's version of SEI for 30 days minimum, preferably one year maximum.[8] This aligns with and carries forward Prop. 227's and Prop. 203's assumption that young ELs can learn English 'easily' and continues the idea that language can be learned 'rapidly'. Ten years later, scant research has been done to document the implementation effects and the outcomes of ELs in Massachusetts (Uriarte *et al.*, 2010). In one of the few existing studies, Uriarte *et al.* found that in the four years after the passage of Question 2, ELs were more likely to be enrolled in special education, dropout rates had increased and the overall achievement gap was not being addressed.

Review of the English-only trajectory and its impact on laws that specifically identify SEI as the program model for instruction of all language minority students is not complete without understanding its origins. The next section discusses how SEI as a program model was defined by scholars and practitioners previous to its use as an alternative to bilingual education, including its initial emergence in the field.

The Genesis of SEI

The abbreviation 'SEI' generally refers to either *Structured English Immersion* or *Sheltered English Immersion*. It first emerged in the literature as *Structured Immersion*, or SI, in a report written as a policy recommendation by Keith Baker, a sociologist, and Adriana de Kanter, a management intern, working for the Office of Planning, Budget and Evaluation (OPBE) during the Carter and Reagan administrations (Baker & de Kanter, 1981, 1983; see also Crawford, 2004). Baker and de Kanter were assigned the task of evaluating the efficacy of TBE programs versus alternatives to TBE. The main goal of TBE programs is the transition of ELs into mainstream English settings over a several-year period. Unlike *maintenance bilingual* programs, the goals of TBE typically do not involve native language maintenance. Baker and de Kanter initially reviewed 28 programs (Baker & de Kanter, 1981) and published a later, revised version based on a review of 39 programs (Baker & de Kanter, 1983). Their initial findings were published in a 1981 report commonly referred to as the Baker and de Kanter Report.

Research conducted and findings presented in Baker and de Kanter focused on the following two research questions:

(1) Is there a sufficiently strong case for the effectiveness of TBE for learning English and non-language subjects to justify a legal mandate for TBE?; and
(2) Are there any effective alternatives to TBE? That is, should one particular method be exclusively required if other methods also are effective? (Baker & de Kanter, 1983: 33; also Baker, 1987: 353)

According to Baker and de Kanter, the efficacy of SI as superior to TBE was demonstrated by four successful cases: three in Québec (Barik & Swain, 1975; Barik *et al.*, 1977; Lambert & Tucker, 1972) and a case in Texas

(Peña-Hughes & Solis, 1980). SI was also considered by Baker and de Kanter to be more supportive of ELs in ESL classrooms as based on two cases (Barik *et al.*, 1977; Lambert & Tucker, 1972). It is notable that three of the four cases cited as demonstrating the superior effectiveness of SI over TBE were researching French-Canadian models of immersion.

One fundamental flaw in the claims made in Baker and de Kanter is that the model of SI they proposed, for US settings, involves the instruction of native Spanish speakers in English as a second language. However, the French model on which the majority of their research was based immerses native English speakers in French settings (Genesee, 1985; Secada, 1987). Because of these very different target audiences, considerable debate over the projection of the French model into contexts in the United States has been extensively documented (Becker & Gersten, 1992; Collier, 1992; Collier & Thomas, 1989; Crawford, 2004; Cummins, 1981, 1992, 1996, 2000; Faltis, 2001, 2006; Gersten & Woodward, 1985; Ramírez *et al.*, 1991; Thomas, 1992; Thomas & Collier, 1995, 1997, 2001; Verhoeven, 1991).

Although the Baker and de Kanter model of SI is only generally discussed in the report, over the past 30 years it has been further explicated primarily by Baker, Christine Rossell, a professor of Political Science at Boston University, and Rosalie Pedalino Porter (Baker & de Kanter, 1981, 1983; Porter, 1996; Rossell, 2002, 2003; Rossell & Baker, 1996). Below, Baker and de Kanter (1983) describe the context of SI implementation, including medium of instruction, its curricula, and practitioner knowledge of first (L1) and second language (L2):

> Structured Immersion: Instruction is in the second language (L2), as in the case of submersion, but there are important differences. The immersion teacher understands L1, and students can address the teacher in L1; the immersion teacher, however, generally replies only in L2. Furthermore, the curriculum is structured so that prior knowledge of L2 is not assumed as subjects are taught. Content is introduced in a way that can be understood by the students. The students in effect learn L2 and content simultaneously. Most immersion programs also teach L1 language arts for thirty to sixty minutes a day. Structured immersion differs from TBE in that L1 is rarely used by the teacher (except where it is a subject) and subject-area instruction is given in L2 from the beginning of the program. (Baker & de Kanter, 1983: 34)

Based on the 1983 definition of SI, which ultimately became SEI, several key distinctions are notable: (a) SI teachers are proficient in students' native languages; (b) native language clarification requests are available for content learning; and (c) SI programs often include native language arts coursework (see Faltis & Arias, 2012: 29, for a concise chart depicting the differences). SEI in English-only states does not require teachers' proficiency in languages other than English. Though much current English-only legislation allows for native language support, school-based interpretation and teacher use of the L1 are not part of the SEI program models. Arizona's current SEI model does not include native language arts curricula. The disconnect between early definitions of SI and today's versions of SEI have significant implications on program model implementation, curriculum and teacher qualifications (Krashen & McField, 2005; McField, 2007).

Research responding to Baker and de Kanter

A range of researchers responded to the Baker and de Kanter Report with claims that the studies reviewed were flawed, and that the support of SI as a program model for the instruction of ELs was not appropriate for the context of ELs in US schools (Thomas & Collier, 1995, 1997; Willig, 1985). In response to Baker and de Kanter, Willig (1985) conducted the first meta-analysis of the programs included in Baker and de Kanter (1981), for which she reviewed 23 of the previously reviewed 28 evaluations.[9] She wrote:

> A major result of the current synthesis has been the revelation that bilingual education has been badly served by a predominance of research that is inadequate in design and that makes inappropriate comparisons of children in bilingual programs to children who are dissimilar in many crucial respects. In every instance where there did not appear to be crucial inequalities between experimental and comparison groups, children in the bilingual programs averaged higher than the comparison children on criterion instruments. (Willig, 1985: 312)

In response, Baker (1987) claimed that the Willig meta-analysis was flawed because it was not sufficient to warrant the application of findings for federal policy recommendations regarding the instruction of ELs. Specifically, he argued the following: (a) the questions that each study addressed were different; (b) the 39 programs reviewed by Baker and de Kanter (1983) were not fully represented in Willig's analysis; (c) meta-analysis as a method for analyzing the studies included is inappropriate; and (d) Willig's analysis lacks generalizability. Further, Baker argued, 'there is no reason to modify any of Baker and de Kanter's conclusions based on Willig's results. ... There are some successful TBE programs, and the overall quality of the literature is poor; better studies are highly desirable' (Baker, 1987: 357). Another prominent critique was a quantitative comparison analysis of different program models for EL instruction conducted by Ramírez et al. (1991) and published in the Ramírez Report. Their report concluded that students in TBE programs achieve at comparable levels to their counterparts in SI, and that students in maintenance BLE programs outperform their counterparts in each of the other two models (ESL and SI) reviewed in Baker and de Kanter. Ultimately,

Ramírez *et al.* found that, of the programs reviewed, students in SI settings were the least successful as compared with TBE, maintenance BLE and ESL. The Ramírez Report has been widely cited for its comprehensive review and well-founded critique of findings in Baker and de Kanter (August & Hakuta, 1997; Baker, 2011; Cummins, 1992; Romaine, 2001; Thomas, 1992; Willig, 1982, 1985; Wiley, 2005).

Reviews on the efficacy of both bilingual education and the imposition of SEI as the primary means of educating ELs, especially in reference to Arizona, assert opposition to English-only models' effects on EL achievement levels (Mahoney & MacSwan, 2005; Rolstad *et al.*, 2005; Wright, 2005; Wright & Choi, 2006). Rolstad *et al.* (2005) conducted a meta-analysis of studies on the effectiveness of bilingual education following the same model adopted in Willig's (1985) study and found 'a positive effect for bilingual education on all measures, both in English and the native language of English language learners, when compared to English-only instructional alternatives' (Rolstad *et al.*, 2005: 43). MacSwan and Pray (2005: 653), based on research regarding the relationship between age and language acquisition, as applied to approaches to bilingual education, 'suggest that children in bilingual education programs learn English as fast or faster than children in all-English programs', and concluded that:

> schools should consider a broad range of issues before placing children in mainstream [all English] classrooms – not only should they have achieved a reasonable level of proficiency in English, but they should also be ready to engage texts and perform classroom assignments at grade level. (MacSwan & Pray, 2005: 673)

Debates surrounding program models for ELs have largely been constructed around medium of instruction. Advocates for bilingual education believe that ELs should have the opportunity to maintain their native language and culture, and that native language maintenance should be supported by public schooling as a civil right. In Arizona, for a range of reasons, including the conflation of several court cases and Prop. 203, the issues have become much broader than access to native language maintenance.

English Learner Education in Arizona

Since the passage of Prop. 203, Arizona's definition of SEI has been unclear, and its implementation of the model has been inconsistent – realities that are evident in Arizona's classrooms. The statutes defined in Arizona resulting from Prop. 203 and the emanating House Bill (HB) 2064, in conjunction with the passage of NCLB (2001) and the ongoing saga of the *Flores* case, mean that policies implemented in Arizona schools have created a hotbed of confusion, controversy and, in the situation with ELs, inequality.

Flores, the Consent Order and HB 2064

Since 1992, the question of proper funding for language programs and the students enrolled in them (and thus, ultimately, the education of ELs) has been challenged in a case known as *Flores v. Arizona* (see Hogan, Chapter 2, for a thorough description). The case was brought forth by Miriam Flores in Nogales, Arizona as a class action lawsuit wherein it was declared that Arizona was not providing an equal education to ELs on the basis of the Equal Educational Opportunities Act (EEOA) of 1974, claiming the state was failing to provide 'appropriate action to overcome language barriers' (20 U.S.C. §1703(f.)). The argument was that the instruction ELs were receiving was not helping them to become proficient in English and therefore help them master the curriculum. Centrally, the case had to do with whether EL programs were receiving adequate funding. Almost eight years after *Flores* started, US District Court Judge Marquez determined that the funding of EL programs was 'arbitrary and capricious' and that there were insufficient materials, a shortage of qualified teachers, too few classrooms and not enough tutoring or after-school programs to help ELs succeed.

In June of 2000, five months before Prop. 203 was passed, the Flores Consent Order was established based on Marquez's decree. The purpose was to determine the EL program to be used in order to be able to address the funding concerns (although it did not decide which *type* of instruction was to be used in those programs, e.g. bilingual, pull-out/push-in, SEI). In short, the Consent Order (2000) required the following three key points:

> daily instruction in English Language Development appropriate to the level of English proficiency of the student including listening and speaking, reading and writing skills, and cognitive and academic development in English;

> daily instruction in basic subject areas that is understandable and appropriate to the level of academic achievement of the LEP student, and is in conformity with accepted strategies for teaching LEP students; and

> the curriculum of all bilingual education and ESL programs shall incorporate the Board's Academic Standards and shall be comparable in amount, scope, and quality to that provided to English proficient students. (Consent Order, 2000: 4–5)

HB 2064 emerged in 2006, partly in response to the Flores Consent Order from six years earlier. It decreed that a *statewide* model of sheltered/structured English immersion be established in which *every* EL student in Arizona schools would participate. Having one model would help eliminate the variation of programs in existence since Prop. 203 was passed, and it would also help contribute to a better understanding of the per pupil costs associated with implementation. During the *Flores* trial, the Ninth Circuit Court of Appeals noted three flaws in HB 2064: (1) the increase in funding is not rationally related to effective EL programs; (2) there is an irrational two-year limit on funding; and (3) it violates federal law by using federal money to supplant (not supplement) state funds[10] (*Flores v. Arizona*, 2006, 2009; see also *Horne v. Flores*, 2009: 5). Although HB 2064 did not prescribe how SEI should look in schools, it did, however, require the establishment of an English Language Learner Task Force (see A.R.S. §15-756.01), which ultimately led to the creation of the four-hour block as it stands today.

The nine-person Task Force was mostly appointed by Arizona's conservative legislature and the Arizona Department of Education (ADE) Superintendent. There were only two appointees (by the then Governor Janet Napolitano) who had experience in educational policy (Faltis & Arias, 2012; Moore, 2008). The Task Force was charged to develop and establish cost-effective, 'research-based models [*sic*] of structured English immersion programs' (A.R.S. §15-756.01, C.26). The plan was to adopt a model by 1 September 2006, statewide. The Task Force thus created the four-hour SEI model, comprised of daily English language development (ELD) classes. SEI implementation did not occur statewide, however, until the 2008/2009 school year; from 2006–2008 there was wide variation across the state regarding implementation and understanding of the newly designed model (Davenport, 2008; Moore, 2008).

The *Flores* case went before the US Supreme Court as *Horne v. Flores* (2009), wherein the Supreme Court reversed and remanded earlier decisions. The majority opinion stated that 'both of the lower courts focused excessively on the narrow question of the adequacy of the state's incremental funding for ELL instruction instead of…the broader question…[of if] the State was fulfilling its obligation [under EEOA] by other means' (*Horne v. Flores*, 2009: 10). The opinion remarked that the lower courts had not engaged in a proper analysis under Rule 60 (b)(5), noting that since the earlier decisions there had been major implementation changes (e.g. Prop. 203, the institution of the Task Force). Alito's opinion also sided with the ADE and refuted what academic scholars know in the effectiveness debate on bilingual education when he stated:

> Research on ELL instruction indicates there is documented, academic support for the view that SEI is significantly more effective than bilingual education. Findings of the Arizona State Department of Education in 2004 strongly support this conclusion. (*Horne v. Flores*, 2009: 19)

Therefore, based on the assenting decision, *Flores* was sent back to Arizona to be further argued with the parties instructed to consider the 'improvements' the state had made in the way schools were instructing ELs. On 11 January 2011, the court adjourned. On 29 March 2013, a final decision was reached in favor of Arizona. The final federal district court's decision will likely have major implications for education in the entire United States (see, for example, Rios-Aguilar & Gándara, 2012; Hogan, Chapter 2, this volume). An appeal has been filed.

Arizona's Structured English Immersion Model

The results of the Task Force's work culminated in the SEI model in place today, as guided by policy demanding a uniform structure and prescribed classroom practices (ADE, 2008). This SEI model further defined and established SEI Endorsements, a Discrete Skills Inventory (DSI), and the SEI classroom curricula. In short, every EL enrolled in Arizona schools must take four hours, every day, of ELD classes until they are no longer designated as an EL student (see Lillie & Markos, Chapter 7, this volume).

SEI for Teachers: The endorsements

Based on the A.R.S. and school board rules (SBE Rules, R7-2-613, see J, I and H), all certified personnel (and students in pre-service teacher preparation programs) were required to complete 15 seat hours of SEI training, equivalent to one university credit, by 31 August 2006 (see Moore, Chapter 4 and Markos & Arias, Chapter 5, this volume). Practitioners who completed the initial 15 hours of training were awarded a Provisional SEI Endorsement. Since 2006, the Provisional SEI Endorsement was expanded to 45 hours. When SEI training was *first* introduced, many teachers with ESL and bilingual endorsements were told they, too, would be required to complete the 15-hour training, despite the fact that most held these endorsements (the equivalent of 315 seat hours) as the result of completing graduate-level coursework or degrees in the ESL field.[11] Practitioners who did not obtain the Provisional SEI Endorsement through the completion of training by 31 August 2006 were threatened with the revoking of their teaching certificates. In addition, the state eventually required 45 seat hours of training to be completed by 31 August 2009, which led teachers to obtaining Full SEI Endorsements (45 seat hours is equivalent to a three-credit university course).

Defining SEI for the classroom

On 15 June 2007, the Task Force published a document entitled 'Draft SEI Models' based on testimony and consultation with Kevin Clark, one of six experts who testified.[12] Clark first testified on 30 November 2006 as an 'expert' and advocate for English immersion. Among the six experts, Clark was the only person to present a 'model' of SEI in practice and later was a regular presenter before the Task Force, further explicating the model he initially outlined in November 2006. Although presented to the public as an 'objective' expert, Clark has a long history as a strong proponent of English immersion models and opponent of bilingual education (Clark, 2000).

The result of Clark's analyses and presentations was a document entitled 'Structured English Immersion Models of the Arizona English Language Learners Task Force' (ADE, 2008). SEI for Arizona was now defined. Specifically, SEI was defined as the program model put in place for ELs which was claimed to be 'research-based and include three major components: policy, structure, and classroom practices' (ADE, 2008: 2).

SEI Fully Implemented

Arizona's SEI model is an attempt to address both Prop. 203 and HB 2064. It is unique in that it is literally unlike any other interpretation of 'SEI' in the United States and is functionally distinctive from what was initially outlined in Baker and de Kanter's (1981) version of SI. In Arizona, SEI stands for *'structured* English immersion', and while the ADE claims this is a 'research-based' model, researchers and scholars have shown that the interpretation, applications and implementation of SEI in the classrooms conflict with findings from rigorous research (Krashen *et al.*, 2007; Lillie *et al.*, 2012; Rios-Aguilar *et al.*, 2012).

The process for placement in SEI settings is as follows. First, students are given a primary home language survey, called the PHLOTE,[13] which determines whether or not students take the AZELLA. Initially, students were asked three questions. This was the case until 2009, when the policy suddenly changed and students were asked only one question: *What is the primary language spoken by the student?* It is notable that when the PHLOTE shifted to one question, countless numbers of ELs who might otherwise have qualified for services were excluded from receiving language support (Goldenberg & Rutherford-Quach, 2012). The Department of Justice (DOJ) conducted a review with the Office of Civil Rights (OCR) and the US Department of Education, and found that the identification process in Arizona was fundamentally flawed and in violation of Title VI of the Civil Rights Act of 1964 (Rios-Aguilar & Gándara, 2012). Therefore, as of April 2011, the three-item PHLOTE was reinstated, asking:

(1)   What is the primary language used in the home regardless of the language spoken by the student?
(2)   What is the language most often spoken by the student? and
(3)   What is the language that the student first acquired?

If an answer of anything other than English is given to just one of these questions, the student is automatically tested via the AZELLA to determine the level of English proficiency and thus identification as an EL. The AZELLA determines both entry and exit from the ELD classrooms. Its validity has been questioned by researchers (Florez, 2012).

The SEI model designed by Clark, now known as the *four-hour block* by many school personnel, requires that all teachers are 'highly qualified' and hold an SEI Endorsement (see earlier discussion; also Moore, Chapter 4 and Markos & Arias, Chapter 5, this volume). ELD settings ensure reduced exposure to native-English-speaking children, and often have limited access to age, grade and content-area appropriate materials; at the secondary level, this results in preclusion from graduation within a typical four-year time frame (see also Lillie & Markos, Chapter 7, this volume; also Lillie *et al.*, 2012).

Arizona's classrooms are now pockets of ELs segregated into highly prescriptive classrooms – across the entire K–12 system, statewide. The Arizona model of SEI implemented in classrooms is designed around the ADE's 'model principles'. These are that (1) in order to fully understand content, one must know English; (2) grouping students by their language proficiency will help 'facilitate [*sic*] rapid language learning'; (3) students should spend most of their time learning English in English to better 'increase academic learning' (time-on-task); and (4) that discrete language skills will help ELs learn English better (OELAS, 2009, slide 42). In short, all students will enter these ELD classrooms via the AZELLA and will remain there until their scores demonstrate successful mastery of the English language, unless excluded from ELD classes via a parental waiver.

For four strictly defined hours every day, ELs are required to take an hour each of grammar, reading, writing and conversational/academic English (oral skills). Class sizes are not to exceed 20–25 students and they are grouped, preferably, by language proficiency levels. There are no native English-speaking peers in the ELD classroom. Classrooms are not to focus on content – the ADE stresses that the English language is a 'vehicle' through which content can be learned. ADE's OELAS has trained teachers to focus on four key areas that must be done in ELD classrooms to 'accelerate' ELs' learning of English; if monitored, teachers are expected to be observed using these four concepts.

The first concept revolves around *error correction*, in which a teacher must immediately correct children with the proper form of English when they make a mistake. Second, it is 'English only in the classroom' in order to 'maximize language production, practice, and competence' (Castellano *et al.*, n.d.). Therefore, although A.R.S. §15-751 states that minimal use of the native language may be used to assist with comprehension, teachers are trained to use only English. Third, all students must consistently *use complete sentences* when they speak, which conflicts with natural language production. Fourth is a *50/50 rule*, wherein teachers and students equally share the talking time for each of the four hours. Amidst the tension of English-only sentiment in Arizona and the strict ADE monitoring and oversight of ELD compliance, many teachers are teaching English in this prescribed manner, focusing on English-only and discrete skills.

Discrete skills

Arizona's policy also involves what is known as the 'discrete skills inventory' (DSI), which has been criticized by academic scholars (Krashen *et al.*, 2007, 2012). In order to address the goal of one-year proficiency within his defined SEI model, Clark devised the DSI which was to be taught overtly and in conjunction with the English language proficiency (ELP) standards (Combs, 2012). The DSI is a 'sequential series of English language skills' (OELAS, 2009, slide 68) to be used as a 'tool' to help support teachers in their instruction of the English language. The ADE's definition of *language*, however, is very narrow and is comprised of five areas: phonology, morphology, syntax, lexicon and semantics. ADE and OELAS define these five 'elements' as points on the 'language star' (OELAS, 2009). When looking at the broad, misinformed definitions of the five 'points' from OELAS (e.g. 'syntax is defined as the word order rules for language. It combines the meaningful parts of the language', OELAS, 2009, slide 62 notes), it is apparent that while the ADE defends the SEI model as being 'research-based' they themselves do not have a clear understanding of language. However, these five elements are to be 'systematic, focused, and consistent' and 'reinforced on a daily basis' (OELAS, 2009, slide 62).

The DSI is presented as 'the specific teaching/learning objectives derived from the Arizona K–12 English Language Learner Proficiency Standards … and refined as needed to remain synchronized with the Arizona K–12 Academic English Language Arts Standards' (ADE, 2008: 1–2). Further, the DSI was prepared to better assist teachers in making sure that grammar is the 'foundation' that all ELs must have in order to be 'successful'. The DSI specifically states that ELs will not be successful in learning English if they are not able to 'skillfully employ words according to the grammatical rules that govern their use' (ADE, n.d.: 1). Made up of benchmarks by which teachers can help plan their lessons, it is comprised of three sections: parts of speech, grammar, and a standards link which shows how the DSI is explicitly linked to the ELP standards. With the assumption that language must be learned in a concrete, sequential order, teachers are given a sort of checklist for what students need to know and the order in which they must learn them. The DSI presents the linear order of concepts by 'increasing levels of difficulty' (Castellano *et al.*, n.d.). For example, it is suggested that a child needs to learn a singular common noun (e.g. *bird*) before they can learn a proper noun (e.g. *Tucson*). While studies in second language acquisition have pointed to some predictable developmental sequences in which all L2 learners appear to move, this is not to say that all learners move through these stages at the same time nor in a linear, concrete and compartmentalized fashion (Lightbown & Spada, 2006). In fact, learners may show evidence of multiple stages simultaneously. This explicit focus on language skills alone means that ELs are limited in exposure to important content material which they need once they exit the model. They are, in essence, segregated academically from the rest of the school.

Segregation of students

The inequality in access to a well-rounded education is not only resulting from the ELD classes and the DSI-prescribed curriculum. ELs are often segregated physically from the mainstream school body (e.g. Lillie *et al.*, 2012). Since ELD classrooms are constructed based on proficiency groupings, ELs are not only separated from non-ELs, they are also removed from other ELs who have tested at higher or lower levels of English proficiency. This model conflicts with long-standing research regarding language acquisition, as well as teaching models and methods that promote language learning (August *et al.*, 2010; García *et al.*, 2011; Gifford & Valdés, 2006).

The SEI model imposes a 'two-fold' segregation in which students are not only segregated from the rest of their peers within the classrooms, but also from the rest of the school (Gándara & Orfield, 2012). To be clear, this is a case of language-based segregation, in the sense that since all of the students in ELD classrooms are learning English, they have been separated from the mainstream by virtue of their linguistic abilities. Segregating ELs within schools based on English language ability into non-native language groups exacerbates the problems that are inherent in school/district-wide segregation cases. These ELs are in what Gifford and Valdés (2006) and Valenzuela (1999) deem to be *ESL Ghettos*, wherein students continually fall behind their non-EL peers. Students who face segregation may reach overall lower academic achievement due to fewer educational opportunities, and they may not then complete school (Rumberger & Tran, 2010; Valencia *et al.*, 2002).

Rios-Aguilar *et al.* (2012) surveyed English language coordinators in districts across Arizona, and the topic of segregation was *the most often mentioned concern* throughout phone surveys. According to Rios-Aguilar *et al.*, 75% of those surveyed have this concern, particularly in relation to the missing academic content. Social segregation was also a worry, with 65% of the participants mentioning that ELs are not able to associate with non-ELs. More and more recent studies are documenting that ELs are not receiving an equitable education due to the fact that not only are they removed from much of what goes on within the school but also because so much of their time is devoted to four hours of English-only every day. Older ELs are missing out on significant course opportunities which hinder them from meeting graduation deadlines, while younger ELs are also missing out on content. Since the focus of ELD classrooms is only to be the instruction of English, this results in students not being taught material that it will be imperative to know when they exit the SEI model and move into the mainstream. Ultimately, the academic achievement gap is further widened.

Conclusions

The impact of English-only ideologies and state-based initiatives (e.g. English for the Children) is now longstanding and broad based, having affected children for over a decade, particularly in certain states. Arizona's 'English-only' adoption constitutes the most restrictive and potentially damaging case. For over 20 years, Arizona ELs have been presented with upheavals in policy that have influenced their education. Ultimately, its SEI model is flawed in its design, conception and implementation. With the new decision on *Flores* this year, and the upcoming appeal to the Ninth Circuit Court of Appeals (Wright, 2013), it still remains to be seen whether there will be a change in the way Arizona educates ELs. In the meantime, however, with this March 2013 decision the SEI model will remain. The implications from Arizona's SEI model are long-lasting and have impacted thousands of ELs whose only fault was attending school.

Students in Arizona who are designated ELs are force-fed a program that is not based on sound pedagogical theory, and they languish in these classrooms for more than the expected 'one year' goal as set forth by the A.R.S. and ADE. Many teachers are not prepared well enough to successfully implement Arizona's SEI program, and there appears to be continual change within the ADE in its approach to both the SEI model and ELD in classrooms. This only further prevents good teachers from the ability to do what they do best: educate their students.

Students are not given the opportunity for a well-rounded education while enrolled in the SEI program, which likely limits their capacity for reasonable academic progress after mainstreaming. The plight of students in Arizona should stand as a warning to stakeholders in other states, whose children's education in today's system of schooling is under the mercy of state governance, and clearly not always protected by federal oversight. The policies described in this chapter and book demonstrate that, under Arizona's state-based leadership, segregationist policies that violate access to equal educational opportunity have been allowed to thrive, therefore begging the ultimate question – how far should states' rights go?

Notes

(1) Tanton was an ophthalmologist and 'immigration-restriction activist' (Crawford, 2004: 133).
(2) See http://usenglish.org/view/3. Accessed March 23, 2014.
(3) For a more complete description of these law cases, see the following: Del Valle, 2003; Faltis & Arias, 2012; Mahoney *et al.*, 2010; Wiley, 2013.
(4) Del Valle (2003) provides a clear discussion on language rights as argued under the 14th Amendment.
(5) Since NCLB, any terminology related to 'bilingual' has been replaced and removed (Gándara *et al.*, 2010; Wiley & Wright, 2004; Wright, 2011). Title III is *Language*

Instruction for Limited English Proficient and Immigrant Students (Crawford, 2004; García, 2005; Johnson, 2009).

(6) For a discussion of the California waivers, see Wiley and Wright (2004).

(7) The same night Question 2 passed, an English-only initiative (Amendment 31) was struck down in Colorado (Escamilla *et al.*, 2003; Mitchell, 2002). Colorado's win signaled the first time an 'Unz-led effort' was struck down (Benz, 2005: 265).

(8) Uriarte *et al.* (2010) present a clear picture of the issue of waivers in Massachusetts.

(9) Willig's selection criteria eliminated five of the 28 programs included in Baker and de Kanter (1981). Criteria 'required that the programs that were the object of any study be located in the United States and that the programs be regular school programs representing kindergarten, primary, or secondary grades. These added restrictions had the effect of excluding 5 studies from the pool of 28 that were addressed in the Baker and de Kanter review. The excluded studies were 3 Canadian reports (Barik & Swain, 1975; Barik *et al.*, 1977; Lambert & Tucker, 1972) on total or structured immersion programs, 1 review of bilingual education in the Philippines (Ramos *et al.*, 1967), and 1 U.S. study (McConnell, 1980)' (Willig, 1985: 272).

(10) See No. CV-92-596-TUC-RCC, 2006 U.S. Dist. LEXIS 97364, pp. 4–8 (April 25, 2006), App. to Pet. for Cert. in No. 08-294, pp. 176a, 181a–182a.

(11) This requirement is no longer. Holding an ESL/BLE Endorsement waives the requirement for the SEI Endorsement. See 'SEI: Fast Facts' at http://www.azed.gov/educator-certification/ Accessed March 23, 2014.

(12) The Task Force heard 'expert' testimony from three bilingual education advocates and three SEI advocates on two separate days. The first round included: Dr Christian J. Faltis, professor at Arizona State University; Dr Richard Ruiz, professor at the University of Arizona; and Dr Norbert Francis, professor at Northern Arizona University. The testimony on behalf of SEI was given by: Kevin J. Clark; Rosalie Pedalino Porter, a teacher from Amherst, Massachusetts; and Ken Noonan, Superintendent of Riverside Unified School District in California.

(13) The PHLOTE can be found here via the ADE website, at http://www.azed.gov/wp-content/uploads/PDF/HomeLanguageSurvey-English.pdf. Accessed March 23, 2014.

References

ADE (2008) *Structured English Immersion Models of the Arizona English Language Learners Task Force*. Phoenix, AZ: Arizona Department of Education. See https://www.azed.gov/wp-content/uploads/PDF/SEIModels05-14-08.pdf. Accessed March 23, 2014

ADE (n.d.) *Discrete Skills Inventory (DSI)*. Phoenix, AZ: Arizona Department of Education. See https://www.azed.gov/wp-content/uploads/PDF/DSIAllLevels.pdf. Accessed March 23, 2014.

Arizona Voter Initiative (2000) Proposition 203, *English for the Children*. http://www.azed.gov/wp-content/uploads/PDF/PROPOSITION203.pdf. Accessed March 23, 2014.

A.R.S. (2000) Arizona Revised Statute. Articles 3.1 §15-751 to §15-757: *English Language Education for the Children in Public Schools*. Phoenix, AZ: Arizona State Legislature. See http://www.azleg.state.az.us/ArizonaRevisedStatutes.asp?Title=15. Accessed March 23, 2014.

August, D. and Hakuta, K. (eds) (1997) *Improving Schooling for Language-minority Children: Research Agenda*. Washington, DC: National Academy Press.

August, D., Goldenberg, C. and Rueda, R. (2010) Restrictive state language policies: Are they scientifically based? In P. Gándara and M. Hopkins (eds) *Forbidden Languages: English Learners and Restrictive Language Policies* (pp. 139–158). New York: Teachers College.

Baker, C. (2011) *Foundations of Bilingual Education and Bilingualism* (5th edn). Bristol: Multilingual Matters.

Baker, K.A. (1987) Comment on Willig's 'Meta-analysis of selected studies in the effectiveness of bilingual education'. *Review of Educational Research* 57 (3), 351–362.

Baker, K.A. and de Kanter, A.A. (1981) *Effectiveness of Bilingual Education: A Review of Literature*. Washington, DC: Office of Planning, Budget and Evaluation, US Department of Education.

Baker, K.A. and de Kanter, A.A. (1983) *Bilingual Education*. Lexington, MA: Lexington Books.

Barik, H. and Swain, M. (1975) Three year evaluation of a large scale early grade French immersion program: The Ottowa study. *Language Learning* 25 (1), 1–30.

Barik, H., Swain, M. and Nwandudnobi, E.A. (1977) English–French bilingual education: The Elgin Study through grade five. *Canadian Modern Language Review* 33 (4), 459–475.

Becker, W.C. and Gersten, R. (1992) A follow-up of follow through: The later effects of the direct instruction model on children in fifth and sixth grades. *American Educational Research Journal* 19 (1), 75–92.

Benz, B. (2005) Amendment 31 in Colorado. In J. Cohen, K.T. McAlister, K. Rolstad and J. MacSwan (eds) *ISB4: Proceedings of the 4th International Symposium on Bilingualism* (pp. 259–266). Somerville, MA: Cascadilla Press.

Bill Emerson English Language Empowerment Act of (1996) H.R. 123. 104th Cong., 2nd Session (1996) Retrieved from http://www.languagepolicy.net/archives/hr123d.htm. Accessed March 23, 2014.

California Voter Initiative (1998) Proposition 227, *English for the Children*.

Cashman, H.R. (2006) Who wins in research on bilingualism in an anti-bilingual state? *Journal of Multilingual and Multicultural Development* 27 (1), 42–60.

Castañeda v. Pickard (1981) No. 79-2253, 989, United States Court of Appeals, Fifth Circuit. Unit A, 648 F.2d 989; US App. LEXIS 12063.

Castellano, J.A., Meza Downs, S., Eide, S., Gamboa-Lopez, C., Goldstein, M., Harvey, L. and Santa Cruz, A. (n.d.) *Structured English Immersion Teacher Training*. Phoenix, AZ: Arizona Department of Education, Accountability Division, Office of English Language Acquisition Services.

Clark, K. (2000) The design and implementation of an English immersion program. *The ABCs of English Immersion: A Teacher's Guide*. Washington, DC: Center for Equal Opportunity.

Collier, V.P. (1992) A synthesis of studies examining long-term language minority student data on academic achievement. *Bilingual Research Journal* 16 (1–2), 187–212.

Collier, V.P. and Thomas, W.P. (1989) How quickly can immigrants become proficient in school English? *Journal of Educational Issues of Language Minority Students* 5, 26–38.

Combs, M.C. (2012) Everything on its head: How Arizona's structured English immersion policy re-invents theory and practice. In M.B. Arias and C. Faltis (eds) *Implementing Educational Language Policy in Arizona: Legal, Historical, and Current Practices in SEI* (pp. 59–85). Bristol: Multilingual Matters.

Crawford, J.W. (2000a) *Anatomy of the English-only Movement*. Retrieved December 13, 2006, http://www.smkb.ac.il/privweb/Teachers/Chaim_Tir/nurit/Anatomy%20 of%20the%20English.doc. Accessed March 23, 2014.

Crawford, J.W. (2000b) *At War with Diversity: US Language Policy in an Age of Anxiety*. Clevedon: Multilingual Matters.

Crawford, J.W. (2004) *Educating English Learners: Language Diversity in the Classroom* (5th edn). Los Angeles, CA: Bilingual Education Services.

Crawford, J.W. (2007) Hard sell: Why is bilingual education so unpopular with the American public? In O. García and C. Baker (eds) *Bilingual Education: An Introductory Reader* (pp. 145–160). Clevedon: Multilingual Matters.

Crawford, J. and Krashen, S. (2007) *English Learners in American Classrooms: 101 questions 101 answers*. New York: Scholastic.

Cummins, J. (1981) The role of primary language development in promoting educational success for language minority students. In California State Department of Education, Office of Bilingual Education (ed.) *Schooling and Language Minority Students: A Theoretical Framework* (pp. 3–49). Los Angeles, CA: California State University Evaluation, Dissemination, and Assessment Center.

Cummins, J. (1992) Bilingual education and English immersion: The Ramírez Report in theoretical perspective. *Bilingual Research Journal* 16 (1–2), 91–104.

Cummins, J. (1996) *Negotiating Identities: Education for Empowerment in a Diverse Society.* Ontario, CA: California Association for Bilingual Education.

Cummins, J. (2000) *Language, Power, and Pedagogy: Bilingual Children in the Crossfire.* Clevedon: Multilingual Matters.

Davenport, D.K. (2008) *Baseline Study of Arizona's English Language Learner Programs and Data, Fiscal Year 2007.* Phoenix, AZ: State of Arizona Office of the Auditor General. See http://www.auditorgen.state.az.us/Reports/School_Districts/Statewide/2008_April/ELL_Baseline_Report.pdf. Accessed March 23, 2014.

Davenport, D.K. (2011) *Arizona English Language Learner Program, Fiscal Year 2010.* Report No. 11-06. Phoenix, AZ: State of Arizona Office of the Auditor General. See http://www.azauditor.gov/Reports/School_Districts/Statewide/2011/ELL_Report.pdf. Accessed March 23, 2014.

Del Valle, S. (2003) *Language Rights and the Law in the United States: Finding our Voices.* Clevedon: Multilingual Matters.

Escamilla, K., Shannon, S., Carlos, S. and García, J. (2003) Breaking the code: Colorado's defeat of the anti-bilingual education initiative (Amendment 31). *Bilingual Research Journal* 27 (3), 357–382.

Faltis, C.J. (2001) *Joinfostering: Teaching and Learning in Multilingual Classrooms* (3rd edn). Upper Saddle River, NJ: Merrill.

Faltis, C.J. (2006) *Teaching English Language Learners in Elementary School Communities: A Joinfostering Approach* (4th edn). Upper Saddle River, NJ: Merrill.

Faltis, C. and Arias, M.B. (2012) Research-based reform in Arizona: Whose evidence counts for applying the Castañeda test to structured English immersion models? In M.B. Arias and C. Faltis (eds) *Implementing Educational Language Policy in Arizona: Legal, Historical, and Current Practices in SEI* (pp. 21–38). Bristol: Multilingual Matters.

Farrington v. Tokusighe (1927) 273 US 284.

Flores v. Arizona (2000) *Consent Order.* U.S. District Court of Arizona, *CIV 92-596 TUC ACM.*

Flores v. Arizona (2006) No. CV 92-596-TUC-RCC, United States District Court for the District of Arizona, 2006 U.S. Dist. LEXIS 97364.

Flores v. Arizona (2009) No. 07-15603, No. 07-15605, 1014, United States Court of Appeals for the Ninth Circuit, 577 F.3d 1014; 2009 U.S. App. LEXIS 18092.

Florez, I.R. (2012) Examining the validity of the Arizona English language learners assessment cut scores. *Language Policy* 11 (1), 33–45; doi: 10.1007/s10993-011-9225-4.

Gándara, P. and Orfield, G. (2012) Segregating Arizona's English learners: A return to the 'Mexican room'. *Teachers College Record* 114 (9), 1–27.

Gándara, P., Losen, D., August, D., Uriarte, M., Gómez, M.C. and Hopkins, M. (2010) Forbidden language: A brief history of U.S. language policy. In P. Gándara and M. Hopkins (eds) *Forbidden Language: English Learners and Restrictive Language Policies* (pp. 20–33). New York: Teachers College Press.

García, O. (2005) Positioning heritage languages in the United States. *Modern Language Journal* 89 (4), 601–605.

García, O. (2009) *Bilingual Education in the 21st Century: A Global Perspective.* West Sussex: Wiley-Blackwell.

García, E.E., Wiese, A. and Cuéllar, D. (2011) Language, public policy, and schooling. In R.R. Valencia (ed.) *Chicano School Failure and Success: Past, Present, and Future* (3rd edn) (pp. 143–159). New York: Routledge.

Genesee, F. (1985) Second language learning through immersion: A review of U.S. programs. *Review of Educational Research* 55 (4), 541–561.

Gersten, R. and Woodward, J. (1985) Structured immersion for language minority students: Results of a longitudinal evaluation. *Educational Evaluation and Policy Analysis* 7 (1), 75–79.

Gifford, B.R. and Valdés, G. (2006) The linguistic isolation of Hispanic students in California's public schools: The challenge of reintegration. *Yearbook of the National Society for the Study of Education* 105 (2), 125–154; doi: 10.1111/j.1744-7984.2006.00079.

Goldenberg, C. and Rutherford-Quach, S. (2012) The Arizona home language survey: The under-identification of students for English language services. *Language Policy* 11 (1), 21–31; doi: 10.1007/s10993-011-9224-5.

Horne v. Flores (2009) No. 08-28, No. 08-294, Supreme Court of the United States, 557 U.S. 433; 129 S. Ct. 2579; 174 L. Ed. 2d 406; 2009 U.S. LEXIS 4733; 77 U.S.L.W. 4611; 21 Fla. L. Weekly Fed. S 1020.

Johnson, D.C. (2009) The relationship between applied linguistic research and language policy for bilingual education. *Applied Linguistics* 31 (1), 72–93; doi: 10.1093/applin/amp011.

Kloss, H. (1998 [1977]) *The American Bilingual Tradition*. Washington, DC and McHenry, IL: Center for Applied Linguistics and Delta Systems. Original work published (1977) Rowley, MA: Newbury House.

Krashen, S. and McField, G. (2005) What works? Reviewing the latest evidence on bilingual education. *Language Learner* 1 (2), 7–10, 34.

Krashen, S., Rolstad, K. and MacSwan, J. (2007) Review of 'Research summary and bibliography for structured English immersion programs' of the Arizona English language learners task force. Tempe, AZ: Arizona State University. See www.asu.edu/educ/sceed/azell/review.doc. Accessed March 23, 2014.

Krashen, S., MacSwan, J. and Rolstad, K. (2012) Review of 'research summary and bibliography for structured English immersion programs' of the Arizona English language learners task force. In M.B. Arias and C. Faltis (eds) *Implementing Educational Policy in Arizona: Legal, Historical and Current Practices in SEI* (pp. 107–118). Bristol: Multilingual Matters.

Lambert, W.E. and Tucker, G.R. (1972) *Bilingual Education of Children: The St. Lambert Experiment*. Rowley, MA: Newbury House.

La Morte, M.W. (2008) *School Law: Cases and Concepts* (9th edn). Boston, MA: Pearson.

Lau v. Nichols (1974) No. 72-6520, U.S. Supreme Court, 414 U.S. 563; 94 S. Ct. 786; 39 L. Ed. 2d 1; 1974 U.S. LEXIS 151.

Lightbown, P. and Spada, N. (2006) *How Languages Are Learned* (3rd edn). Oxford: Oxford University Press.

Lillie, K.E., Markos, A., Arias, M.B. and Wiley, T.G. (2012) Separate and not equal: The implementation of structured English immersion in Arizona's classrooms. *Teachers College Record* 114 (9), 1–33.

Lippi-Green, R. (2012) *English With an Accent: Language, Ideology and Discrimination in the United States* (2nd edn). Abingdon: Routledge.

MacSwan, J. and Pray, L. (2005) Learning English bilingually: Age of onset exposure and rate of acquisition among English language learners in a bilingual education program. *Bilingual Research Journal* 29 (3), 653.

Mahoney, K.S. and MacSwan, J. (2005) Reexamining identification and reclassification of English language learners: A critical discussion of select state practices. *Bilingual Research Journal* 29 (1), 31–42.

Mahoney, K., MacSwan, J., Haladyna, T. and García, D. (2010) Castañeda's third prong: Evaluating the achievement of Arizona's English learners under restrictive language policy. In P. Gándara and M. Hopkins (eds) *Forbidden Languages: English Learners and Restrictive Language Policies* (pp. 50–64). New York: Teachers College.

McCarty, T. (2004) Dangerous difference: A critical-historical analysis of language education policies in the United States. In J.W. Tollefson and A.B.M. Tsui (eds) *Medium of Instruction Policies: Which Agenda? Whose Agenda?* (pp. 71–93). Mahwah, NJ: Lawrence Erlbaum.

McCarty, T. (2013) *Language Planning and Policy in Native America: History, Theory, Praxis.* Bristol: Multilingual Matters.

McField, G.P. (2007) What is Structured English Immersion? Variations on a theme. *International Journal of Foreign Language Teaching* 3 (3), 2–22.

Mitchell, N. (2002) Colorado hands English immersion backer his first loss. *Rocky Mountain News* 6 November, p. 29A.

Moore, S.C.K. (2008) Language policy implementation: Arizona's SEI training. Doctoral dissertation, Arizona State University.

NCLB (2001) *No Child Left Behind* Act. Pub. L. No. 107–110.

OELAS (2009) *Administrators Model Implementation Training* [PowerPoint], 4 June. Phoenix, AZ: Office of English Language Acquisition Services, Arizona Department of Education. See https://www.azed.gov/english-language-learners/presentations/ Accessed March 23, 2014.

Parrish, T.B., Merickel, A., Pérez, M., *et al.* (2006) *Effects of the Implementation of Proposition 227 on the Education of English Learners, k–12: Findings from a Five-year Evaluation.* Washington, DC: American Institutes for Research. See http://www.air.org/files/227Report.pdf Accessed March 23, 2014.

Peña-Hughes, E. and Solis, J. (1980) Abcs. Unpublished report. McAllen, TX: McAllen Independent School District.

Porter, R. (1996) *Forked Tongue: The Politics of Bilingual Education* (2nd edn). New Brunswick, NJ: Transaction Publishers.

Ramírez, J., Pasta, D., Yuen, S., Ramey, D. and Billings, D. (1991) *Final Report: Longitudinal Study of Structured English Immersion Strategy, Early-exit and Late-exit Bilingual Education Programs for Language-minority Children*, Vol. I. No. 300-87-0156. Prepared for US Department of Education. San Mateo, CA: Aguirre International.

Rios-Aguilar, C. and Gándara, P. (2012) *Horne v. Flores* and the future of language policy. *Teachers College Record* 114 (9), 1–13.

Rios-Aguilar, C., González-Canche, M.S. and Moll, L.C. (2012) Implementing structured English immersion in Arizona: Benefits, challenges, and opportunities. Teachers College Record 114 (9), 1–18.

Rolstad, K., Mahoney, K. and Glass, G. (2005) The big picture: A meta-analysis of program effectiveness research on English language learners. *Educational Policy* 19 (4), 572–594.

Romaine, S. (2001) *Bilingualism* (3rd edn). Malden, MA: Blackwell Publishers.

Rossell, C.H. (2002) *Dismantling Bilingual Education, Implementing English Immersion: The California Initiative.* San Francisco, CA: Public Policy Institute.

Rossell, C.H. (2003) The near end of bilingual education. *Education Next* 3 (4), 44–52.

Rossell, C.H. and Baker, K. (1996) The educational effectiveness of bilingual education. *Research in the Teaching of English* 30 (1), 7–74.

Rumberger, R.W. and Tran, L. (2010) State language policies, school language practices, and the English learner achievement gap. In P. Gándara and M. Hopkins (eds) Forbidden Languages: English Learners and Restrictive Language Policies (pp. 86–101). New York: Teachers College.

Secada, W.G. (1987) This is 1987, not 1980: A comment on a comment. *Review of Educational Research* 57 (3), 377–384.

Smith, J.M., Coggins, C. and Cardoso, J.M. (2008) Best practices for English language learners in Massachusetts: Five years after the question 2 mandate. *Equity & Excellence in Education* 41 (3), 293–310; doi: 10.1080/10665680802179485.

Thomas, W.P. (1992) An analysis of the research methodology of the Ramírez Study. *Bilingual Research Journal* 16 (1–2), 213–246.

Thomas, W.P. and Collier, V.P. (1995) *Language Minority Student Achievement and Program Effectiveness. Research Summary.* Fairfax, VA: George Mason University.

Thomas, W.P. and Collier, V.P. (1997) *School Effectiveness for Language Minority Students.* Washington, DC: National Clearinghouse for Bilingual Education.

Thomas, W.P. and Collier, V.P. (2001) *A National Study of School Effectiveness for Language Minority Students' Long-term Academic Achievement: Final Report Executive Summary.* Washington, DC: Center for Applied Linguistics. See http://www.usc.edu/dept/education/CMMR/CollierThomasComplete.pdf Accessed March 23, 2014.

Tollefson, J.W. (1991) *Planning Language, Planning Inequality.* London: Longman.

Uriarte, M., Tung, R., Lavan, N. and Diez, V. (2010) Impact of restrictive language policies on engagement and academic achievement of English learners in Boston public schools. In P. Gándara and M. Hopkins (eds) *Forbidden Language: English Learners and Restrictive Language Policies* (pp. 65–85). New York: Teachers College Press.

Valencia, R.R., Menchaca, M. and Donato, R. (2002) Segregation, desegregation, and integration of Chicano students: Old and new realities. In R.R. Valencia (ed.) *Chicano School Failure and Success: Past, Present, and Future* (2nd edn) (pp. 70–113). New York: Routledge.

Valenzuela, A. (1999) *Subtractive Schooling: U.S.–Mexican Youth and the Politics of Caring.* Albany, NY: State University of New York Press.

Verhoeven, L. (1991) Acquisition of biliteracy. *AILA Review* 8, 61–74.

Weinberg, M. (1995) *A Chance to Learn: The History of Race and Education in the United States* (2nd edn). Long Beach, CA: California State University, The University Press.

Wentworth, L., Pellegrin, N., Thompson, K. and Hakuta, K. (2010) Proposition 227 in California: A long-term appraisal of its impact on English learner student achievement. In P. Gándara and M. Hopkins (eds) *Forbidden Language: English Learners and Restrictive Language Policies* (pp. 37–49). New York: Teachers College Press.

Wiley, T.G. (2004) Language planning, language policy, and the English-only Movement. In E. Finegan and J. Rickford (eds) *Language in the U.S.A.: Themes for the 21st Century* (pp. 319–338). Cambridge: Cambridge University Press.

Wiley, T.G. (2005) *Literacy and Language Diversity in the United States.* Washington, DC: Center for Applied Linguistics.

Wiley, T.G. (2007) Accessing language rights in education: A brief history of the U.S. context. In O. García and C. Baker (eds) *Bilingual Education: An Introductory Reader* (pp. 89–107). Clevedon: Multilingual Matters.

Wiley, T.G. (2010) Language policy in the U.S.A. In K. Potowski (ed.) *Language Diversity in the U.S.A.* (pp. 255–271). Cambridge: Cambridge University Press.

Wiley, T.G. (2013) A brief history and assessment of language rights in the United States. In J.W. Tollefson (ed.) *Language Policies in Education: Critical Issues* (2nd edn). New York: Routledge.

Wiley, T.G. and Wright, W.E. (2004) Against the undertow: Language-minority education policy and politics in the 'age of accountability'. *Educational Policy* 18 (1), 142–168; doi: 10.1177/0895904803260030.

Willig, A.C. (1982) The effectiveness of bilingual education: Review of a report. *NABE Journal* 6 (2–3), 1–19.

Willig, A.C. (1985) A meta-analysis of selected studies on the effectiveness of bilingual education. *Review of Educational Research* 55 (3), 269–317.

Wilson, W.H. (2014) Hawaiian – A Native America language official for a state. In T. Wiley, J.K. Peyton, D. Christian, S.C.K. Moore and N. Liu (eds) *Handbook of Heritage and Community Languages in the United States: Research, Educational Practice, and Policy.* (pp. 219–228) New York: Routledge.

Wright, W.E. (2005) English language learners left behind in Arizona. *Bilingual Research Journal* 29 (1), 1–29.

Wright, W.E. (2011) Historical introduction to bilingual education: The United States. In C. Baker (ed.) *Foundations of Bilingual Education and Bilingualism* (5th edn) (pp. 182–205). Bristol: Multilingual Matters.

Wright, W.E. (2013) Recent Flores decision is not an endorsement of Arizona's ELL policies and programs. Blog post, 15 July. See http://www.niusileadscape.org/bl/?p=1376#more-1376. Accessed March 23, 2014.

Wright, W.E. and Choi, D. (2006) The impact of language and high-stakes testing policies on elementary school English language learners in Arizona. *Education Policy Analysis Archives* 14 (13), 1–75. See http://epaa.asu.edu/ojs/article/viewFile/84/210. Accessed March 23, 2014.

2 *Flores v. Arizona*

Tim Hogan

It was a different world over 20 years ago when *Flores v. State of Arizona* was filed (1992). Funding for education in Arizona wasn't great, but it wasn't pathetic. And, of course, anti-immigration hysteria had not yet swept the country, and particularly Arizona, eventually making the state a lightning rod for the new nativism.

At the time of *Flores*, in 1992, the US Supreme Court had just added its newest member, Clarence Thomas, after motivated Senate hearings over his nomination. His appointment marked the beginning of a new judicial ideology in the country. Over the next 20 years, the Court would add Chief Justice Roberts and Samuel Alito, Jr. The law, education policy and politics would intersect in a way that would have significant consequences for students identified as 'Limited English Proficient'.

Arizona at the Beginning of the *Flores* Lawsuit

In 1992, when the *Flores* lawsuit was filed, Arizona public education was not a very controversial topic, nor was the instruction of English learners (ELs). In 1992, Arizona Statutes allowed for a variety of English instructional methodologies and programs to be chosen by school districts for the education of ELs. A district could choose from English as a second language (pull-out or push-in), bilingual education, bilingual-bicultural or a transitional bilingual model (Former ARS §§15-751 to 15-756). Different methodologies could be used at different schools within a district and at different grade levels within schools. The system provided for a great deal of flexibility, but very little accountability (Rolstad *et al.*, 2005). It was largely unknown how long it was taking students to learn English in each of the programs and how well they were performing academically.

The issue of funding allocations for program models designed for the instruction of ELs was more of an afterthought than anything else. Arizona, like many states, used the foundation method for supporting its school finance system. Under the foundation method, minimum funding was determined by multiplying the number of students times a base-level amount. The number of students was weighted to account for the different costs associated with educating particular groups of students. For example, high school students received a higher weight than elementary school students, just as students with disabilities received higher weights than non-disabled students.

With regard to funding for ELs, the state had conducted a study in 1988 (ADE, 1988) to determine the amount that six school districts with large numbers of ELs were spending on respective programs and methodologies for instruction. It was determined that, on average, the school districts were spending approximately $450 over and above base-level funding for EL students. The legislature determined, somewhat arbitrarily, that it would fund a third (or roughly $150) of that amount through the school funding system. As a result, EL students in 1992 were counted as 1.06 students, meaning that the school district would receive 6% over and above base-level funding for each EL student in its population.

The 6% additional weight for EL students equated to approximately $150 for EL students in 1992. The lawsuit filed by the Plaintiffs in the *Flores* case asserted that the amount of funding provided by the state was inadequate to implement any of the programs and methodologies the state authorized to educate EL students (*Flores v. Arizona*, 1999). The legal claim was that the Equal Educational Opportunities Act (EEOA, 1974) requires states to take 'appropriate action' to help students overcome language barriers, and that appropriate action included funding adequate to implement the programs and methodologies authorized by the state.

The *Flores* Lawsuit From 1992 Until 2000

The *Flores* lawsuit was filed as a class action on behalf of EL students and their parents and guardians in the Nogales Unified School District. The Defendants were the State of Arizona, the Superintendent of Public Instruction and the members of the State Board of Education. The complaint generally alleged that the state had violated the Equal Educational Opportunities Act (EEOA, 1974) in the oversight, administration and funding of federally mandated instruction for limited English proficient students enrolled in the Nogales Unified School District. The Plaintiffs contended that the Defendants had failed to provide limited English proficient students with a program of instruction calculated to facilitate proficiency in speaking, listening, reading and writing English, while enabling mastery of the standard academic curriculum required of all students.

The claims brought by the Plaintiffs fell into two categories. First, there were programmatic violations of the EEOA alleged by the Plaintiffs. The complaint alleged that:

(1) The Arizona Department of Education did not maintain sufficient staff to monitor and enforce federal requirements for EL students.

(2)   The state did not systematically audit school districts' EL programs.
(3)   The reporting requirements for school districts on their EL programs were inadequate and failed to include any kind of evaluation of the actual content or delivery of curriculum in EL classes.
(4)   40% of the school district faculty teaching English as a second language classes lacked even the provisional certifications required by state regulations.
(5)   The test for measuring English proficiency required less proficiency to exit an EL program than to enter it, resulting in students not receiving necessary supports and services. (*Flores v. Arizona*, 2000c)

These programmatic issues were ultimately addressed through a Consent Order that was agreed to by the state and approved by the court in 2001 (*Flores v. Arizona*, 2001).

Although the parties were able to agree on the appropriate resolution for the programmatic issues, they were unable to reach any agreement on the financial issues raised by the complaint. As a result, the court held a three-day trial in 1999 to determine whether the state was providing sufficient resources to school districts to adequately implement EL programs and methodologies (*Flores v. Arizona*, 1999).

At the trial, the Plaintiffs presented evidence about Arizona's school finance system and the constraints it placed on school districts like Nogales. The Plaintiffs also offered evidence about Nogales' EL programs and whether the district had sufficient resources to properly implement them.

The 2000 *Flores* Decision

In January 2000, US District Court Judge Alfredo Marquez issued his decision in the *Flores* case (*Flores v. Arizona*, 2000a, 2000b), finding that the Defendants were violating the EEOA because the state's funding for EL programs was arbitrary and capricious and bore no relation to the actual funding needed to insure that EL students in the Nogales School District were achieving mastery of required essential skills. In so holding, the Judge first examined Arizona's school finance system in detail and particularly its impact on the Nogales Unified School District. The Judge noted that Arizona's financing scheme is basically a foundation program and that the state guarantees a minimum level of funding for each student to insure that each student receives a basic education. He noted that the state's funding had not kept pace with inflation and also that the state's finance formula increases funding for certain factors such as the type of student, experience of the teaching faculty, and size and type of school district.

The factor accounting for EL students in calculating district budgets was put in place in 1989–1990 based on the cost study that had been done showing that school districts were spending approximately $450 extra per EL student. Judge Marquez cited testimony in which a Department of Education witness reported that the cost study was not reflective of the actual cost of operating a successful language acquisition program for a variety of reasons, including the fact that costs had not been measured in the same way across school districts, and that the costs of the school districts differed based upon the differences among the types of programs they operated.

Although the state had never updated or revised the cost study, the state legislature ordered that another cost study be done and created the English as a Second Language (ESL) and Bilingual Education Study Committee. It was appointed to conduct a cost study to determine the cost of educating EL students versus current expenditures, with the goal of determining the best practices in bilingual education and ESL and evaluate ways to improve bilingual education in school districts across the state.

The court observed that the EL weight per student was 0.02 in 1989–1990, which meant that school districts received approximately $50 more for each EL student. The weight was increased in 1991–1992 to the then current amount of 0.06, which meant that $150 was being allocated for each EL student. (The base-level amount per student at the time was approximately $2500.) The judge noted that state funding to school districts was generally provided in the form of block grants, which enabled districts to spend the amounts they received as they saw fit. In other words, districts have discretion regarding decisions on spending more or less on EL students than the amount provided by the state.

The court then examined other methods by which school districts could generate additional revenues to help support programs for ELs. The court compared the ability of high valuation school districts to generate 'override' money with little additional tax burden. Override money is funding accessible in districts with residents of higher socioeconomic status. As compared with Nogales, in which it would take a substantially higher tax effort to generate funds, high valuation districts' ability to generate 'override' money was deemed significant. As a result, the judge found that the impact of financing EL programs through an override is greater in low valuation districts because they have heavier concentrations of EL students. In any event, the judge noted Nogales did not have an override in place. In other words, Nogales did not have access to additional funding sources to supplement the monies allocated for EL per pupil funding.

Without a voter-approved override, the only way Nogales could increase funding for its EL programs was by shifting money away from non-EL student apportionments. For example, funding Nogales' EL program at $450 per EL student resulted in a loss of $270 to the mainstream programs' operating budget because the state was only providing $180 per EL student. Shifting the funds to support EL programs, therefore, impacted all students because it resulted in a lower base level of financial support for all students, including EL students.

After describing the constraints imposed on Nogales by Arizona's school finance system, Judge Marquez described the EL programs in place at Nogales' schools. At the time, Nogales had 10 schools with a student population close to 6000. The student population was approximately 95% Hispanic and 60% of the students were identified as EL students.

Nogales elementary schools used a transitional bilingual education (TBE) model. Nogales' middle schools used an ESL model. However, the majority of EL students in the middle schools were not in ESL programs and were mainstreamed because the state allowed students who could communicate orally in English to be placed in mainstream English medium of instruction classrooms. The high school also used an ESL model. However, similarly, EL students who demonstrated oral English proficiency were placed in mainstream classrooms even if their English reading or writing abilities were limited.

Most EL students in middle and high school in mainstream classes received no English language development (ELD) instruction because Nogales lacked qualified teachers for that purpose. The court noted that Nogales did not have enough money to hire the number of teachers it needed, and that its salary level was not competitive enough to retain endorsed teachers or to hire new endorsed teachers. In order to adequately implement EL programs in Nogales, the district would have to hire at least 60 more teachers with either bilingual or ESL elementary-level endorsements.

The witness from Nogales testified that the District spent more on its EL programs than the amount of money provided by the state. She testified that in order to acquire funding for the programs, Nogales had to 'rob Peter to pay Paul'. She also indicated the availability of some federal funding to support the programs, adding that those funds were insufficient and, regardless, had expired without replacement by the state.

Judge Marquez analyzed the evidence within the structural framework provided by *Castaneda v. Pickard*, a Court of Appeal's decision arising out of Texas in 1981 (*Castañeda v. Pickard*, 1981). The Court in *Castañeda* established a three-pronged test for determining compliance with the EEOA. First, there has to be an educational theory recognized as sound by experts in the field or, at least, deemed a legitimate experimental strategy. (The Plaintiffs agreed that the state prescribed, and that Nogales adopted, models generally regarded by experts as sound designs for effective language acquisition.)

The second factor is whether the programs and practices actually used by a school system are reasonably calculated to implement effectively the educational theory that is adopted. On this point, Judge Marquez determined that, for the state to adopt appropriate practices and allocate adequate resources, it must first establish minimum standards for providing EL funding and program oversight. He cited the Arizona Supreme Court's finding that it could only determine the adequacy of the state's school finance system once minimum standards had been set.

In Arizona, the state had established minimum academic standards called the 'Arizona Essential Skills', which eventually became the Arizona Common Core Standards (ADE, 2012). The state had developed a test for measuring attainment of the skills, and the judge concluded that the Arizona Essential Skills were therefore the minimum standards which must be taught in all schools and that all students, including EL students, must master the essential skills. Judge Marquez then determined that Arizona's funding level for EL programs was arbitrary and capricious and bore no relationship to the actual funding needed to insure that EL students in Nogales were achieving mastery of the essential skills. He noted that the study authorized by the legislature to more accurately assess EL program costs might provide a basis for the state to set a minimum-based funding level per EL student which would not be arbitrary and capricious.

From Judgment to the United States Supreme Court

Between the issuance of the judgment by Judge Marquez in early 2000 (*Flores v. Arizona*, 2000a, 2000b) and the US Supreme Court's decision in the *Flores* case in 2009 (*Flores v. Arizona*, 1992/*Horne v. Flores*, 2009), a number of issues emerged both inside and outside of the courtroom that impacted the *Flores* case. It would make sense to start first with the one notable issue that was not addressed. The state decided not to appeal the judgment in the *Flores* case. That meant that at least until the US Supreme Court decided otherwise in 2009, the state was obligated to comply with Judge Marquez's finding that funding in Nogales was 'arbitrary and capricious'.

The Plaintiffs in *Flores* contacted each member of the Arizona state legislature, as well as the Governor, during the early part of 2000 to encourage completion of the cost study that the legislature had previously authorized so that adequate funding could be provided for EL programs. Responses from legislators and the Governor were not received. As a result, later in 2000, Plaintiffs filed a motion to require that a cost study be performed and that the legislature take appropriate action to comply with the judgment. Judge Marquez granted that motion and between late 2000 and early 2001 the Arizona Department of Education commissioned an expedited cost study (Arizona Legislature, 2001). However, the timeline converged with the November 2000 election, in which Arizona voters approved Proposition 203, establishing English-only instruction as the primary methodology for language acquisition in the state (Arizona Voter Initiative, 2000).

When Prop. 203 passed, there were only a handful of schools in Arizona that used English immersion as the methodology for teaching ELs. Consultants retained by the Department of Education, therefore, reviewed several of these schools and also programs outside of Arizona to identify the costs associated with a now statewide required English-only program as the primary means of instructing EL students. The average incremental cost per EL student to implement Prop. 203's English immersion requirement in the school systems studies was slightly over $1200. The Arizona legislature was not swift to increase EL funding from $150 per student to $1200 per student. At the time, Arizona had approximately 50,000 EL students, so increasing funding by $1000 per student would have meant an appropriation of $50 million annually.

Instead, the legislature enacted interim legislation which, for no apparent reason, increased the funding from $150 to approximately $350 per student. The weight in the school finance formula for EL students was increased from 0.06 to 0.115 (HB, 2001).

The legislation was called interim because the legislature determined that it needed more data upon which to base funding decisions. It decided to authorize a comprehensive study of costs for EL programs and, ultimately, retained the National Conference of State Legislatures (NCSL) for that purpose (NCSL, 2005). The assigned study was never actually completed. Instead, the NCSL submitted, in draft form, findings to the Arizona legislature in August 2004, which identified cost levels ranging from $700 for low-need high school EL students to over $2500 for high-need elementary school students (NCSL, 2005). True to form, the legislature ignored the NCSL cost study because it had 'grave doubts' about its validity (Laws, 2006).

By this time, in 2005, another judge, Ranier Collins, had been assigned to the *Flores* case. The Plaintiffs asked him to impose fines on the state for failing to comply with the judgment. He did so and, by the end of February 2006, some $20 million in fines had been assessed against the state. By this time, the *Flores* case had been swept up by an increasing wave of anti-immigration sentiment in the state. Recoiling at the prospect of a federal judge imposing fines on the state to promote the cause of non-English speaking children, the Arizona legislature decided to intervene in the case. Meanwhile, during the 2006 legislative session, the legislature enacted a controversial measure requiring ELs, no matter their proficiency level, to spend four hours out of every school day in ELD classes (ADE, n.d.; see Grijalva & Jimenez-Silva, Chapter 6 and Markos & Arias, Chapter 7, this volume).

Citing House Bill 2064 (HB, 2006), which required the four hours of daily ELD instruction, as well as a number of other factors, the legislature and the Superintendent of Public Instruction asked the court to determine that they were no longer required to comply with the judgment that had been issued in 2000.

The Plaintiffs were initially confounded by the state's claim that it was no longer equitable to require compliance with the judgment. After all, the state had done nothing since 2001 to make funding for EL programs any less arbitrary. The funding scheme basically remained the same, and still bore no relationship to the actual cost of equitably educating EL students.

Without regard for the aspect of the court's judgment noting the arbitrary and capricious nature of funding for ELs, the Defendants contended that circumstances had changed since 2000, such that it was no longer appropriate to require compliance by the legislature with the 2001 Marquez judgment. They cited Congress' enactment in 2001 of *No Child Left Behind* (NCLB, 2001) and the additional funding it provided as one of the changes in circumstances eliminating required compliance. To be sure, the requirements in NCLB requiring the collection of data on the performance of various student groups including ELs was necessary and would later become helpful for placing emphasis on states' and districts' responsibility for meeting the needs of ELs, but it had very little to do with the judgment in the *Flores* case.

Likewise, the Defendants cited the adoption by Arizona voters of English immersion in 2000 (Prop. 203: Arizona Voter Initiative, 2000) as another changed circumstance excusing them from compliance with the judgment. Although structured/sheltered English immersion (SEI), the specific phrase for English immersion written into Prop. 203, represented a different methodology, it nevertheless qualified as a program for language acquisition and, therefore, still involved the costs identified in the Marquez ruling.

The Defendants also cited changes that had occurred in the Nogales School District since the judgment was entered in 2000. A new superintendent had imposed fiscal discipline on the district and the structure of the district's EL programs. Although these were positive developments, they did not ultimately affect the district's allocation of insufficient funds from the state to adequately support the operation of its EL programs.

Overall, the Defendants' main argument was that the District had sufficient funds available to it from its entire budget including federal, state and local sources to finance the district's EL programs. And, of course, in some ways that was true. If all federal and state aid was considered available to support EL programs, then the Marquez judgment should never have been entered in the first place. Indeed, the Defendants had argued when the judgment was entered that it was not appropriate to look only at state funding for EL students, but instead to determine the full amount of funding available to Nogales for *all* its students, including ELs. The court had rejected that argument, focusing instead on the funding specifically associated with EL students.

After an eight-day trial in 2006, Judge Collins ruled against the Defendants, who then appealed to the Ninth Circuit Court of Appeals. In February 2008, the Court of Appeals issued a lengthy opinion affirming Judge Collins and denying any relief to the Defendants (*Flores v. Arizona*, 2008). In effect, the Court of Appeals held that the Defendants were invoking changed circumstances as a device to escape the fact that they had failed to appeal the judgment that was entered against them in 2000 (*Flores v. Arizona*, 2008, 516 F.3d at 1171). In effect, the Defendants were arguing that the Judge was wrong in 2000 when he focused only on state funding associated with EL students, rather than all of the funding available to school districts to support their EL programs, because the focus did not account for federal and other sources of funding.

The Court of Appeals noted that the Defendants had not appealed either that judgment, or the orders issued after the judgment to enforce compliance. The Appeals court stated that:

> Underlying the declaratory judgment and post-judgment orders is the basic determination under the EEOA that, given Arizona's educational funding structure, EL programs require substantial state funding in addition to that spent on basic educational programming. That conclusion rests, in turn, on the recognition that EL students require additional attention to bring their language skills to the point where they can fully benefit from instruction in English. (*Flores v. Arizona*, 516 F.3d at 1168)

As a consequence, the court said that the superintendent and legislature would have to demonstrate one of the following: that the basic factual premises of the district court's incremental funding determination had been swept away, or that there had been some change in the legal landscape that made the original ruling now improper.

As for the Defendants' claim that even if EL programming costs exceed EL-specific funding there is ample state funding to cover them, the court cited the EEOA's requirement that the state take 'appropriate action' to overcome the language barriers of students that impede equal participation. The court held that taking money away from basic educational programs and thereby hurting all students in an attempt to equalize opportunities for EL students was not 'appropriate action'.

There was only one place left for the Defendants to go. They petitioned the United States Supreme Court for review of the Court of Appeal's decision later in 2008, and in January 2009 the US Supreme Court granted review.

The Supreme Court Decision

In a five:four decision, the Supreme Court held that the Court of Appeal's inquiry was too narrow, focusing almost exclusively on the sufficiency of EL incremental funding (*Horne v. Flores*, 2009). The majority asserted that the Court of Appeals attributed undue significance to the failure to appeal the district court's 2000 order and, in doing so, failed to engage in the appropriate inquiry surrounding circumstances that had changed since 2000, when the judgment was entered. The Court remanded the case for a proper examination of at least four factual and legal changes that it said might warrant the granting of relief from the judgment. Those factors were: the state's adoption of a new EL instructional methodology in 2000 (SEI); Congress' enactment of *No Child Left Behind*; structural and management reforms in Nogales; and increased overall education funding in Arizona. The purpose of examining these factors was to ascertain whether ongoing enforcement of the original 2000 order was supported by an ongoing violation of federal law, namely the EEOA (1974).

With respect to the first factor, the majority erroneously stated that EL instruction in Nogales had been based primarily on 'bilingual education'. That was not the case. In fact, ESL was the predominant methodology in place in Nogales schools at the time the judgment was rendered in 2000. Nevertheless, the majority stated that research on EL instruction indicates documented academic support for the view that SEI is significantly more effective than bilingual education and that, as a result, on remand, the Court should include further factual findings regarding whether Nogales' implementation of SEI methodology constituted a 'significantly changed circumstance' that warrants relief.

The court also discussed Congress' enactment of *No Child Left Behind* as another potentially significant 'changed circumstance'. Fortunately, the court rejected the argument that compliance with NCLB was the equivalent of compliance with the EEOA. Even so, the majority determined that NCLB was relevant to the changed circumstance inquiry because it prompted the state to institute significant structural and programming changes in its delivery of EL education and because of the increased federal funding for education in general, and EL programming in particular. Finally, the majority stated that NCLB's reporting requirements could provide persuasive evidence about the current effectiveness of Nogales' EL programming.

The majority also held that the lower courts had erred by refusing to consider that Nogales might be taking 'appropriate action' to address language barriers without having satisfied the original order. The Court said that the EEOA seeks to provide 'equal educational opportunity' and that its ultimate focus is on the quality of educational programming provided to students, not the amount of money spent on them. A proper analysis, said the Court, should include an inquiry into whether, as a result of structural and managerial improvements in Nogales, the district was now providing equal educational opportunities to EL students.

The final factor was an overall increase in education funding available in Nogales. It was true that overall education funding for Nogales, as well as other school districts in Arizona, had increased in the nine years between the judgment and the Supreme Court's decision. The majority held that the Court of Appeals was wrong when it stated that diverting base-level education funds would necessarily hurt other state educational programs and was not therefore an 'appropriate step'. To this, the majority stated that the EEOA's 'appropriate action' requirement does not necessarily require any particular level of funding and, to the extent that funding is relevant, the EEOA certainly does not require that money come from any particular source. The Court stated:

> It is unfortunate if a school, in order to fund EL programs, must divert money from other worthwhile programs, but such decisions fall outside the scope of the EEOA. (*Horne v. Flores*, 2009)

According to this line of thinking, the proper analysis on remand should evaluate whether the state's budget for general education funding, in addition to any local revenues, is currently supporting EEOA-compliant EL programming in Nogales.

Based on the majority's decision, the case was remanded to the district court to analyze the four factors identified by the majority to determine whether Nogales was providing EL programs that comply with the EEOA and whether the state was violating the EEOA on a statewide basis. According to the Court, if the state was not committing statewide violations of the EEOA, the injunction against it ordering compliance should be vacated.

Arizona's Four-hour ELD Requirement

The Arizona legislature's enactment of HB 2064 in 2006 became relevant after the US Supreme Court decision remanding the case to the district court to determine whether the EL programs in Arizona complied with the EEOA.

HB 2064 established an English Language Learners Task Force, the appointments to which would be made by the governor, the president of the senate, the speaker of the house and the superintendent of public instruction (ARS 15-756.01(A)). The principal function of the Task Force was to develop SEI models incorporating the requirement that the first year in which a student is classified as an EL include a minimum of four hours per day of ELD (ARS, 15-756.01(C)). The models ultimately approved by the Task Force required four hours of daily ELD, not only for first year EL students, but for all EL students until their test scores reflect English proficiency, regardless of how many years that takes (ADE, 2008).

The motivation for HB 2064 was not very clear. It was used by the Defendants in court as evidence that the state had established a rational funding system for EL programs. That is because HB 2064 contained provisions for funding the incremental costs of the four-hour models (ARS, 15-756.01(I)). Indeed, in enacting HB 2064, the legislature acknowledged the *Flores* litigation and rejected the cost study performed by the NCSL (Laws, 2006).

Separate and apart from the funding provisions of HB 2064, it is equally clear that the idea for a uniform program that included four hours of daily ELD came from the Arizona Department of Education. Ever since Arizona voters approved English immersion in 2000 (Prop. 203), and particularly after the election of Superintendent Tom Horne in 2003, the Department was unhappy with what it thought was a failure on the part of school districts to implement immersion with fidelity. To the extent that English immersion had been implemented in school districts across the state, implementation was uneven and varied significantly from district to district.

The requirement for four hours of ELD came from a Department consultant, Kevin Clark, who advised the Task Force and testified in court that there was little point in providing ELs with academic instruction until they were fully proficient in English and the way to achieve proficiency was by increasing time spent on the task of learning English. As a result, the four-hour models adopted by the Task Force are quite detailed about the amount of time within the four-hour block that should be spent on various language components like vocabulary, grammar, reading and writing. The time allocations vary by proficiency and grade level, but must always equal four hours daily (ADE, n.d.).

When *Flores* came back from the US Supreme Court to the District Court in late 2009 (*Horne v. Flores*, 2009), the question for the district court was whether Nogales now had in place EL programming that complied with the EEOA and, likewise, whether the state itself was violating the EEOA. The Plaintiffs contended that the four-hour daily ELD requirement violated the EEOA in several ways. The Plaintiffs' primary contention was that the four-hour ELD requirement unnecessarily denies EL students access to the academic curriculum. Additionally, the Plaintiffs alleged that the four-hour model was premised on the notion that students would rapidly acquire English within the legislature's goal of one year, after which EL students would have full access to the academic curriculum. However, implementation of the four-hour model limits access to academic curricula for more than one year for ELs not rapidly reclassified. Many EL students continue to be stuck in the program for years. Therefore, the Plaintiffs contended that the four-hour model was not the least segregative program necessary to achieve the state's goal of reclassification within one year.

Finally, the four-hour model denies EL students access to the academic curriculum not only while they are classified as EL, but even after they exit the program because there the state does not require school districts to provide exited EL students with the academic content they missed while participating in the four-hour ELD program. Under *Castañeda v. Pickard*, temporary segregation of EL students is only permissible if the academic deficits that EL students incur while learning English are rectified. According to the Court in *Castañeda*:

> In order to be able ultimately to participate equally with the students who entered school with an English language background, the limited English speaking students will have to acquire both English language

proficiency comparable to that of the average native speakers and to recoup any deficits which they may incur in other areas of the curriculum as a result of this extra expenditure of time on English language development. We understand §1703(f) to impose on educational agencies not only an obligation to overcome the direct obstacle to learning which the language barrier itself poses, but also a duty to provide limited English speaking students with assistance in other areas of the curriculum where their equal participate may be impaired because of deficits incurred during participation in an agency's language remediation program. (*Castañeda v. Pickard*, 1981)

The state said that it was the school district's responsibility, not the state's, to ensure that some form of compensatory instruction was provided to EL students to remedy academic deficits incurred while spending most of their school day in ELD classes.

The district court conducted a 23-day trial concerning the factors identified by the US Supreme Court and the Plaintiffs' contention that the four-hour model violated the EEOA. The Plaintiffs' evidence showed that the four-hour model was having virtually no impact on the reclassification of EL students. In Nogales, the reclassification data before and after implementation of the four-hour model are shown below in Figure 2.1.

As the data for Nogales indicate (Hogan & Herr-Cardillo, 2011), there was no appreciable difference in the reclassification rates for EL students after implementation of the four-hour model. Prior to the implementation of the four-hour model, Nogales used a two-hour ESL pull-out model at most of its schools. If a shift in EL reclassification rates did occur after the implementation of the four-hour model, the time it took for exiting from the ELD program was actually lengthened.

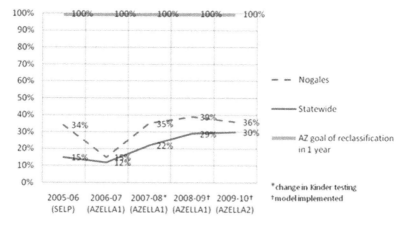

Figure 2.1 Reclassification rates before and after four-hour model

Results of implementation of the four-hour model in Nogales were comparable to data from Tucson Unified School District (TUSD), one of the largest school districts in Arizona (see Figure 2.2) (Hogan & Herr-Cardillo, 2011). Because of its size, TUSD had a range of different programs in place for EL instruction prior to implementation of the four-hour model. The programs and reclassification rates are shown below.

During the trial in the lower court following the Supreme Court decision, a witness from TUSD testified that, prior to the implementation of the four-hour model, regardless of the program EL students participate in, reclassification rates 'turned out to be about the same'. If that were true, then there was very little point in segregating EL students for four hours a day.

The Plaintiffs also produced evidence that students placed in four-hour ELD classes were stigmatized and regarded as being in 'dumb' classes. The principal at Nogales High School talked about how the four-hour ELD class isolated the EL students at the high school, adding that the four-hour ELD class negatively affected their self-esteem. The principal, himself an EL who was educated in the Nogales District, testified that he would not have wanted to be segregated from his fellow students when he was an EL student in Nogales because mixing with other students motivated him to achieve more than he could have if he were separated from them.

In late March 2013, more than two years after the trial concluded, the district court judge finally issued his ruling. Judge Rainer Collins rejected the Plaintiffs' claims and granted the Defendants' request to be relieved from complying with the original judgment from 2000. Basically, Judge Collins terminated the case, concluding that 'this lawsuit is no longer the vehicle to pursue the myriad of educational issues in this state' (*Flores v. Huppenthal*, 2013: 23).

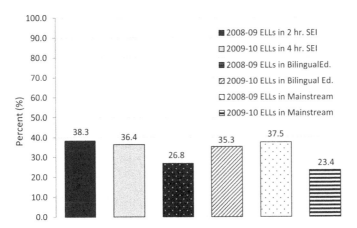

Figure 2.2 Reclassification data by method of instruction

With regard to the Plaintiffs' claim that the four-hour model denied EL students access to the academic curriculum, the Judge agreed with the Plaintiffs that:

> The state does not require school districts to provide ELL students with an opportunity to recover the academic content that they missed while they were in the four hour model and makes no effort to determine whether ELL students have been deprived of academic content as a result of being placed in four hours of ELD. (*Flores v. Huppenthal*, 2013: 10)

He cited the testimony of the chairman of the English Language Learner Task Force for the proposition that 'it was impossible for ELLs to be taught science and social studies because they were ELL students and were not English proficient' (*Flores v. Huppenthal*, 2013: 8). Additionally, the Judge determined that 'even at school districts that claim to teach academic content as part of the four hours of ELD, the witnesses acknowledge that the academic content provided to ELL students is not the same, and is less than, what is provided to English proficient students' (*Flores v. Huppenthal*, 2013: 9).

Despite these findings, incredibly, the Judge concluded that there was no violation of the Equal Educational Opportunities Act without any explanation.

As for the Plaintiffs' claim that the four-hour model unlawfully segregates EL students, the Judge cited *Castañeda* for the proposition that the EEOA permits 'ability grouping' of EL students (*Flores v. Huppenthal*, 2013: 21). This reference neglected the statement in *Castañeda* indicating that such segregation should be temporary and followed by 'compensatory and supplemental education to remedy deficiencies in other areas which they may develop during this period' of segregation (*Castañeda v. Pickard*, 1981, quoted in *Flores v. Huppenthal*, 2013: 19).

Judge Collins completely ignored the undisputed fact that the segregation imposed by the four-hour model was anything but 'temporary'. He noted that the Arizona Department of Education was unable to provide him with information regarding the average length of time it takes for EL students to test proficient on the state's language assessment test (*Flores v. Huppenthal*, 2013: 18). However, he failed to mention the undisputed evidence in the record from Nogales and Tucson school districts that on average students remain classified as ELs for approximately four years. He also failed in his order to mention that the classification rates under the four-hour model in the Nogales and Tucson districts are no better, and in some cases worse, than under alternative models of instruction.

The Judge ended his order with this comment:

> Education in this state is under enormous pressure because of lack of funding at all levels. It appears that the state has made a choice in how

it wants to spend funds on teaching students the English language. It may turn out to be pennywise and pound foolish, as at the end of the day, speaking English, and not having other educational gains in science, math, etc. will still leave some children behind. (*Flores v. Huppenthal*, 2013: 22–23)

How the Judge could come to that conclusion without finding that the four-hour model violates EEOA is a mystery. For this reason, Plaintiffs have appealed the Judge's order to the Ninth Circuit Court of Appeals in hopes of correcting some of the very fundamental mistakes made by the District Court Judge.

What will become of the four-hour model of ELD as it relates to *Flores* remains to be seen. However, as is illustrated in later chapters in this text, its segregationist nature and approach to discrete language instruction removed from content learning has already anecdotally demonstrated negative effects on principals, teachers, students and schools.

References

ADE (1988) *Limited English Proficient (LEP) Cost Study, Fiscal Year 1987–1988*. Phoenix, AZ: Arizona Department of Education.

ADE (2008) *Structured English Immersion Models of the Arizona English Language Learners Task Force*. Phoenix, AZ: Arizona Department of Education. See https://www.azed.gov/wp-content/uploads/PDF/SEIModels05-14-08.pdf Accessed March 21, 2014.

ADE (2012) *Arizona Common Core Standards*. Phoenix, AZ: Arizona Department of Education. See http://www.azed.gov/azcommoncore/files/2012/08/accs_ela_math_generaloverview_updated_081912.pdf Accessed March 7, 2012.

ADE (n.d.) *Discrete Skills Inventory (DSI)*. Phoenix, AZ: Arizona Department of Education. See https://www.azed.gov/wp-content/uploads/PDF/DSIAllLevels.pdf Accessed March 22, 2014.

Arizona English Language Learners Task Force (n.d.) See http://www.ade.az.gov/ELLTaskForce Accessed March 22, 2014.

Arizona Legislature (2001) *The Cost of Educating Arizona's English Learners*. Phoenix, AZ: Arizona State Agency Publications. See http://azmemory.azlibrary.gov/cdm/singleitem/collection/statepubs/id/8484/rec/19 Accessed March 22, 2014.

Arizona Revised Statutes §§15-751 to 15-756.

Arizona Revised Statutes, Title 15, Chapter 7, Article 3.1 and A.R.S. §15-943.

Arizona Voter Initiative (2000) Proposition 203, *English for the Children*.

Castañeda v. Pickard (1981) 648 F.2d 989, 1011 (5th Cir., 1981).

EEOA (1974) Equal Educational Opportunities Act, 20 United States Code Section 1703.

Flores v. Arizona (1992) No. CV 92-596.

Flores v. Arizona (1999) 48 F.Supp.2d 937 (D. Ariz. 1999).

Flores v. Arizona (2000a) 172 F.Supp.2d 1225–1239 (D. Ariz. 2000).

Flores v. Arizona (2000b) 160 F.Supp.2d 1043 (D. Ariz. 2000).

Flores v. Arizona (2000c) *Consent Order*. CIV 92-596. (D. Ariz. 1992).

Flores v. Arizona (2001) (not reported) F.Supp.2d (D. Ariz. 2001).

Flores v. Arizona (2005) 405 F.Supp.2d 1112 (D. Ariz. 2005).

Flores v. Arizona (2008) 516 F.3d 1140 (9th Cir. 2008).

Flores v. Huppenthal et al. (2013) (not reported). 29 March.

HB (2001) 2010, 45th Leg., 2nd Spec. Sess., Ch. 9. (Ariz. 2001).

HB (2006) 2064, 57th Leg., 2nd Spec. Sess. (Ariz. 2006).

Hogan, T.M. and Herr-Cardillo, J. (2011) Plaintiff's post-hearing brief. Case No. CIV 92-596-TUC-RCC, 18 March.

Horne v. Flores (2009) 557 U.S. 433, 129 Sup. Ct. 2579, 174 Lawyer's Edition 2nd 406.

Laws (2006) Ch. 4, Sec. 14 (C).

NCLB (2001) *No Child Left Behind,* Act. Pub. L. No. 107–110.

NCSL (2005) *Arizona English Language Learner Cost Study.* Denver, CO: National Conference of State Legislatures.

Rolstad, K., Mahoney, K.S. and Glass, G.V. (2005) Weighing the evidence: A meta-analysis of bilingual education in Arizona. *Bilingual Research Journal* 29 (1), 43–67.

3 Proposition 203 and Arizona's Early School Reform Efforts: The Nullification of Accommodations[1]

Wayne E. Wright

In the United States, the number of children classified as English learner (EL)[2] students is increasing rapidly, especially in southwestern states such as Arizona (National Clearinghouse, 2010). In past educational reform efforts, the needs of EL students were seldom recognized (Deschenes *et al.*, 2001; Gándara & Contreras, 2009; Wiley & Wright, 2004). However, greater attention has been paid to EL students in more recent educational language and assessment policy initiatives. There is general agreement on the need for high standards and achievement expectations, and a consensus that EL students need to learn English and have access to the core curriculum in order to succeed academically. Nevertheless, there is strong disagreement on how best to bring about high academic achievement for all students, especially EL students, and how to help EL students obtain high levels of proficiency and literacy in English (Cook *et al.*, 2011; Crawford, 2000).

One common educational accommodation for ELs is transitional bilingual education (TBE), in which students are provided with a few years of content-area instruction in their primary language(s), while also providing English as a second language (ESL) until the students attain enough proficiency in English to transition into a mainstream English-only classroom. Other bilingual approaches are based on the same principle, but may extend beyond a few years to ensure students develop and maintain high levels of proficiency and literacy in both languages. Research has shown that when properly implemented, these programs are effective in helping EL students learn English and achieve academic success (August & Hakuta, 1997; Crawford, 2004; Krashen, 1996; Krashen & Biber, 1988; Slavin & Cheung, 2003). When bilingual education is not provided, schools typically try to accommodate their EL students through a wide variety of ESL program designs (Peregoy & Boyle, 2000; Wright, 2010). In the climate of school reform efforts in the early 2000s, however, these approaches and methods came into conflict with newly imposed state restrictions on bilingual and ESL programs, e.g. Prop. 227 in California (California Voter Initiative, 1998), Prop. 203 in Arizona (Arizona Voter Initiative, 2000) and Question 2 in Massachusetts (Massachusetts Voter Initiative, 2002).

In addition, these restrictions occurred at a time when other state and federal policies were also being adopted, including high-stakes achievement testing as required by *No Child Left Behind* (NCLB, 2001) and individual state accountability programs. Federal policy then and now requires the full inclusion of EL students in these high-stakes tests, and students, their teachers and their schools are held accountable for the test results. In recognition that students' lack of proficiency in English may affect their performance, these policies require accommodations for ELs who take the tests.

Interpreting and implementing these intersecting language and assessment policies created significant challenges for educators attempting to accommodate the linguistic and academic needs of EL students (Wright, 2004). This difficulty was especially true in Arizona, which is the focus of this study. Along with the rapid growth of the EL student population, there were three major educational assessment and language policies being interpreted and implemented in the state at that time: (a) AZ LEARNS (2001), Arizona's statewide school accountability and assessment program; (b) NCLB (2001); and (c) Prop. 203 (2000). Each of these policies had specific mandates for EL students, as well as allowances for certain types of accommodation for ELs in meeting these requirements. Several issues emerged as the requirements of each policy became intertwined and as each was interpreted and implemented by various policy actors at the state level. Within this intersection, many of the accommodations become nullified; that is, an accommodation allowed by one policy was canceled out by the mandates (or interpretation of the mandates) of another. In addition, accommodations allowed or created by previous policy actors were nullified by subsequent policy actors based on their own interpretation and implementation of these intersecting policies. Furthermore, new accommodations were created that may have been more beneficial to the policy actors themselves than to the EL students.

This study is a policy analysis of the nullification of accommodation-oriented policies for ELs within the context of the intersection of Prop. 203, AZ LEARNS and NCLB in the early 2000s. This analysis is based on frameworks of educational language policies, which I briefly describe in the next section. I will then provide a brief description of the methodology used in this study, followed by an overview of the basic requirements of these three policies, particularly as they relate to EL students. I will then analyze these policies, and their intersection, using the language policy frameworks. Finally, I will describe and analyze the nullification of many of the accommodations for ELs within these policies as they have been interpreted and implemented by various policy actors at the state level.

Language Policy Frameworks

Corson (2001), reflecting on the type of diversity found in multilingual countries such as the United States, argues that three policy principles are essential for meeting the linguistic and academic needs of language-minority students. The first principle states that children should have the right to 'be educated whenever possible in the same variety of language that is learned at home or is valued most by them' (Corson, 2001: 32). When this is not possible, the second principle applies, which states that students should have the right to 'attend a school that shows full respect for the language variety that is learned at home or valued most by them' (Corson, 2001: 32). The third principle states that students have the right 'to learn, to the highest level of proficiency possible, the standard language variety of wider communication used by the society as a whole' (Corson, 2001: 32).

Corson acknowledges that there are settings where many languages exist, thus 'the second principle becomes the second-best alternative for most schools' (Corson, 2001: 33). Nevertheless, he makes a strong case for the first principle:

> Just valuing the minority language does not go far enough for many students, such as the signing Deaf, or users of native languages, or indeed children in general for whom loss of their minority first language would create academic difficulties. These children, and many others, will always need the support that the first policy principle offers. (Corson, 2001: 33)

Corson (2001) also provides a framework (from Churchill, 1986) for classifying minority-language policies in education. There are six ascending levels or rankings that reflect a policy's recognition of minority languages, and its implementation of suitable educational policies. A modified version of this framework appears in Table 3.1.

Absent from this framework is a category in which the needs of language minority students are simply ignored (i.e. sink-or-swim mainstream instruction), which Corson (2001) acknowledges is not uncommon. Corson deems Levels 4–6 as the 'fairer language policies', as they meet the three principles outlined previously. My analysis of Prop. 203, NCLB and AZ LEARNS will determine the level in which these policies (and their intersection) fall.

Kloss (1998 [1977]) developed a framework that is useful in identifying the overarching purposes of specific policies. Macias and Wiley (1998) and Wiley (2002) added two additional categories to the framework (numbers 5 and 6) to address what they identified as limitations in Kloss's original

Table 3.1 Classification of language policies in education

Recognition of students' needs	Policy response
(1) Students lack English.	Provide extra teaching in English as a second language.
(2) Students' need for English also linked to family status.	Provide assistance in adjusting to the majority society (aids, tutors, psychologists, social workers, career advisors, etc.)
(3) Students' need for English linked to disparities in esteem between their group's culture and the majority culture.	Provide multicultural education; sensitize teachers to minority needs.
(4) Premature loss of native language inhibits transition to English.	Provide transitional bilingual education.
(5) The minority groups' languages are threatened with extinction if they are not supported.	Provide developmental and maintenance bilingual education or native-language immersion programs.
(6) The minority and majority languages have equal rights in society, with special support available for the less viable languages.	Give minority language official status; provide opportunities for all children to learn both languages voluntarily; provide support beyond educational systems.

Notes: Adapted from Corson (2001: 102–103).

framework. Kloss's framework, as expanded by Macias and Wiley (1998), is as follows:

(1) *Promotion-oriented policies*: Active government agenda in which state resources are committed to advancing the official use of minority languages.
(2) *Accommodation (expediency)-oriented policies*: Accommodations to the use of a minority language without the intent of promoting it.
(3) *Tolerance-oriented policies*: Laissez faire. The significant absence of state interference in the linguistic life of the language-minority community.
(4) *Restricted-oriented policies*: Restrictions on the use of minority languages. May be accomplished by placing conditions on the attainment of social, political and economic benefits, rights and opportunities by tying them to the ability to use the dominant language.
(5) *Repression-oriented policies*: The state actively seeks the eradication of non-dominant languages.
(6) *Null policies*: The significant absence of policy recognizing minority languages or language varieties.

I utilize this framework to analyze the overall purposes, or results, of Prop. 203, NCLB and AZ LEARNS, and their intersection in Arizona's early school reform efforts.

Wiley (2000, 2002) makes an important distinction between explicit language policies and implicit or covert policies, which 'may not start out to be language policies, but have the effect of policy' (Wiley, 2002: 51). He argues that implicit or covert policies and informal practices 'can have the same, or even greater force than official [explicit] policies' (Wiley, 2002: 51). This distinction is important for analyzing how educational assessment policies such as NCLB and AZ LEARNS, while not explicitly language policies per se, nonetheless can have the same impact as or greater impact than explicit language policies such as Prop. 203.

Method

Data sources for this study include official policy texts and documents connected to the implementation of Prop. 203, AZ LEARNS and NCLB, media coverage of the implementation of these policies, and first-hand observations of policy-relevant events. Policy texts and documents were obtained from the US Department of Education, state and federal courts, and Arizona governmental offices, including the Department of Education, State School Board, State Legislature and Office of the Attorney General. Newspaper articles were gathered through extensive searches of the national and Arizona press using the LexisNexis and Newsbank databases. Policy documents and newspaper articles cover the years 1997–2004. Observations of policy events took place between 2000 and 2004 and include political debates, State Board of Education meetings, public hearings, official and informal presentations made by Arizona education officials, and training seminars offered by the Arizona Department of Education (ADE). Digital audio recordings and field notes of these observations were created. Electronic copies of all documents and news articles were obtained or created through scanning. These data were then imported into NVivo, a qualitative analysis software program. Analysis procedures followed those outlined by Yanow (2000) and Miles and Huberman (1994).

Background and Implementation of AZ LEARNS, *No Child Left Behind* and Proposition 203

In this section I briefly describe the requirements of each of the three policies and how these policies were being interpreted and implemented in Arizona in the early 2000s.

AZ LEARNS

AZ LEARNS was authorized by Arizona Revised Statutes (A.R.S.) §15241 in 2001. The individual components of AZ LEARNS predate the official authorization of the program by several years, including the Arizona's Instrument to Measure Standards (AIMS) test, the Stanford Achievement Test, 9th edn (SAT-9) and the Measure of Academic Progress (MAP). AZ LEARNS encompassed these and used their results to label schools and to provide a system of rewards and sanctions (ADE, 2003a).

The AIMS is a criterion-referenced test designed to measure the achievement in meeting state academic standards in math, reading and writing. The AIMS was first administered in the 1998–1999 school year. Prior to 2004 it was only administered in Grades 3, 5 and 8, and once in high school.

The state began developing Spanish-language versions of the AIMS test for Grades 3, 5 and 8, with a policy stating that eligible EL students could only take the test in Spanish once; thus, they would have to take the AIMS in English in subsequent administrations. However, the Spanish AIMS was abandoned following the passage of Prop. 203 (Associated Press, 1998). No efforts were made to develop a Spanish version of the AIMS at the high school level.

The high school AIMS test also functions as a graduation test (Associated Press, 1998). However, the use of AIMS as a high school exit exam had to be postponed several times due to substantially high failure rates (Kossan, 2000a, 2001b). In the first year, 88% of all sophomores and 97% of Hispanic, Black and Native American sophomores failed at least one section of the AIMS (Barrett & Pearce, 1999). Testing experts found that the state rushed the development and use of the AIMS, resulting in numerous problems, including overly difficult items, testing students on material they had not yet had the opportunity to learn, errors on the test, ambiguous questions, errors in scoring, and inappropriately set passing scores (Barrett & Pearce, 1999; Kossan, 2000b, 2004a; Pearce, 2000a, 2000b). As a result, the AIMS test has undergone numerous changes (Arizona State Board of Education, 2004; Kossan, 2004).

One superintendent of public instruction, Jaime Molera (who inherited the AIMS crisis from his predecessor), began efforts to create an alternative means for students who did not pass the AIMS to demonstrate proficiency in the state standards in order to obtain a high school diploma (Kossan, 2001a). This effort was dubbed the AIMS-Equivalency Demonstrated (AIMS-ED). However, the AIMS-ED, although never fully developed or implemented, was highly criticized by Molera's 2002 election opponent, Tom Horne, who ran on a platform of reinstating the AIMS as a high school exit exam as quickly as possible (Horne, 2001). Horne defeated Molera and immediately eliminated the AIMS-ED. Horne instituted other changes in an effort to make the AIMS test 'more reasonable' (Horne, 2003b, 2004), and AIMS became a high school graduation requirement again in 2006.[3]

The SAT-9 is a norm-referenced test that was used in Arizona from 1996 to 2005. Arizona students took the math, language and reading sections of the exam. Unlike the AIMS, no changes were made to the content of the SAT-9, although there was variation in terms of which grades were required to take it and which students must be included. Up until 2004, it was given to students in Grades 2–9, and first-graders only took the language section. For ELs with less than four years of enrollment, school districts used to have the option of administering the Spanish-language version called the Aprenda (2nd edn) or simply excluding ELs altogether and providing some form of alternative assessment (Keegan, 1999, 2000). Few districts actually provided this accommodation, and this option was no longer viable following the passage of Prop. 203.

The MAP, initiated in 2000, was calculated using SAT-9 scores and attempted to measure growth over time (Garcia & Aportela, 2000). While viewed as a fairer measure of progress, particularly for schools in low socio-economic status neighborhoods, calculating MAP proved to be problematic for many inner-city schools as well as charter schools, which traditionally had high rates of student mobility.

AZ LEARNS required the ADE to use data from the AIMS and SAT-9 (via MAP) to compile an 'annual academic achievement profile' and assign a label for each public school (ADE, 2003a; A.R.S. §15-241). The names of the labels have changed over time, but essentially consisted of a hierarchy of five classifications ranging from 'Underperforming' to 'Excelling', with schools obtaining a label of 'Underperforming' for two consecutive years obtaining the label of 'Failing'. 'Underperforming' schools were required to submit a school improvement plan to the ADE and to notify all residents in the school's neighborhood of the label and plan, and also were required to work with a state-assigned 'solutions team' (ADE, 2003a; A.R.S. §15-241). These solutions teams, according to the law, were comprised of master teachers, fiscal analysts and curriculum assessment experts. If a school failed to improve after working with the solutions team, it was subject to state take-over (ADE, 2003a).

When the first labels were assigned in 2002, only three schools in the state received the highest classification of 'Excelling', while 276 schools were designated as 'Underperforming'. State policy actors were uncomfortable with these results for a number of reasons, but particularly because of concern about the high costs involved in providing assistance to schools as required by the law (Kossan, 2003b). The following year, the state made several changes to the formulas and procedures used to assign labels, which made it easier to obtain the 'Excelling' label and more difficult to obtain the 'Underperforming' label. As a result, in 2003, 132 schools received the 'Excelling' designation, while the number of 'Underperforming' schools was reduced to 135 – a decrease of over 50% (Arizona State Board of Education, 2003; Kossan, 2003b).

A key component of the new formula was a change in how EL test scores affect a school's designation. For schools' aggregate AIMS test scores and MAP calculations, scores for ELs enrolled for three years or less were excluded (ADE, 2004). This policy change eliminated the scores of the majority of EL students – particularly, and most importantly, those at the lowest levels of English language proficiency. AZ LEARNS continued to undergo a number of changes to bring it into compliance with NCLB.

No Child Left Behind Act

NCLB is President George W. Bush's reauthorization of the Elementary and Secondary Education Act (ESEA). It was signed into law by President Bush in January 2002 as Public Law 107–110. The stated purpose of the act is 'to close the achievement gap with accountability, flexibility and choice, so that no child is left behind' (preamble to Section 1). NCLB is a highly complex law, comprising nearly 700 pages of federal regulations for states that accept federal education funding (which all currently do). While President Obama and members of Congress from both major parties have publically acknowledged that NCLB has proven to be deeply flawed and ineffective, at the time of this writing the law remains in effect despite the fact that it is long overdue for reauthorization. In this study, I focus only on the testing and accountability components of NCLB.

Title I and Title III of NCLB

Title I mandates annual student testing of all students in Grades 3–8, and once in high school. Rather than creating a national test, Title I requires each state to create its own academic content and achievement standards, create assessments to measure those standards, and use the results to hold schools accountable. Assessments must cover math, reading or language arts, and science. The state must issue individual student reports, and also school and district 'report cards' annually that include the results of these tests. NCLB does not require a high school exit exam. However, a non-regulatory guidance document issued by the US Department of Education (2003b) indicates that states may use their tests for this purpose if they so desire.

All students are expected to meet or exceed the state's academic standards by 2014. In other words, by 2014, it is expected that 100% of students will pass their state's test. Test score data must be disaggregated into different subgroups, including 'gender, each major racial and ethnic group, migrant status, students with disabilities, students with limited English proficiency, and economically disadvantaged students' (US Department of Education, 2003b: 11). For each of these subgroups, states and local education agencies must establish baseline data, and then set annual measurable achievement objectives (AMAOs) relative to ensuring that all subgroups will be 100% proficient in the standards by 2014. A subgroup is deemed as making adequate yearly progress (AYP) if it meets or exceeds that year's AMAO. In addition, to be deemed as making AYP, at least 95% of the students in the subgroup must be tested each year. Thus, if a subgroup does not reach the AMAO, or if fewer than 95% of the students in that group take the test, that subgroup is deemed as 'Failing' to make AYP. Furthermore, schools and school districts are held accountable for ensuring that each subgroup reaches the AMAO. If any one of its subgroups does not, then the entire school or district is deemed as 'Failing' to make AYP. If the school continues to be deemed as 'Failing', the state may ultimately take it over.

Title I originally required that students classified as limited English proficient (LEP) be included in state testing, regardless of their English-language proficiency or how long they have been in the United States. This mandate was eventually loosened a little for LEP students who had been in the US for less than one year; they could be excluded from the state reading test and, while still required to take the state math test, their scores could be excluded from school AYP calculations. All other LEP students, however, were required to take all state tests and their scores did count for AYP purposes. States are required to assess LEP students 'in a valid and reliable manner' and must also provide 'reasonable accommodations'. The non-regulatory guidelines (US Department of Education, 2003b) suggest that accommodations for LEP students may include extra time, small-group administration, flexible scheduling, simplified instructions, audio-taped instructions in the native language or English, or additional clarifying information.

'Reasonable accommodations' for LEP students also include, 'to the extent practicable, assessments in the language and form most likely to yield accurate data on what such students know and can do in academic content areas, until such students have achieved English language proficiency' (Title I, p. 115, Stat. 1451). After the first three years of LEP students' enrollment in a US school, they must be assessed in English on reading or language arts. However, schools may extend testing in the native language for two additional years on an individual case-by-case basis, if they determine this would 'yield more accurate and reliable information' (Title I, p. 115, Stat. 1451). The non-regulatory guidelines (US Department of Education, 2003b) make clear that native language assessments are only required 'to the extent practicable', but otherwise states must offer 'other appropriate accommodations in order to yield accurate and reliable information on what those students know and can do in subjects other than English' (US Department of Education, 2003b: 20).

Title III, 'Language Instruction for Limited English Proficient and Immigrant Students', provides block grants to states, and each state in turn provides subgrants to all districts (and charters) that submit applications for the funds. Title III requires that LEP students be placed in a 'language instruction educational program', defined as an instructional course

> in which a limited English proficient child is placed for the purpose of developing and attaining English proficiency, while meeting challenging State academic content and student academic achievement standards, ... and that may make instructional use of both English and a child's native language to enable the child to develop and attain English proficiency, and may include the participation of English proficient children if such course is designed to enable all participating children to become proficient in English and a second language. (Title III, p. 115, Stat. 1730–1731)

Thus, without referring to these programs by name, Title III permits TBE and dual immersion programs. It also allows for a wide variety of other approaches that do not necessarily make use of a student's first language. This flexibility, along with compliance with state law, is stressed in the non-regulatory guidance document for Title III (US Department of Education, 2003a: 4):

> [A local education agency] may select one or more methods of instruction – consistent with the requirements of State law – to be used in assisting LEP students to attain English proficiency and meet State content and student academic achievement standards. However, the language instruction curriculum used must be tied to scientifically based research on teaching LEP students and must have demonstrated effectiveness.

Title III requires states to develop English-language proficiency standards and English-language proficiency assessments designed to measure LEP students' progress in attaining those standards. The English-language proficiency assessments must be given annually. As with the content assessments, states, districts and schools must set AMAOs and are held accountable for students making AYP in achieving those objectives.

To comply with NCLB, Arizona had to revamp its academic standards, develop science tests, create EL standards and develop a statewide English language proficiency exam. As the AIMS test was only given in Grades 3, 5 and 8 and high school, the state had to create new tests for Grades 4, 6 and 7. Rather than continuing to give both the AIMS and the SAT-9, the state decided to create a combined criterion-referenced and norm-referenced test, called the AIMS-Dual Purpose Assessment (DPA) (Arizona State Board of Education, 2003). The state rushed the development of the AIMS-DPA and administered it for the first time in 2004. As with the previous AIMS exams, the failure rates were extremely high: 70% of high school juniors (who were required to pass the test to graduate in 2006) failed one or more sections of the AIMS (Kossan, 2004d). This led to renewed concerns about the use of the test as a graduation requirement, but the state resisted pressure from parents and educators to postpone this requirement.

While NCLB requires that LEP students be included in statewide tests, the ADE adopted a special rule on minimum group size, which impacts the calculation of AYP for LEP students and other subgroups. This special rule was approved by the State Board of Education and reads as follows:

> A group or subgroup was not evaluated [for AYP] if it had less than 30 test scores that met the selection criteria. Thirty is the sample size conventionally considered large enough to provide statistically meaningful results. (ADE, 2003b: 19)

In other words, a school would not be required to track a subgroup's progress on meeting AYP if the subgroup (at each grade and for each test section) had fewer than 30 students. Thus, for example, if a school had 29 or fewer LEP students in third grade, the school would not have to calculate AYP for the LEP subgroup, and thus the LEP subgroup would not be included in the determination of the school's AYP. According to the Arizona Republic, this change alone prevented around 680 Arizona schools from being designated as 'Failing' under NCLB (Kossan, 2004b). In addition, 'the state doesn't count the test scores of students who are in their first three years of learning English' (Kossan, 2004b: B1). This allowance did not appear in any official documents, but Arizona officials claimed it was negotiated with federal education officials (Kossan, 2004b: B1) – a claim later denied by the US Department of Education who found the state out of compliance with the EL testing mandate in 2005. Nonetheless, Arizona continued to illegally use the same exclusion mechanism for EL test scores for NCLB that it did for AZ LEARNS (upon appeal from the schools).[4] Thus, EL students with less than four years of enrollment were still required to take the AIMS test, but their scores were excluded from both AZ LEARNS and NCLB accountability and labeling calculations.

Proposition 203

Prop. 203, 'English for the Children' (also known as the 'Unz Initiative'), is a voter initiative passed on 7 November 2000, by 63% of the electorate. It replaced statutes authorizing bilingual and ESL programs. The law's most basic requirement is as follows:

> Children in Arizona public schools shall be taught English by being taught in English and all children shall be placed in English language classrooms. Children who are English learners shall be educated through sheltered English immersion during a temporary transition period not normally intended to exceed one year. (A.R.S. §15-752)

The law's definition states:

> [Sheltered (or structured) English immersion (SEI) is] an English language acquisition process for young children in which nearly all classroom instruction is in English but with the curriculum and presentation designed for children who are learning the language. Books and instructional materials are in English and all reading, writing, and subject matter are taught in English. (A.R.S. §15-751)

This definition merely emphasizes the language of instruction. For several years, the state failed to provide a working definition of SEI other than just teaching ELs in English.

One misconception is that Prop. 203 does not allow any use of a student's native language. However, accommodation in the form of primary language support is allowed. The law states that 'teachers may use a minimal amount of the child's native language when necessary', with the qualification that 'no subject matter shall be taught in any language other than English, and children in this program learn to read and write solely in English' (A.R.S. §15-751).

Bilingual education for ELs is allowed through waiver provisions in which parents can request that their children be waived from the requirements outlined above. In order to obtain a waiver, the parent(s) must visit the school in person each year to apply. The school is required to provide parents with a full description of the different program choices and the materials used in those programs. If a waiver is granted, then the child is to be transferred to 'classes teaching English and other subjects through bilingual education techniques' (A.R.S. §15-753). Schools are required to offer a bilingual class when 20 or more waivers have been granted to students at the same grade level. If the school does not have enough waivers to offer a bilingual class, the student may transfer to a school where bilingual classes are offered. There are three circumstances in which waivers may be granted:

(1)   Children already know English.
(2)   Children are 10 years or older.
(3)   Children have special individual needs.

Qualification for waiver Provision 1 is determined by English-language proficiency tests. A student is deemed as possessing 'good English language skills' if the child 'scores approximately at or above the state average for his grade level or at or above the 5th grade average, whichever is lower' (A.R.S. §15-753). For waiver Provision 3, the law clarifies that the special individual needs must be 'above and beyond the child's lack of English proficiency' (A.R.S. §15-753). Furthermore, 'a written description of no less than 250 words documenting these special individual needs for the specific child must be provided' (A.R.S. §15-753). The waiver must be approved via signatures of both the school principal and local superintendent. Even if parents go through all this trouble, the law declares that 'teachers and local school districts may reject waiver requests without explanation or legal consequence' (A.R.S. §15-753). Thus, while bilingual education is technically possible, these waiver provisions were designed to make it extremely difficult, if not impossible, for parents to receive this accommodation for their children (see below).

Prop. 203 also requires the administration of a national norm-referenced test each year – in English – to all students in Grades 2–9. ELs must be included, and only students with severe learning disabilities may be excluded. The state is required to release the results to the public and to provide disaggregated scores for students classified as 'limited-English'. The law does not specify how the results are to be used other than 'monitoring educational progress', but it authorizes state and local officials to use the results for other purposes 'if they so choose' (A.R.S. §15-755). Arizona previously used the SAT-9 for this purpose, but later used the AIMS-DPA, which includes a norm-referenced component. However, as the AIMS-DPA test is not given in Grades 2 or 9, the state adopted the TerraNova, just for these grades, to comply with this mandate.

Until around 2006, the implementation of Prop. 203 varied greatly (Wright, 2005). When it first passed, then-Superintendent of Public Instruction Lisa Graham Keegan showed little interest in it, issued little guidance to school districts in terms of how to comply with the law, and literally told school district leaders that they could interpret it any way they liked (Arizona Republic, 2001). As a result, implementation varied widely across the state (Zehr, 2001). Keegan resigned in 2001 and was replaced by Jaime Molera, who was appointed by the governor. Molera recognized the ambiguous nature of the poorly written law, but nonetheless he answered the call from school districts for state guidance in implementing Prop. 203. Molera (2001) issued a substantive guidance document, and the ADE provided assistance to school districts in complying with the law. These guidelines made it clear, however, that bilingual programs were allowed through the waiver process outlined in the law, and thus several districts were able to continue their programs.

The situation in Arizona changed dramatically, however, following the election of Superintendent Tom Horne, who took office in January 2003. Horne received the endorsement of Ron Unz and local leaders of English for the Children (Davenport, 2002), and he ran an aggressive media campaign accusing Molera of refusing to enforce Prop. 203 (Corella, 2002). Once in office, Horne appointed Margaret Garcia Dugan – the local co-chair of Prop. 203 – as an associate superintendent with responsibility over EL programs (Horne, 2003c). Thus, Prop. 203's chief proponent became its chief enforcer.

Horne and Dugan (2003) issued new guidelines regarding waivers for bilingual education, which essentially made it impossible for EL students in Grades K–3 to qualify for a waiver. They made it clear that these new guidelines also applied to charter schools, which by definition are generally free from most state school regulations. Despite two opinions issued by the state Office of the Attorney General that questioned both the legality of Horne and Dugan's interpretation (Goddard, 2003b) and the guidelines' application to charter schools (Goddard, 2003a), Horne and Dugan managed to enforce strict compliance by threatening to withhold EL funds from any district that did not comply with their new guidelines (Associated Press, 2003; Kossan, 2003a). Furthermore, Horne and Dugan announced the hiring of 45 monitors to 'police bilingual' (Horne, 2003a). These monitors, and Dugan herself, personally visit schools and classrooms to ensure strict compliance (Ruelas, 2003).

Horne and Dugan have also attempted to skirt around a previous Attorney General opinion (Napolitano, 2001) exempting public schools on Indian reservations from Prop. 203. This opinion recognized these schools' efforts to revitalize endangered Native American languages that are protected by federal law. Nonetheless, Dugan issued her own interpretation of the Attorney General opinion, claiming that these schools are still subject to Prop. 203 (Donovan, 2004). Tribal leaders contested Dugan's efforts to shut down their programs.

As a result of Horne and Dugan's strict interpretation and implementation of Prop. 203, only a handful of bilingual programs remain. Most of the surviving programs are dual immersion classes. The irony is that ELs under 10 cannot be in a bilingual program unless they are designated as fluent English proficient (FEP), meaning they are no longer EL students. And if they are not EL students, there is no need to obtain a waiver, as waivers are only for ELs. Thus, the waiver provisions create the illusion of an accommodation that simply does not exist, and the few remaining bilingual programs in Grades K–3 do not contain any EL students. A few bilingual programs for students 10 years and older remain. However, Dugan attempted to go after these programs as well (see Judson & Dugan, 2004).

Analysis

My analysis of the formality or explicitness and the goals and effects of the various mandates and implementations of Prop. 203, NCLB and AZ LEARNS are summarized in Table 3.2.

Prop. 203, as a whole, is clearly an explicit and restricted-oriented language policy. The requirement for sheltered English immersion means that instruction in any language other than English for ELs is prohibited. The waiver provisions appeared to be an accommodation-oriented policy;

Table 3.2 Formality or explicitness and policy goals and effects of Prop. 203, AZ LEARNS and NCLB

Policy	Formality	Goal/Effect
Prop. 203		
Sheltered English immersion	Explicit	Restricted-oriented
Waiver provisions	Explicit and implicit (covert)	Restricted-oriented
Horne and Dugan's waiver regulations	Explicit	Restricted-oriented
Norm-referenced testing in English (Stanford Achievement Test, 9th edn/TerraNova)	Null and implicit	Restricted-oriented
Monitors	Explicit	Restricted-oriented
Allowances for bilingual programs for fluent English proficient students	Explicit and implicit (covert)	Tolerance-oriented
Attorney General opinion – Native Americans	Explicit	Tolerance-oriented
Attorney General opinion – Charter schools	Explicit	Tolerance-oriented
Enforcement on Indian Reservations	Explicit and implicit	Restricted- and repression-oriented
NCLB and Title III		
English language proficiency (ELP) standards	Explicit	Restricted-oriented
English language proficiency assessment	Explicit	Restricted-oriented
High-quality language instruction program	Explicit	Accommodation-oriented and restricted-oriented
Academic testing requirements of AZ LEARNS and NCLB		
High school graduation test (Arizona's Instrument to Measure Standards [AIMS])	Null and implicit (embedded)	Restricted-oriented
Initial allowances for native-language testing, exclusions	Explicit	Accommodation-oriented
High-stakes testing in English (AIMS)	Null and implicit (embedded)	Restricted-oriented
Native-language testing to the extent practicable	Explicit	Accommodation-oriented

(continued)

Table 3.2 (*Continued*)

Policy	Formality	Goal/Effect
Reasonable accommodations	Explicit	Accommodation-oriented
AIMS-Equivalency demonstrated	Null	Accommodation-oriented
Solution teams	Null	Restricted-oriented?
Exclusion of EL test scores in accountability formulas	Explicit and implicit (covert)	Accommodation-oriented and restricted-oriented

however, they were written in a manner that made them extremely difficult to obtain. In reality, the waiver provisions were implicitly and covertly a restricted-oriented policy. Horne and Dugan's new guidelines, which attempt to close the loopholes in the waiver provisions, are explicitly restricted oriented, as was their use of monitors to enforce strict compliance. The requirement to include ELs in norm-referenced tests was in part a null policy, as these tests were not developed for or normed on EL students. However, I argue that this policy is implicitly and covertly a restricted-oriented policy. Previous research in California showed that the pressure to prepare EL students for English-language high-stakes tests led many districts to reduce or eliminate their bilingual programs (Garcia, 2000; Wright, 2003). Hence, mandating this in Arizona would further encourage school districts toward English-only programs.

The Attorney General opinions excluding charter schools and Native American students from Prop. 203 represented attempts at more tolerance-oriented policies, even though these opinions were ignored by ADE leaders. Given the fact that Native American languages are endangered and school programs represent one of the few hopes of preventing the death of these languages, I classify Dugan's attempt to enforce Prop. 203 on the Indian reservations as a repression-oriented policy. Finally, the allowances for bilingual programs to serve FEP students represents an explicit tolerance-oriented policy. Nonetheless, I also classify it as an implicit (covert) policy, given the fact that bilingual programs were initially designed for EL students. This new policy means that dual language programs now consist of English-only students and students who are already bilingual and proficient in English. As the original intent of dual language programs is to help both ELs and English-only students become bilingual, it appears now that the benefit is mostly going to the English-only students, given the fact that the other students are already bilingual.

Title III of NCLB, in general, is an explicit restricted-oriented policy. I classify it as such because its focus is clearly on English, as evidenced by the requirements for EL standards and English-language proficiency assessments, rather than developing or promoting bilingualism. This stands in contrast to its predecessor, Title VII (the Bilingual Education Act), in which funds were provided specifically for bilingual education programs. While Title III's definition of high-quality language instruction programs does not preclude transitional or dual immersion bilingual programs, it can be considered an accommodation-oriented policy. However, it is better classified as restricted oriented as it avoids the term 'bilingual education' altogether and gives states leeway to restrict bilingual approaches.

The testing requirements of AZ LEARNS and Title I of NCLB are also, for the most part, restricted-oriented policies. Earlier assessment policy in Arizona contained explicit accommodation-oriented policies, including possibilities for native-language testing (which NCLB also allows) on both the AIMS test and the SAT-9, and the ability to exclude ELs from the SAT-9 for up to the first three years of enrollment. However, the use of the English-only high school AIMS test as a graduation requirement in high school functions as null language policy because it fails to take into consideration the needs of EL students. It also functions as an implicit restricted-oriented language policy because ELs will nonetheless have to pass it in order to obtain a high school diploma. Thus, this policy is creating a situation where students who are not yet fluent in English may not only be denied a high school diploma but also all of the social benefits that come with it, such as higher paying jobs and the ability to pursue higher education. Furthermore, given the high stakes associated with the AIMS, teachers may be more prone to spending classroom time teaching to the test rather than providing linguistically and culturally appropriate instruction for their EL students (Wright, 2002). The use of 'solutions teams' to assist 'underperforming schools' is null policy at best. These teams are spending minimal amounts of time at the schools they are assigned to help, and many of these schools have large EL student populations, yet the law does not require team members to have any relevant experience or expertise with EL students (Wright, 2005).

NCLB's requirement to provide reasonable accommodations is obviously an explicit accommodation-oriented policy. However, the law does not specify what 'reasonable' means or what accommodations are allowed. In addition, states are under no obligation to report what accommodations they provide for ELs. Thus, with no enforcement mechanisms, there is no guarantee that ELs will be accommodated on the tests. Arizona did not have a well-articulated statewide accommodation policy for ELs, and instead placed the onus on individual school districts. As a result, practice varied widely across the state, with many districts providing no accommodations whatsoever.

Regardless, the issue of providing accommodations is problematic in several ways. First, accommodations are very difficult to provide, and those viewed as the most beneficial are typically the most expensive (LaCelle-Peterson & Rivera, 1994). Second, providing accommodations can affect the validity and reliability of the test scores, as the accommodation may provide an unfair advantage over those students who do not receive the accommodation (Gottlieb, 2003; Linn, 2002). Finally, to date, research simply has not been able to show which accommodations are the most beneficial without affecting validity. Thus, the testing accommodation policy of NCLB requires schools to implement practices for which there is no research base (Abedi, 2003, 2004; Menken, 2008; Rivera, 2002; Rivera *et al.*, 1997). In other words, NCLB's mandate to assess ELs in a 'valid and reliable manner' is nearly impossible.

Ironically, the ADE currently provides the most extensive explicit, accommodation-oriented policy to date, in terms of the inclusion of ELs on high-stakes tests, with its policy to exclude the test scores of EL students with less than four years of enrollment. This policy ensures that EL test scores have a minimal impact on the schools' accountability calculations, which means the labels assigned to schools are not reflective of how effective these schools are with their EL student populations. In addition, the exclusion of LEP subgroups smaller than 30 in each grade level tested at each school means the school's AYP designation ('makes' or 'fails') may likewise be completely unreflective of the school's progress with its ELs.

With this policy, the ADE acknowledged that test scores of EL students on tests administered only in English are not valid and should not be used in judging the quality of a school. Thus, it may be a worthwhile accommodation. However, the question must be asked, whom does this policy actually accommodate and benefit? The EL students are still subjected to hours of testing in a language in which they are not yet proficient, even when the state has little interest in and places little value on their scores. The students and their parents still receive individual student reports that claim to make some sort of statement about the children's achievement and ability, even though the state considers their scores invalid. In addition, few classroom teachers realize most EL scores are excluded. Nonetheless, they feel great pressure to spend hours of classroom instruction to prepare their EL students for the test, rather than providing instruction that is more attuned to their linguistic and academic needs (Wright & Choi, 2006).

If the scores of most ELs do not count, then why make them take the tests? It appears this accommodation mostly benefits state-level policy actors. Superintendent Horne frequently declared that enforcing Prop. 203 to eliminate bilingual education would ensure that EL students would 'soar academically' (Wright & Pu, 2005). That didn't happen. However, the dramatic changes in the AZ LEARNS accountability formula – in which the exclusion of EL scores plays a key role – resulted in a much rosier picture of education in Arizona. Besides a less embarrassing number of 'Underperforming' schools that the state has to pay money to assist, there is one other important benefit. The elimination of bilingual education (and ESL), the imposition of the ill-defined SEI model, and the efforts to legally legitimize the placing of EL students in mainstream classrooms indeed had a negative impact on the academic achievement of EL students (Wright & Pu, 2005). However, the exclusion of EL scores from the accountability program enabled state education leaders to mask this failure. In other words, the negative impact of the ADE's early policies were not immediately reflected in school test scores or labels. Thus, the ADE leaders at the time could to point to rising (aggregate) test scores and schools with impressive-sounding labels, and declare these as evidence that their restricted-oriented policies were improving the education of EL students (Wright & Pu, 2005).

Nullification of Accommodations

In the intersection of Prop. 203, AZ LEARNS and NCLB, most of the accommodation- and tolerance-oriented provisions in each of these policies became nullified. Table 3.3 provides a summary of the nullification of these accommodations, and additional accommodations that were introduced but nullified under the subsequent interpretations and implementations of these policies.

Prop. 203 had few accommodation-oriented policies to begin with. As mentioned earlier, the waiver provisions are an illusion of an accommodation that does not exist. The Attorney General opinions excluding charter schools and schools on Native American reservations were nullified by Horne and Dugan's interpretation and enforcement. Finally, the law's allowance for primary-language support is rarely mentioned by ADE officials, to the point that many teachers believe that Prop. 203 outlaws any use of the students' native language(s) (Wright & Choi, 2006). Evidence of this emerged in the case of a Scottsdale middle school teacher who was fired for hitting students who were speaking Spanish (Ryman, 2004). In defense, the teacher claimed she was enforcing Prop. 203. In response to this incident, Superintendent Horne stated that if the teacher did indeed hit children, she deserved to be fired, but nonetheless declared that she was correct in insisting her EL students speak English (Ryman & Madrid, 2004). This further perpetuated the view that languages other than English were not allowed in the classroom. Furthermore, Prop. 203 monitoring teams from the ADE observed classroom teachers to make sure that their instruction was only in English, and also to ensure that students in the class were only speaking in English (despite the fact that Prop. 203 only addresses the language used by the teacher).

Prop. 203 has also nullified many of the accommodation-oriented policies of AZ LEARNS and NCLB. Previous policies allowing Spanish versions of the AIMS and SAT-9 were discontinued after the passage of Prop. 203, and even though NCLB allows for native-language testing up to five years, this option is no longer viable in Arizona. Title III's allowance for transitional and dual immersion programs for ELs is also nullified by Prop. 203. While testing accommodations for ELs are left up to individual school districts, those

Table 3.3 Reality and nullifications of accommodation- or tolerance-oriented policy provisions of Prop. 203, AZ LEARNS and NCLB

Accommodation- or tolerance-oriented policy provisions	Reality	Nullification	Comments
Prop. 203			
Waivers for bilingual education	Made intentionally difficult to get	Horne and Dugan's waiver regulations	Local Prop. 203 chairperson becomes chief enforcer
Does not apply to charter schools	Opinion of Attorney General	Horne's threat to withhold funds	
Does not apply to Indian Reservations	Opinion of Attorney General	Dugan's letter, Horne's threat to withhold funds	Tribal leaders challenged Dugan
Primary language support	Not stressed by ADE	Prop. 203 monitors discourage it	Many teachers unaware of option
AZ LEARNS			
Exclusions from Stanford Achievement Test, 9th edn (SAT-9) up to 3 years	Most ELs were still included	Prop. 203	
SAT-9 in Spanish (Aprenda)	Less than 15% of ELs took it	Prop. 203	
Arizona's Instrument to Measure Standards (AIMS) in Spanish, Grades 3, 5 and 8	Quality issues, never fully developed, small percentage took it	Prop. 203	
Testing accommodations	Absence of clear state policy	Prop. 203 (nullifying native-language linguistic accommodations)	Required by NCLB but not specified
Exclusion of EL scores under 4 years of enrollment	Benefits the state-level policy actors, not the ELs	N/A	Masks the harmful effects of restricted-oriented policies

Table 3.3 (*Continued*)

Accommodation- or tolerance-oriented policy provisions	Reality	Nullification	Comments
NCLB			
Transitional, dual immersion programs	High-stakes test in English discourage it	Prop. 203	
Testing in native language	Allowed 'to the extent practicable'	Prop. 203	
'Reasonable' testing accommodations	Not defined, left up to state; no research to support practice; validity problems	Prop. 203 (nullifying native-language linguistic accommodations)	Least beneficial non-linguistic accommodations remain
Minimum subgroup size = 30 for adequate yearly progress	Benefits the state-level policy actors, not the ELs	N/A	
Exclusion of EL scores under 4 years of enrollment	Benefits the state-level policy actors, not the ELs	N/A	

accommodations that directly address the language issues of ELs are no longer viable options. The remaining accommodations districts may choose to use are mainly non-linguistic and, thus, less helpful. The other remaining accommodation of excluding EL scores from school accountability formulas, as described previously, is of little benefit to the EL students.

Conclusions

The purpose of education reform is to improve schooling for all students. The language and assessment policies of NCLB, AZ LEARNS and Prop. 203 are major components of early educational reform efforts in Arizona, each of which had a direct impact on the education of EL students. The analysis above reveals that, from the perspective of language policy frameworks, most of the mandates associated with these policies fall under the category of restricted-oriented language policies. These policies did little to promote, or even tolerate, the native languages of EL students, but rather served to restrict their use in instructional settings. The restrictive nature of these policies was intensified as the policies intersected at the level of interpretation and implementation.

These increased restrictions were due particularly to the fact that accommodations for EL students allowed by one policy became nullified by restrictions in others. Further nullifications were created as subsequent policy actors at the state level implemented their own strict interpretations of these policies. The result was that EL students in Arizona classrooms were afforded far fewer accommodations than allowed previously, at a time when the stakes had never been higher for EL students and their schools.

Although ELs were still forced to take the tests, and schools and teachers were still required to prepare them for these tests, the state created the means by which the majority of EL test scores were removed from school accountability formulas under both AZ LEARNS and NCLB. This accommodation was of little benefit to the ELs themselves. Rather, this accommodation benefited state-level policy actors who are able to mask the harm being done to EL students through their restricted-oriented policies and nullification of meaningful accommodations. Thus, while an illusion had been created of a greater number of 'Excelling' schools and a decrease in the number of 'Underperforming' and 'Failing' schools, a large number of EL students were, and still are, being left behind. Accordingly, Arizona ranks at the bottom (Level 1) of Corson's (2001) classifications of educational language policies (if ELs lack English, provide ESL instruction). A strong case can be made, however, that in reality the initial implementation of SEI instruction was actually nothing more than sink-or-swim mainstream instruction (Wright & Choi, 2006), and thus Arizona fails to even qualify for Level 1 status.

The effects of many of these policy gimmicks to mask inadequate education for ELs, however, have proved to be temporary. For example, Arizona recently experienced a major spike in the number of its schools designated as failing to make AYP under NCLB – 814 schools in 2011 compared to 563 schools the year before (Kossan & Konig, 2011).[5] Even before this spike, however, Arizona education officials could no longer ignore the widespread underachievement of its EL students. In addition, the *Flores v. Arizona* case continued to draw attention to the state's failure to adequately meet the needs of its EL students (see Hogan, Chapter 2, this volume). The state was compelled to move away from its previous ill-conceived SEI model, which essentially had been defined as simply 'teaching ELs in English', to a highly structured SEI four-hour block model, which they hoped would make ELs learn English faster so they could better handle English-only instruction and pass the AIMS test sooner. This new SEI model has also proved to be highly problematic, as will be detailed in subsequent chapters of this book (see Moore, Chapter 4, Markos & Arias, Chapter 5, Grijalva & Jimenez-Silva, Chapter 6, and Lillie & Markos, Chapter 7, this volume). Nonetheless, this change provides evidence of the failure of these earlier school reform efforts, and the desperation educational leaders must have felt in attempting to undo some of the damage. After all, if ELs were truly 'soaring academically' as Horne had promised, why would radical changes to the SEI model be needed?

Unfortunately, Arizona's more recent efforts to make Prop. 203, SEI and high-stakes testing work are as ill-informed as the earlier school reform efforts. The situation for ELs in Arizona could be improved easily if Prop. 203 were eliminated, or at least if state education leaders stopped interpreting it so narrowly and allowed schools greater flexibility in terms of offering quality ESL and bilingual education programs. The state's policy of removing most EL scores from school accountability formulas could have been used in a manner more beneficial to ELs. For example, the policy could have been clearly articulated to school leaders and classroom teachers so that they did not feel undue pressure to dedicate so much classroom instruction time to preparing ELs for tests in which the students could not reasonably perform well. Combined with the elimination of Prop. 203, this would have allowed schools to instead focus on the language, literacy, academic and cultural needs of their EL students. This also would have given EL students the gift of time to learn English and academic content before their scores on high-stakes English-only tests really count.

Better yet would be the repeal of the high-stakes testing policy as well, or at least the repeal of the high stakes associated with the tests. Researchers have long pointed out fundamental flaws within NCLB that had the potential of eventually labeling most schools as 'Failing', particularly those schools with EL students (Abedi, 2003; Wiley & Wright, 2004). Policymakers are now facing this reality. In 2011, US Secretary of Education Arne Duncan warned Congress that, unless changes were made to NCLB, 'the country is on track to see 82% of its schools labeled "failing" this year' (McNell, 2011: 1). At the time of this writing, the serious work of 'fixing NCLB' through the reauthorization of the ESEA has yet to be done. Initial proposals from the Obama administration have not, unfortunately, backed away from the reliance on high-stakes tests, and their insistence that test scores be tied directly to teacher evaluations could make the problem even worse. Nonetheless, there does appear to be general agreement about the need to address the technical flaws in the accountability provisions of the law and to make the law more flexible in terms of how ELs are included in state testing programs.

If Prop. 203 were to be repealed, if the flaws in NCLB were to be removed, and if the pressure to teach to an English-only test were to be eliminated, Arizona schools and teachers would have an opportunity to focus on providing the types of quality educational programs that meet the three policy principles outlined by Corson (2001), which would provide students the opportunity to become fully bilingual and biliterate in both their native language(s) and English. Such policy changes would move Arizona near the top of Corson's classification system, and thus represent better quality and more equitable education programs for EL students.

Notes

(1) The original version of this study was published in the *Bilingual Research Journal*. It has been revised and updated for this chapter. Original publication: Wright, W.E. (2005) English language learners left behind in Arizona: The nullification of accommodations in the intersection of federal and state policies. *Bilingual Research Journal* 25 (1), 1–29.
(2) In this article, the terms English Language Learners (EL) and Limited English Proficient (LEP) students will be used interchangeably. While EL is a much preferred label over the deficit-oriented LEP label, the LEP term is used when discussing federal policy documents as this is the official label used within these documents.
(3) While Superintendent Horne made a political showcase of shutting down efforts to develop an alternative to passing the AIMS test to earn a high school diploma, four different alternatives to the AIMS were eventually authorized via state statutes during Horne's term in office. See http://www.azed.gov/wp-content/uploads/PDF/AIMSHSGraduationOverview.pdf.
(4) The ADE's failure to comply with NCLB's mandate for including EL scores in AYP calculations resulted in the US Department of Education rejecting Arizona's proposal for a growth-based accountability model pilot project in 2006. See the rejection letter at http://www2.ed.gov/admins/lead/account/growthmodel/az/azgmdecltr.pdf.
(5) The large spike in schools failing to make AYP is also the result of Arizona's early efforts to delay the impact of NCLB by setting low AMAOs for several years, in the hope that the law would be changed prior to the point when the vast majority of students would be required to pass the AIMS test in order to be deemed as making AYP toward the goal of 100% proficiency by 2014. While the growing failure rate is just as much an indication of the unrealistic expectations of NCLB, the poor academic achievement of EL students whose needs have been ignored are likely contributing to the rapidly increasing number of failing schools.

References

Abedi, J. (2003) Standardized achievement tests and English language learners: Psychometric issues. *Educational Assessment* 8 (3), 231–258.
Abedi, J. (2004) The No Child Left Behind Act and English learners: Assessment and accountability issues. *Educational Researcher* 33 (1), 4–14.
ADE (2003a) *Arizona LEARNS: A Step-by-step Guide to Calculating an Achievement Profile*. Phoenix, AZ: Arizona Department of Education Research & Policy.
ADE (2003b) *State of Arizona Consolidated State Application Accountability Workbook*. Phoenix, AZ: Arizona Department of Education.
ADE (2004) *Arizona's School Accountability System Technical Manual: Vol. I. Arizona Learns Achievement Profiles*. Phoenix, AZ: Arizona Department of Education.
Arizona Republic (2001) Editorial. Bilingual legal muddle has schools under fire: Federal intimidation, lack of local leadership. *Arizona Republic*, 23 January.
Arizona State Board of Education (2003) *State Board of Education Minutes, 17 November*. Phoenix, AZ: Arizona Department of Education.

Arizona State Board of Education (2004) *State Board of Education Minutes, 26 January*. Phoenix, AZ: Arizona Department of Education.

Arizona Voter Initiative (2000) Proposition 203, *English for the Children*. See http://www.azed.gov/wp-content/uploads/PDF/PROPOSITION203.pdf.

A.R.S. (2001) AZ LEARNS. School Accountability, Arizona Revised Statutes §15-241.

Associated Press (1998) High school AIMS test to be in English, board says. *Arizona Republic*, 27 October, p. B3.

Associated Press (2003) Bilingual classes ending in Tucson. *Arizona Republic*, 1 September.

August, D. and Hakuta, K. (1997) *Improving Schooling for Language-minority Children: A Research Agenda*. Washington, DC: National Academy Press.

Barrett, J. and Pearce, K. (1999) Some items not covered in class. *Arizona Republic*, 17 November, p. A1.

California Voter Initiative (1998) Proposition 227, *English for the Children*.

Churchill, S. (1986) *The Education of Linguistic and Cultural Minorities in OECD Countries*. Clevedon: Multilingual Matters.

Cook, H.G., Boals, T. and Lundberg, T. (2011) Academic achievement for English learners: What can we reasonably expect? *Phi Delta Kappan* 93 (3), 66–69.

Corella, H.R. (2002) Horne raises AIMS, bilingual ed issues in commercial. *Arizona Daily Star*, 2 September.

Corson, D. (2001) *Language Diversity and Education*. Mahwah, NJ: Lawrence Erlbaum.

Crawford, J. (2000) *At War with Diversity: US Language Policy in an Age of Anxiety*. Clevedon: Multilingual Matters.

Crawford, J. (2004) *Educating English Learners: Language Diversity in the Classroom* (5th edn). Los Angeles, CA: Bilingual Education Services.

Davenport, P. (2002) English education backer endorses Horne, criticizes Molera. *Associated Press State & Local Wire*, 11 July.

Deschenes, S., Cuban, L. and Tyack, D.B. (2001) Mismatch: Historical perspectives on schools and students who don't fit them. *Teachers College Record* 103 (4), 525–547.

Donovan, B. (2004) AG: Public schools not exempt from Prop. 203. *Navajo Times*, 19 February.

Gandara, P. and Contreras, F. (2009) The Latino education crisis: The consequences of failed social policies. Cambridge, MA: Harvard University Press.

Garcia, D. and Aportela, A. (2000) Arizona Measure of Academic Progress: A first look at growth in Arizona schools. Technical Report. Phoenix, AZ: Arizona Department of Education.

Garcia, E.E. (ed.) (2000) *Implementation of California's Proposition 227: 1998–2000* (Special Issue). *Bilingual Research Journal* 24 (1 & 2).

Goddard, T. (2003a) *Attorney General Opinion No. 103-002 (R03-010), Re: Application of Proposition 203 to Charter Schools*. Phoenix, AZ: Office of the Attorney General. See https://www.azag.gov/sgo-opinions/I03-002 (accessed 31 January 2005).

Goddard, T. (2003b) *Attorney General Opinion No. 103-001(R03-014), Re: Guidelines Governing Waivers from English Immersion Programs*. Phoenix, AZ: Office of the Attorney General. See https://www.azag.gov/sgo-opinions/I03-001 (accessed 31 January 2005).

Gottlieb, M. (2003) *Large-scale Assessment of English Language Learners: Addressing Educational Accountability in K-12 Settings*. Alexandria, VA: Teachers of English to Speakers of Other Languages.

Horne, T. (2001) Molera shortcuts would only lead us all to failure. *Arizona Republic*, 18 November.

Horne, T. (2003a) *Superintendent Tom Horne Vindicated on Bilingual Guidelines: 45 Monitors to Police Bilingual* [Press release, 22 July]. Phoenix, AZ: Arizona Department of Education.

Horne, T. (2003b) Arizona education not dumbing down. *Arizona Republic*, 13 October, p. B9.

Horne, T. (2003c) *Media Advisory: Superintendent of Public Instruction Tom Horne Begins Year With New Leadership Team* [Press release]. Phoenix, AZ: Arizona Department of Education.

Horne, T. (2004) *First Annual State of Education Speech.* See http://repository.asu.edu/attachments/77563/content/2004StateofEducation.pdf (accessed 6 January 2004).

Horne, T. and Dugan, M.G. (2003) *Implementation of Arizona English Language Immersion Laws.* Phoenix, AZ: Arizona Department of Education.

Judson, E. and Dugan, M.G. (2004) *The Effects of Bilingual Education Programs and Structured English Immersion Programs on Student Achievement: A Large-scale Comparison.* Phoenix, AZ: Arizona Department of Education.

Keegan, L.G. (1999) English acquisition services: A summary of bilingual and English as a second language program for school year 1997–1998. Report of the Superintendent of Public Instruction to the Arizona Legislature. Phoenix, AZ: Arizona Department of Education.

Keegan, L.G. (2000) English acquisition services: A summary of bilingual and English as a second language program for school year 1998–1999. Report of the Superintendent of Public Instruction to the Arizona Legislature. Phoenix, AZ: Arizona Department of Education.

Kloss, H. (1998 [1977]) *The American Bilingual Tradition.* Washington, DC: Center for Applied Linguistics and Delta Systems. Original work published (1977) Rowley, MA: Newbury House.

Kossan, P. (2000a) Keegan puts AIMS test on hold indefinitely, cites high failure rate. *Arizona Republic*, 21 November.

Kossan, P. (2000b) By trying too much too quick, AIMS missed mark. *Arizona Republic*, 27 November.

Kossan, P. (2001a) Alternate to AIMS is possible. *Arizona Republic*, 22 August.

Kossan, P. (2001b) Tamer AIMS on the way; Molera wants 4-year delay, eased graduation rates. *Arizona Republic*, 24 August.

Kossan, P. (2003a) Charters bypass English-only law. *Arizona Republic*, 26 July.

Kossan, P. (2003b) Doubts cloud school rankings. *Arizona Republic*, 12 October.

Kossan, P. (2004a) 8th-graders'AIMS math to get easier; state admits error in scoring. *Arizona Republic*, 25 January, p. BI.

Kossan, P. (2004b) Ariz easing fed's rules for school standards. *Arizona Republic*, 4 April, p. B1.

Kossan, P. (2004c) Standardized tests changing. *Arizona Republic*, 11 April, p. BI.

Kossan, P. (2004d) $4.5 mil may shift for AIMS; Horne seeks funds for boosting scores. *Arizona Republic*, 14 September.

Kossan, P. and Konig, R. (2011) Arizona schools fail to hit test targets in record numbers. *Arizona Republic*, 27 July.

Krashen, S.D. (1996) *Under Attack: The Case Against Bilingual Education.* Culver City, CA: Language Education Associates.

Krashen, S.D. and Biber, D. (1988) *On Course: Bilingual Education Success in California.* Sacramento, CA: California Association for Bilingual Education.

LaCelle-Peterson, M. and Rivera, C. (1994) Is it real for all kids? A framework for equitable assessment policies for English language learners. *Harvard Educational Review* 64 (1), 55–75.

Linn, R.L. (2002) Validation of the uses and interpretations of results of state assessment and accountability systems. In G. Tindal and T.H. Haladyna (eds) *Large-scale Assessment Programs for All Students: Validity, Technical Adequacy, and Implementation* (pp. 27–48). Mahwah, NJ: Lawrence Erlbaum.

Macias, R.R. and Wiley, T.G. (1998) Introduction to the 2nd edition: The American bilingual tradition. In H. Kloss (ed.) *The American Bilingual Tradition.* Washington, DC:

Center for Applied Linguistics and Delta Systems. Original work published (1977) Rowley, MA: Newbury House.

Massachusetts Voter Initiative (2002) Question 2, *English Language Education in Public Schools*.

McNeil, M. (2011) Duncan: 82 percent of schools could be 'failing' this year. *Education Week's Blogs: Politics K-12*. See http://blogs.edweek.org/edweek/campaign-k-12/2011/03/duncan_82_of_schools_could_be.html (accessed 17 November 2011).

Menken, K. (2008) *English Learners Left Behind: Standardized Testing as Language Policy*. Clevedon: Multilingual Matters.

Miles, M. and Huberman, M. (1994) *Qualitative Data Analysis: An Expanded Sourcebook* (2nd edn). Thousand Oaks, CA: Sage Publications.

Molera, J.A. (2001) *Guidance Regarding the Implementation of A.R.S. Section 15-751-755 and Flores Consent Order* (CIV 92-596 TUC ACM). Phoenix, AZ: Arizona Department of Education.

Napolitano, J. (2001) *Attorney General Opinion No. 101-006 (ROO-062), Re: Application of Proposition 203 to Schools Serving the Navajo Nation*. Phoenix, AZ: Office of the Attorney General. See https://www.azag.gov/sgo-opinions/I01-006 (accessed 31 January 2005).

National Clearinghouse (2010) Arizona rate of growth, 1997/1998–2007/2008. [Poster, July]. Washington, DC: National Clearinghouse for English Language Acquisition. Retrieved April 20, 2010, from http://www.ncela.gwu.edu/files/uploads/20/Arizona_G_0708.pdf

NCLB (2001) *No Child Left Behind* Act. Pub. L. No. 107–110.

Pearce, K. (2000a) Tricky math in AIMS test, teachers say. *Arizona Republic*, 25 January, p. A1.

Pearce, K. (2000b) Mistake made in AIMS scoring. *Arizona Republic*, 18 March, p. A1.

Peregoy, S.F. and Boyle, O.F. (2000) *Reading, Writing and Learning in ESL: A Resource Book for K-12 Teachers*. Menlo Park, CA: Addison-Wesley.

Rivera, C. (2002) *Preliminary Findings: State Assessment Policies for English Language Learners 2000–2001*. Paper presented at the National Association for Bilingual Education, Philadelphia, PA.

Rivera, C., Vincent, C., Hafner, A. and LaCelle-Peterson, M. (1997) Statewide assessment programs: Policies and practices for the inclusion of limited English proficient students. *Practical Assessment, Research & Evaluation* 5 (13). See http://pareonline.net/getvn.asp?v=5&n=13 (accessed 29 March 2005).

Ruelas, R. (2003) Checking up on English lesson plan. *Arizona Republic*, 29 December.

Ryman, A. (2004) Teacher faces firing for hitting children. *Arizona Republic*, 16 January, p. A1.

Ryman, A. and Madrid, O. (2004) Hispanics upset by teacher's discipline. *Arizona Republic*, 17 January.

Slavin, R.E. and Cheung, A. (2003) Effective reading programs for English language learners: A best-evidence synthesis. Report No. 66. Baltimore, MD: Center for Research on the Education of Students Placed at Risk, John Hopkins University.

US Department of Education (2003a) *Non-regulatory Guidance on the Title III State Formula Grant Program. Part 1: Preliminary Guidance on the Title III State Formula Grant Program*. Washington, DC: Office of English Language Acquisition, Language Enhancement, and Academic Achievement for Limited English Proficient Students.

US Department of Education (2003b) *Standards and Assessment: Non-regulatory Guidance* (Draft). Washington, DC: US Department of Education.

Wiley, T.G. (2000) Continuity and change in the function of language ideologies in the United States. In T. Ricento (ed.) *Ideology, Politics, and Language Policies: Focus on English*. Philadelphia, PA: John Benjamins.

Wiley, T.G. (2002) Accessing language rights in education: A brief history of the U.S. context. In J.W. Tollefson (ed.) *Language Policies in Education* (pp. 39–64). Mahwah, NJ: Lawrence Erlbaum.

Wiley, T.G. and Wright, W.E. (2004) Against the undertow: The politics of language instruction in the United States. *Educational Policy* 18 (1), 142–168.

Wright, W.E. (2002) The effects of high stakes testing on an inner-city elementary school: The curriculum, the teachers, and the English language learners. *Current Issues in Education* 5 (5). See http://cie.asu.edu/volume5/number5 (accessed 31 January 2005).

Wright, W.E. (2003) The success and demise of a Khmer (Cambodian) bilingual education program: A case study. In C.C. Park, A.L. Goodwin and S.J. Lee (eds) *Asian American Identities, Families, and Schooling* (pp. 225–252). Greenwich, CT: Information Age Publishing.

Wright, W.E. (2004) Intersection of language and assessment policies for English language learners in Arizona. Unpublished doctoral dissertation, Arizona State University.

Wright, W.E. (2005) The political spectacle of Proposition 203. *Education Policy* 19 (5), 662–700.

Wright, W.E. (2010) *Foundations for Teaching English Language Learners: Research, Theory, Policy, and Practice.* Philadelphia, PA: Caslon Publishing.

Wright, W.E. and Choi, D. (2006) The impact of language and high-stakes testing policies on elementary school English language learners in Arizona. *Education Policy Analysis Archives* 14 (13), 1–56. See http://epaa.asu.edu/epaa/v14n13/.

Wright, W.E. and Pu, C. (2005) *Academic Achievement of English Language Learners in Post Proposition 203 Arizona.* Tempe, AZ: Education Policy Studies Laboratory, Language Policy Research Unit. See http://epsl.asu.edu/epru/documents/EPSL-0509-103-LPRU.pdf.

Yanow, D. (2000) *Conducting Interpretive Policy Analysis.* Thousand Oaks, CA: Sage Publications.

Zehr, M.A. (2001) Arizona grapples with bilingual ed. changes. *Education Week* 20 (19), pp. 14, 16.

4 Ensuring Oversight: Statewide SEI Teacher Professional Development

Sarah Catherine K. Moore

The adoption of structured English immersion (SEI) as the primary model of instruction for all English learners (ELs) in Arizona, which resulted from the passage of Proposition 203 (Arizona Voter Initiative, 2000), had a significant impact on EL instruction and resulted in a range of challenges that emerged during the implementation of the new SEI requirement. A key issue in implementing this new, statewide model involved the training of teachers. Findings in this chapter focus on Arizona's statewide SEI training mandate for pre- and in-service certified educational personnel. An important basis for the research described in this chapter involved acknowledging the role of professional development providers functioning as negotiators of informal policymaking vis-à-vis SEI in their professional development sessions and in classrooms. As SEI has been implemented in Arizona over the past nearly 15 years, teachers have, in some ways, become final decision makers in terms of what SEI looks like after its projection from top-down policy into practice (McCarty, 2002). The focus of this study was on the curriculum of Arizona SEI training for pre- and in-service certified educational personnel with the goal of understanding how professional development providers from various backgrounds and organizations responded to their roles and responsibilities for interpreting and communicating SEI to teachers.

The curriculum for Arizona's SEI training was clearly outlined by the Arizona Department of Education (ADE). As of 31 August 2006 all certified personnel were required to complete two SEI training sessions – a 15-hour training and a 45-hour training (ADE, 2013). The curricula for training were initially outlined by hour allocation in two documents distributed by the ADE to administrators and others responsible for the direction of implementation (see Tables 4.1 & 4.2). Known as the SEI Curriculum Frameworks (CFs), they ultimately became the basis for the ADE's oversight of SEI training sessions. Early on in their implementation, the CFs played a key role in guiding SEI content because they essentially became the tool for measuring

Table 4.1 15-hour Curricular Framework

ELL proficiency standards	Assessment	Foundations of SEI	SEI strategies
Minimum: 1 clock hour	Minimum: 1 clock hour	Minimum: 1 clock hour	Minimum: 8 clock hours

Four flex clock hours to be used at the instructor's discretion to augment any combination of the four areas

Table 4.2 45-hour Curricular Framework

ELL proficiency standards	Data analysis & application	Formal & informal assessment	SEI foundations objectives	Learning experiences: SEI strategies	Parent/home/ school scaffolding
Minimum: 1 clock hour	Minimum: 3 clock hours	Minimum: 3 clock hours	Minimum: 1 clock hour	Minimum: 25 clock hours	Minimum: 3 clock hours

Nine flex hours to be used at the instructor's discretion to augment any combination of the four areas

and evaluating fidelity to the 'model' of SEI they represented. Each of the CFs has been revised since its initial publication (see Markos & Arias, Chapter 5, this volume, for additional information on their revision and updated contents). Throughout this chapter, they will be referred to as the CFs.

The challenges associated with Arizona's SEI training implementation were both logistical and conceptual in nature. In terms of logistics, for example, initially the state required *all* certified educational personnel to complete training, a policy which neglected to account for personnel who had already obtained an ESL or BLE credential. As a result, a selection of staff in the state ended up completing the 15-hour SEI workshop, which basically covered an introduction to EL instruction, despite the fact that they were already certified ESL or BLE teachers (and as such considered EL experts). In terms of the conceptual approach to SEI training, the statewide model allowed for any person who had obtained an ESL or BLE credential to submit a syllabus and obtain approval for conducting the training sessions. That policy resulted in tremendous variance across training sessions. It also meant that trainers played an integral role in terms of their interpretation of the SEI CFs and, by extension, the curricula they developed and delivered in SEI training.

Context

The broad issue guiding research conducted for this study involved English-only ideology. In particular, I was interested in understanding how the SEI training policy and its implementation may have been functioning as a vehicle for the promotion of an English-only oriented ideology on behalf of the ADE. In part, the role of the ADE amidst SEI training implementation had to do with its administrative responsibility to public schools in the state. However, it seemed likely at the time that beyond that, SEI provided an opportunity to further postulate and promote English-only ideology by the ADE. For example, the new SEI training requirements (in the form of alignment with the SEI CFs) were written into the ESL methods courses required for all pre-service teachers in Arizona. Because of the relationship between the SEI CFs and pre-service teacher preparation in the state, the SEI training requirements provided an opening for the ADE to use its oversight of SEI training implementation to assess all sessions for fidelity with the SEI CFs. In this way, SEI training oversight by ADE allowed in-depth access and strict scrutiny of educator preparation and professional development that previously would not have been available. Claims that SEI sessions were not aligned well enough to the SEI CFs resulted in threats at ADE-led investigations of the instructors facilitating such sessions (Miller, pers. commun., June 2006). The basis for such threats was established through ADE's promotion of an online survey through which participants in SEI sessions were encouraged to report potential non-compliance with the outlined CFs (the ADE threatened to investigate my course instruction due to an alleged 'political' stance). Essentially, the ADE used its oversight of SEI training as the rationale behind intruding into SEI course content and imposing upon SEI instructors' and trainers' control of their own content and delivery. This new oversight role occupied by ADE was particularly troubling among university instructors, who (though certainly complying with other teacher preparation and university standards) traditionally operate under the security of academic freedom.

On the whole, given the context of swift implementation, strict deadlines and extreme oversight, as well as the association between SEI training and other characteristics of the English-Only Movement at play in the state at the time, it seemed reasonable to presume that the ADE may be utilizing SEI training as a means of furthering English-only ideology. To address the complex policy case of Arizona's SEI training requirements and implementation, I utilized interpretive policy analysis (IPA) (Yanow, 2000), which has been applied largely in social science research and to a variety of settings involving communities with various stakeholders who may share or be in conflict with one another through negotiation or navigation of a particular policy or change. An IPA orientation allows the researcher not only to acknowledge one's own positionality in working through policy implementation, but also to gain a more emic understanding of the knowledge, values and interpretation expressed by those being impacted by a particular policy. In this case, it provided me with an opportunity to break out the discourses voiced by four distinct communities of practice which were each navigating the arduous journey to defining SEI in post-Prop. 203 Arizona through their implementation of SEI training.

Framing: Interpretive Policy Analysis

IPA is best described as more of an orientation than a methodology, and in this way it is compatible with a variety of methodologies (for data collection, analysis, reporting on findings, etc.). These might include, for example, case study research, observation, interviewing, archival data collection and analysis, ethnographically informed methods, among other means of collecting data to research various scenarios, subjects/participants and contexts associated with language policy and education policy (Moore & Wiley, 2014; Yanow, 2000).

IPA provides a useful orientation for researchers who are themselves presently acting in and amidst the policy case at hand. For those who themselves are at once researcher and actor, IPA 'assumes that it is not possible for an analyst to stand outside of the policy issues being studied, free of its values and meanings and of the analyst's own values, beliefs, and feelings' (Yanow, 2000: 6). The interpretive purview for policy analysis includes 'human artifacts and actions, including policy documents, legislation, implementation, are understood here to be not only instrumentally rational but also expressive – of meaning(s), including at times individual and collective identity' (Yanow, 2000: 6).

There are several key components to IPA. These contribute to fleshing out the often multifaceted, perhaps intricate, and usually top-down issues and phenomena in policymaking which may also involve a range of players representing overlapping or conflicting perspectives and agendas. As Yanow (2000) notes, 'the central question, then, for interpretive policy analysts is, How is the policy issue being framed by the various parties in the debate'? (Yanow, 2000: 11). In IPA research, an early step involves identifying interpretive communities – the stakeholders involved in the development, implementation or impact of a policy. The researcher must also identify the various *symbolic artifacts* associated with the policy at hand – these are classified as language, objects or acts. Through data collection and analysis, the researcher engages in the exercise of fleshing out the meanings present among interpretive communities and related symbolic artifacts. Research guided by IPA is not necessarily sequential, but rather involves responding to the communities, artifacts and meanings as they emerge and in association with the researcher's noted positionality in relation to the identified policy. IPA is centrally about interpretation and gaining a better understanding of ways of knowing and knowledge construction. As Yanow (2000: 7) puts it, 'the interpretive approach is less an argument (in the context of policy analysis, at least) contesting the nature of reality than one about the human possibilities of knowing the world around us and the character of that knowledge'.

Guided by an IPA orientation to research, data and findings for this study were categorized into two overarching areas: interpretive communities (and discourses that emerged from interpretive communities) implementing SEI through training sessions, and symbolic artifacts (objects, acts/actors and language) that derived from the ADE through its SEI training directives. This chapter presents findings from the four interpretive communities and their respective discourses in the context of alignment with, or opposition to, symbolic artifacts that emerged from the ADE during its SEI training policy creation and implementation.

Methodology

Based on an IPA-informed perspective, identification of interpretive communities was an important early step in the overall process of 'data collection'. The sources of data for research included interviews, observations and, when available, the identification and collection of documents or other objects related to SEI sessions or the larger policy.

An important note about the participants who agreed to contribute to the research follows. Arizona's SEI training was implemented in two separate phases – the first 15-hour phase and the second 45-hour phase (see Tables 4.1 & 4.2). The deadline for the first phase was 31 August 2006 (to obtain a Provisional SEI Endorsement) and the deadline for the second phase was 31 August 2009 (to obtain a Full SEI Endorsement). Because research began in the fall following the 2006 deadline, participants consisted mostly of those involved with the 45-hour training, but many also had experiences either as trainers or as trainees during the first, 15-hour phase.

The four interpretive communities identified for research were: (1) district facilitators (D); (2) community college instructors (CC); (3) for-profit facilitators (FP); and (4) university instructors (U). University instructors included participants from each of the state's three major universities: Arizona State University (ASU), the University of Arizona and Northern Arizona University. At ASU, given my role at the time as an instructor of the SEI course, I only interviewed one individual from Main campus, in addition to one each from the East and West satellite campuses (these, in many ways function as institutions independent from Main), and I did not previously know those participants. Pseudonyms for research participants, their affiliation(s) with one or more of the four interpretive communities, and the training phase(s) for which they served as session facilitators are displayed in Table 4.3.

Table 4.3 Participants, affiliations, training type

Pseudonym	Affiliation	Type of training
Katie	UU; FP	15; 45
Mary	CC; FP	15; 45
Blanca	U; FP	45
Guillermo	U; CC	15; 45
Irma	D	15
Frank	D; FP	15; 45
Kay	CC	15
Conrado	U	45
Judy	U	15; 45
Saundra	U	15; 45
Beth	U	15; 45
Maggie	D; FP	15; 45
Julie	U; FP	15; 45
Armando	D	15

Discussion

The overall approach to research for the study was driven by the goal of understanding the differences among facilitators from each of the four communities (D, CC, FP, U). During the analysis of interview data, however, it became clear that the most appropriate and manageable way of using IPA for this case was first to tease out the key symbolic artifacts that materialized during the ADE's generation, implementation and oversight of SEI training. Next, these were analyzed to determine their relationship to discourses from the interpretive communities (three outstanding discourses were identified from each of the four communities). Although the majority of this chapter presents salient discourses, a necessary first step and first section regards ADE-derived symbolic artifacts. Given the complexity of the scenario, it was important to situate how the interpretive communities, and the discourses they shared, related back to the larger issue of SEI training requirements. In order to establish these connections (as well as, more broadly, the research question regarding English-only ideology espoused by the ADE), I tracked each of the 12 discourses' relationship to the ADE symbolic artifacts. Tracing the relationships between community discourses and ADE artifacts allowed findings to address the overarching research question regarding to what extent ADE-originated English-only ideology was communicated through respective communities' SEI trainings.

ADE symbolic artifacts

Yanow (2000), in discussing the relationship between interpretive communities, the 'meanings of policies' and symbolic artifacts, reminds the researcher that:

> Interpretive philosophies, such as phenomenology and hermeneutics, contend that human meanings, values, beliefs, and feelings are embodied in and transmitted through artifacts of human creation, such as language, dress, patterns of action and interaction, written texts, or built spaces. In the context of policy analysis, this means focusing on policy or agency artifacts as the concrete symbols representing more abstract policy and organizational meanings. (Yanow, 2000: 14)

In this way, identifying artifacts and tracing their relationships with and to interpretive communities represents a critical step in teasing out the links or disconnects between discourses emerging from the interpreting community members and the symbolic artifacts at play amidst the policy issue. In IPA, symbolic artifacts fall into one of three categories: Language, Objects or Acts. The symbolic artifacts that emerged in relation to this particular case in policy were: the SEI CFs (Object); the Objectives for instruction outlined in the CFs, which drove the curriculum in SEI training sessions (Language); and Course Approval, which was executed by the ADE (Act). These and their relationship to the discourses that emerged from the four interpretive communities are depicted in Figure 4.1, with the symbolic artifacts placed in the upper rectangle, and discourses represented by ovals and squares.

The arrows indicate the relationship between discourses and symbolic artifacts. Each of the three symbolic artifacts tied back to, and originated from, the ADE. I attempted to sketch out the network(s) of values, meaning and beliefs of interpretive communities (as demonstrated in their discourses) as compared with the symbolic artifacts that served as the underpinning of this policy case (SEI CF, Objectives and Course Approval). By delineating the extent to which various discourses did or did not derive from the three symbolic artifacts (originating from the ADE), I hoped to begin to address the issue of whether the ADE was able to utilize SEI training to further English-only ideology.

Interpretive communities and discourses

Table 4.4 illustrates the prominent discourses that emerged from interpretive communities. The following sections summarize the three most salient themes that emerged from each of the four communities, including specific examples and excerpts from interviews.

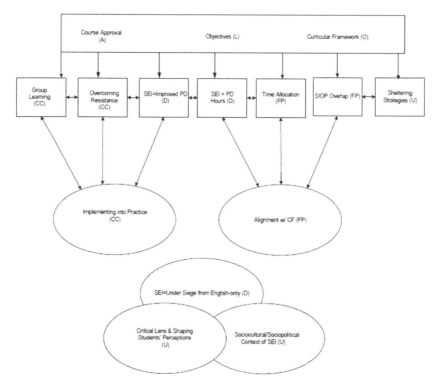

Figure 4.1 Community discourses as derived from symbolic artifacts

District personnel

All participants from the district community mentioned at least one flaw in the initial 15-hour phase of training implementation. Another common

Table 4.4 Interpretive communities' discourses

D	SEI Endorsement = PD hours
	SEI Endorsement = improved PD for ELs
	SEI = under siege from English-only
CC	Overcoming resistance
	Implementing into practice
	Group learning
FP	Time allocation
	Alignment with the Curricular Framework
	SIOP overlap
U	Sociocultural/sociopolitical contexts of SEI
	Critical lens and shaping students' perceptions
	Sheltering strategies

theme among district personnel was their descriptions of communication with the ADE. Blanca, Armando, Mary, Maggie, Julie and Frank all specifically stated that their respective district offices were aware that an SEI CF would be published and a training requirement announced prior to the ADE formal public statement. Because of this early information, several reported that their districts implemented trainings that they believed, based on communication with ADE, would meet SEI requirements, but ultimately did not do so. As a result, Armando's district, for example, was forced to retrain teachers they thought had already completed the SEI training requirements. In general, this scenario, which was common among participants from districts, demonstrates the tight time constraints under which stakeholders were made to implement SEI training. The three discourses that emerged from district facilitators were: (1) SEI training as imposed professional development hours; (2) SEI training as an opportunity to better prepare teachers for supporting ELs; and (3) SEI as feeling under siege from the ADE's English-only policy.

(1) *SEI Endorsement = P.D. hours*

The district personnel overwhelmingly viewed the 15-hour requirement as an additional 15 hours of professional development that could ultimately benefit ELs due to its emphasis on their instruction. However, they also expressed anxiety at its implementation schedule. Due to the tight timeline, Frank's district, for example, made the strategic decision to conduct online training. His initial description was that 'it was 12 hours of online work and then a 3 hour project and then a reflection paper'. Frank emphasized strictly meeting the state's required time allocation and overall mandate and also referred to the content of SLA as 'quick and dirty'. Regarding the selection of online delivery, he described the reason as avoiding 'grumpy teachers' whose time was, as a result of SEI, further burdened by a new, unplanned, additional PD session.

(2) *SEI Endorsement = improved P.D. for ELs*

Despite district personnel's emphasis on time constraints and the logistics of completing SEI training, almost all also acknowledged the positive impact of required SEI training, noting the apparent under-preparation of teachers for working with ELs. Irma remarked that because of preliminary provisional training she suspected an increase in teachers enrolling in ESL/BLE Endorsement coursework through the community college. She specifically stated that, due to the abbreviated timeline and impromptu addition to the district's load, she found the 15-hour to be 'a waste of time'. However, she added that it also did initiate interest in teachers that otherwise would not have had access to professional development aimed at supporting ELs.

(3) *SEI = under siege from English-only*

An overriding characteristic of the discourse emerging from district staff was a sense of feeling attacked by the state due to its enforcement of English-only policy. I was surprised at the frustration expressed by most, and several shared candid opposition to the ADE and its position on English-only. Irma, for example, following up on her negative comments about the initial phase of SEI, said 'and I told Irene Moreno that, too [Assistant Superintendent of Instruction]'. Although only one participant explicitly stated so, Irma's words reflect a sense of resentment and aggression, and point to how harshly SEI training sessions were scrutinized by the ADE. Similarly, Frank compared his perspective about the antagonistic tone in Arizona to what he had previously experienced while working on the East Coast:

> I think living here [in Arizona] and studying here is definitely, this is using the wrong word but it colors our perception of how things have shifted in the field nationally [toward dual-language instruction]. I don't think people feel as under siege on the part of state [in other places]... That's how we feel [in Arizona]; there's a reason that the discourse is aligned with battle.

Although participants from each of the four communities share opposition to the ADE and English-only, district staff seemed the most affected by, and uneasy about, ADE oversight.

Community college instructors

Three study participants were community college instructors: Kay, Guillermo and Mary. The most salient theme across data from them regarded overcoming resistance among teachers in their courses. They also focused on extending and applying content from courses into real-world practice and establishing and promoting group-based learning.

(1) *Overcoming resistance*

All of the community college trainers talked about the importance of initially eliciting engagement from the teachers in their courses as a way of overcoming resistance. Guillermo spoke immediately about the resistance he had to overcome in teaching the SEI course. When I asked him about the differences between his teaching undergraduates versus teachers (he was also a university instructor teaching the undergraduate SEI course), he talked about the fact that in-service teachers did not want to be enrolled in the course. 'Well rule number one... they're only there because the law requires them to be there. They're not there because they're taking it for their personal benefit... So you have to overcome that'. Guillermo added that his strategy for reducing resistance to SEI involved reminders of teachers' responsibility to students' equitable instruction under the law.

(2) *Implementing into practice*

All of the community college instructors also stressed the importance of ensuring that teachers were actually implementing what they learned through the SEI course. Perhaps in part because they were working with certified teachers, they viewed the course as an opportunity to engage with curricula through incorporating learning about SEI into established daily practice.

Mary, for example, stressed attention to teachers' construction of learning through incorporating activities in their own classrooms, collaboration and reflection. 'But what's really critical is teaching or training teachers how to work with these kids, what it really looks like. They have to figure out, okay, how would I use this with my students'. Mary clearly described teachers actually *using* strategies, as opposed to simply being exposed to methodology or the components of the required SEI CFs. She considered this type of engagement and application critical to the likelihood of impacting long-term classroom use of the methods discussed in the SEI course.

(3) *Group learning*

The third point that emerged from community college instructors involved the importance of integrating group learning into SEI course curriculum and instruction. Guillermo, who was most vocal about the resistance he had encountered with CC students, indicated that he emphasized developing a classroom community in which the teachers shared and reflected with one another and with him. Through creating a community with his students, he not only modeled the group learning appropriate for ELs, but also accessed buy-in and acceptance of the SEI content.

Like Guillermo, Kay also talked about her teaching style in terms of 'managing' 'discussions' and 'respecting' what teachers already know, in an attempt at showing her CC students that they bring expertise to the course, and that she knows she can also learn from them. Like Guillermo, Kay described a community of learners in which teachers were actively sharing experiences with others in an effort to construct authentic ways of supporting ELs in their classrooms. She repeatedly mentioned drawing on what teachers already knew and building from the foundation they had already established as educators in developing practical ideas for working with ELs.

For-profit trainers

Emergent themes from the for-profit trainers were similar to those from other interpretive communities in some ways, but in others were very distinct. The for-profit facilitators overwhelmingly indicated alignment with the time allocations outlined in the SEI CFs. The three central themes shared by FP trainers had to do with time allocations, general alignment to the SEI CF, and overlap with the SIOP Model.[1] The for-profit interpretive community included Mary, Katie and Maggie. While both Julie and Blanca had also worked at for-profits, data collected from them were based primarily on roles outside of the for-profit sector.

(1) *Time allocation*

In terms of time allocation, Katie was the most vocal about the imposition of time allotment for covering areas required by the SEI CFs. In particular, she compared her role as a university instructor to how she functions in the for-profit sector. When I asked Katie what it's like to be an SEI trainer working at the for-profit, her response reflected tension around time as a burden.

> I think it's a struggle … it's a tough situation for me … there's constantly this back and forth between what I really feel like they need or what I should be giving them and then the constraints that I have to do that in … If teachers don't believe in what they're doing, why are they gonna do it? And so one of the things that I think we struggle with, or that I struggle with as a trainer is in the limited amount of time that you have with people to cover everything the state's asking you to cover …

Later in our interview, during discussion of session content, this sense of resolute time allotment emerged again. When I asked Katie about questions posed by teachers in her sessions, she responded that often there is very little time to address teachers' inquiries outside of the SEI CFs. She specifically compared her for-profit facilitation to her role as an instructor at the university: 'it's very fast paced … it's not like the class that we do at [the university] where you have a lot of time for that [answering questions] and I don't know if that's just because this is the way they're [the for-profit] doing it … it seems to be more of a I'm the holder of knowledge, I'm giving it to you.'

(2) *Alignment with CF*

Like the district trainers, for-profit instructors were keenly aware of necessary alignment between their sessions and the state frameworks. When asked about what should be included in trainings, each referenced the state SEI CFs. However, some reported more strict alignment than others. Notes from my observation of Maggie's session clearly show how carefully her session explicitly paralleled not only the SEI CF, but also other pertinent areas that could fall under ADE oversight. For example, she not only reviewed the SEI CF, but also professional teacher standards, SIOP objectives, and specific objectives within the state's framework. The most explicit example of alignment with the SEI CF among the for-profit facilitators were the handouts provided in Maggie and Katie's sessions, which were essentially a folder arranged by the same subheadings as in the SEI CF.

(3) *SIOP overlap*

In terms of overlap with the SIOP in SEI trainings, all three of the for-profit trainers indicated the influence of SIOP on SEI curricula. During my interviews with Julie and Mary, they stated that, prior to the development of the SEI CFs, SIOP was adopted to comply with the new SEI model. When I asked Mary if her sessions were based on SIOP, she responded affirmatively. Essentially, she and other FP facilitators equated the SIOP to be 'best practices' for ELs, and hence the foundation of the SEI training sessions.

The organization where Maggie and Katie were employed fundamentally based its SEI curriculum on the SIOP model. In answering a question about what sort of things are addressed during training sessions, Katie responded: 'They highly encourage us to use the SIOP because that's what they used for the first 15 hours…so they versed everybody in the book and all the different components and then now they want us to reflect on and build upon information in the SIOP [for the 45-hour].' Later in her response she added:

> I know that when they wrote their syllabus for [the organization], they wrote that we would be using the SIOP book as our basically reference or resource and so that's what we built, but I think that the connection is so thick…

Later Katie stated that she finds about 80% of the training to be material from the SIOP.

University instructors

Two of the three outstanding ideas that emerged from data sources related to university courses were distinct from the other three communities. They were incorporating in SEI courses the sociocultural/sociopolitical contexts of SEI and the general goal of shaping students' perceptions about language minority schooling through their completion of SEI coursework. University instructors were also concerned with ensuring the delivery of sheltering strategies that students would use with their ELs as teachers. Participants from the universities were: Blanca, Saundra, Conrado, Katie, Judy, Guillermo, Beth and Julie.

(1) *Sociocultural/sociopolitical contexts of SEI*

The university instructors overwhelmingly emphasized providing for students the sociopolitical and sociocultural context of SEI within both the field of language minority education and in schooling more generally. When I asked Julie what she considered to be the most important areas SEI should cover, she replied: 'Legislation, court cases – a lot of teachers have no idea about that. They have no idea why they have to get an SEI Endorsement…we're the only state that has to have endorsements and it's made up by the state department.' Similarly, Judy described a young woman in her course in the excerpt below:

> This girl I'm really seriously considering challenging her about even being in teaching or if she's gonna teach, maybe she should go to another state, I don't know where but since immigrant issues are everywhere…she has big barriers up and that concerns me even if it wasn't about immigration.

Beth's ideas about the impact of pre-service teachers' sociopolitical perspectives on ELs and the world was highlighted when during our interview she suggested that universities and Colleges of Education might consider entry criteria for pre-service teachers interested in working with linguistically diverse learners, based on the bias and misconceptions she had so far encountered during her first semester teaching the SEI course.

(2) *A critical lens and shaping students' perceptions*

Unlike the other communities, university instructors highlighted the importance of shaping students' perceptions about ELs and language minority education through engaging them in critical thinking, reflection and activities. For example, Guillermo shared information about his educational background as a Mexican American in Arizona schools and the prejudice and racism he endured due to ethnicity during his SEI course instruction. He indicated that his course also covered the history of segregationist policies against Mexican and Mexican American students in the southwest. Similarly, Judy illustrated the emphasis she hoped to place on critical inquiry through the SEI course.

> You know what's important is that teachers need to realize that this is only one course and I hope that they will leave the course with more questions about the needs of the students [ELs] than they come into the class with and I also hope that they'll develop a sense of advocacy for their students [ELs] that will help them take their questions and find answers in their community and in their professional organizations.

Julie talked about the importance of 'really getting teachers to start thinking critically about SEI. I don't just say this is a great model or this is the way to do it'. When prompted further, she said she hoped that university courses teach that, 'instead of talking about *these* students and *those* students, they're *our* students'. If a discussion of the notion of *us versus them* weren't critical enough, she continued in the excerpt below:

> ...another [question] is why Hispanic students don't wanna learn English and then we talk about the access to English and it's not necessarily that there's access in the classroom and in the home or the community that we can blame, but the time of access that they have to language... So we start talking about how it's a systematic segregation and they start feeling a little bit more empathetic...

Related to Julie's ideas about access to language and the language of schooling, Beth talked about how she planned to improve her future courses by providing a more critical look at ELs and their background. She talked about several issues she planned to address in upcoming semesters.

> I'm gonna focus more on the social context of the children in ELL or SEI classrooms and sort of talk about their historical reality and probably go into more detail about how those kids were educated here in the past as well as in Mexico, talk a lot about how you define parental support... I

also plan to talk and address, sort of squarely the whole issue of immigration, which you can't really get by. There's no really way, you can't really
talk about education without talking about immigration in Arizona now.

The concerns raised by university instructors were echoed by nearly all participants in this community and stood alone among the other three communities. Ideological issues related to immigration, funds of knowledge,
educational equity and access were rarely voiced by participants from other
communities. Through critically exploring these topics with students, university instructors hoped to impact their students' perceptions of language
minority students, families and communities.

(3) *Sheltering strategies*
The last basic idea that emerged from university instructors involved
emphasizing sheltering strategies (many in this context also referenced the
SIOP). All of the university instructors were either using one of the SIOP texts
for a current course or had used one previously. Although university instructors
were particularly disturbed at the diminished legitimacy of the ESL and BLE
credential in the state as a result of the SEI Endorsement, they also recognized
that required SEI training would in many ways positively impact instruction
for ELs. As such, their SEI curricula heavily emphasized sheltering strategies.

Conclusions

For this investigation, IPA provided a structure for working out the complex characters, issues and symbols at play amidst the Arizona's SEI training
policy. Based on IPA, the three symbolic artifacts identified as derived from
the ADE (see Figure 4.1) were Course Approval, Objectives and the CFs.
Of the total of 12 primary discourses (three from each of the four communities) that emerged, nine were derived either directly or indirectly from one or
more of the three symbolic artifacts originating from the ADE (see Figure
4.1). The primary discourses from interpretive communities that were *not*
derived from ADE symbolic artifacts were: (1) under siege from English-only
(D); (2) critical lens and shaping students' perceptions (U); and (3) sociocul-
tural/sociopolitical context of SEI (U). Only district staff and university
instructors shared discourses incongruent to ADE artifacts.

Therefore, the traced relationships between interpretive communities'
discourses and ADE symbolic artifacts addresses the broad research question
that guided this study: *is the SEI training policy functioning as a vehicle for
promoting English-only ideology?* Based on IPA-situated findings, the answer is
yes – this SEI training policy is functioning as a vehicle for promoting
English-only ideology *if* SEI training sessions are implemented by community colleges or for-profit organizations. However, the content of sessions

conducted by districts and universities will, at least on a minor level, not entirely derive from the ADE (and its symbolic artifacts). Therefore, the values, meanings and beliefs conveyed by D and U facilitators will derive from somewhere other than the ADE.

By utilizing Yanow's (2000) framework for IPA, the findings illustrate the degree to which SEI training requirements abstractly exist among and within the interpretive communities charged with implementation and in the meaning statements communicated through symbolic artifacts. The interplay between dominant discourses voiced by interpretive communities and symbolic artifacts created and applied by the ADE are evidence of the ideological and sociopolitical underpinnings of SEI implementation in Arizona. To be certain, they represent one small manifestation of the much larger issue of equitable access and schooling for EL students in the state, and the degree to which Arizona is allowed authority over a system that may be inconsistent with federal findings with regard to race, language and educational equity.

Note

(1) Originally conceptualized as an observation protocol, the SIOP (Sheltered Instruction Observation Protocol) Model (Echeverría *et al.*, 2008), was co-developed through research funded by the CREDE (Center for Research on Education, Diversity & Excellence) project, which was led by CAL staff and researchers. It is a structured model for delivery of sheltered instruction for ELs. It includes 30 smaller features that are contained in eight overarching components.

References

ADE (2005) Curricular Framework for Full Structured English Immersion (SEI) Endorsement Training (45 Clock Hours). Phoenix, AZ: Arizona Department of Education. See http://www.azed.gov/english-language-learners/files/2011/10/seicurricularframework-completion.pdf. Accessed March 22, 2014.

ADE (2007) *Provisional Structured English Immersion (SEI) Endorsement Training (45 Hours/ Augmented)*. Phoenix, AZ: Arizona Department of Education. See http://www.azed.gov/english-language-learners/files/2011/10/sei-curricularframework-augmented-checklist.pdf. Accessed March 22, 2014.

ADE (2013) *Structured English Immersion, K-12 Endorsements*. Phoenix, AZ: Arizona Department of Education. See http://www.azed.gov/educator-certification/files/2011/09/requirements-for-structured-english-immersion-endorsement.pdf. Accessed March 22, 2014.

Arizona Voter Initiative (2000) Proposition 203, *English for the Children*.

Echevarria, J., Vogt, M.E. and Short, D. (2008) *Making Content Comprehensible for English Language Learners: The SIOP® Model* (3rd edn). Boston: Allyn & Bacon.

HB (2006) 2064, 57th Leg., 2nd Spec. Sess. (Ariz. 2006).

Lau v. Nichols et al. (1974) 414 U.S. No. 72-6520.

McCarty, T.L. (2002) *A Place to be Navajo: Rough Rock and the Struggle for Self-determination in Indigenous Schooling*. Mahwah, NJ: Lawrence Erlbaum.

Moore, S. C. K. and Wiley, T. G. (2014). Interpretive policy analysis for language policy. In F. M. Hult and D. C. Johnson (eds) *Research Methods in Language Policy and Planning: A Practical Guide*. Hoboken, NJ: Wiley-Blackwell.

Yanow, D. (2000) *Conducting Interpretive Policy Analysis*. Thousand Oaks, CA: Sage Publications.

5 (Mis)aligned Curricula: The Case of New Course Content

Amy Markos and Beatriz Arias

In this chapter, we present a critical look at the ways in which pre-service teachers in Arizona are being prepared to teach English learners (ELs), looking specifically at the curricular framework for the state-mandated Structured English Immersion (SEI) Endorsement. As teacher educators who have implemented the endorsement coursework into teacher preparation programs at the university setting, we are concerned that the SEI Endorsement curriculum is misaligned with the literature on preparing teachers for ELs. In teacher preparation, as in all education, it is imperative that practice follows a recognized research base. We assert that Arizona's current SEI Endorsement curriculum is not research based. Our review of the content of the SEI Endorsement program finds that it falls short of adequate preparation for teachers to teach in Arizona's current version of SEI, the four-hour English Language Development (ELD) model. In order that teachers in Arizona be prepared to teach ELs, significant revisions of the current curriculum are necessary.

We begin with an overview of the reasons why all teachers should be prepared to teach ELs and discuss the variety of policies and practices currently in place across the nation's teacher preparation programs. Next, we focus attention on Arizona's mandate that all teachers be prepared to teach ELs. In order to analyze the content of the SEI Endorsement curriculum, we review the literature on preparing teachers for ELs and illustrate the ways in which the content of the SEI Endorsement curriculum is misaligned with the recommendations of scholars, researchers and teacher educators. Knowing that making changes to policy is a hard, slow process, we end the chapter with suggestions for the ways in which teacher educators can make the most of the limited, mandated curriculum currently in place.

The Need to Prepare All Teachers for ELs

In 2000, the numbers of ELs in classrooms was up 105% from 1990 (Kindler, 2002). While colleges have been preparing specialized bilingual education (BLE) and English as a second language (ESL) teachers, the disparities between the academic achievements of ELs and native English-speaking students continue to grow (Wilde, 2010). Efforts focused at preparing a specialized group of BLE and ESL teachers, while well intended, have fallen short of meeting the needs of the growing population of ELs in K–12 classrooms. In 1992, Milk, Mercado and Sapiens foreshadowed the need to move beyond preparing only a specialized group of BLE and ESL teachers, saying:

> in order for the needs of language minority children to be fully met within public schools, it is not sufficient to prepare only bilingual education and ESL teachers to work with them – mainstream teachers must also be prepared to address the special needs of this group. (Milk *et al.*, 1992: 2)

Today, there are three important reasons for preparing all teachers for ELs. First, the EL population is exploding in a way that outnumbers available specialized teachers. Second, when language programs are provided for ELs, they are typically transitional, early-exit programs. When ELs exit out of these models, they are still in need of language development and this demand falls on the mainstream teacher. Third, because of the increase in restrictive language policies, BLE/ESL programs are being dismantled, placing the responsibility to educate ELs on every teacher (Crawford, 1992; Lucas & Grinberg, 2008; Rumberger & Gándara, 2004). While the reasons for preparing all teachers for ELs are consistent across the country, variations exist across state language policies and teacher preparation practices.

Mandated Teacher Preparation for ELs across the United States

Across the United States there is variation in language policy orientation. Some promotion-oriented policy states would describe themselves as 'English Plus' states, stressing the importance of proficiency in more than one language: New Mexico, Oregon, Rhode Island (Menken, 2008). Several states including Illinois and Texas (see Crawford, 2004) promote the expediency model, allowing short-term transitional and developmental BLE, and dual language and ESL programs for ELs. Other states such as Nebraska demonstrate a tolerance model, not mandating or sanctioning BLE programs. Finally, there are the English-only states, Arizona, California and Massachusetts, which display a restrictive language policy orientation, prohibiting and proscribing the use of languages other than English in classrooms. These restrictive language oriented state policies have emerged in the last decade in the US as the English-Only Movement has made its way through ballot measures to the classroom (Wright & Choi, 2006). Of the three states that mandate English as the official language of instruction,

Arizona is the most restrictive, sanctioning the use of students' native language in classrooms and prescribing a teacher preparation endorsement that promotes a restrictive language policy.

Teacher Preparation for ELs in Arizona

Current events in Arizona are prime examples of the reasons why all teachers should be prepared to teach ELs. The numbers of ELs in schools increased by 48% from 1998 to 2008 (Batalova & McHugh, 2010). In 2000 Proposition 203 dismantled Bilingual and ESL language acquisition programs for ELs, replacing them with a quick transition SEI model, not intended to exceed one year. Furthermore, the prescribed SEI model carried with it the directive to prepare all educators for teaching in SEI classrooms (A.R.S. 15-756). To this end, six years after the proposition passed, the state, in conjunction with the Arizona Department of Education (ADE) and the English Language Learner Task Force, set forth the requirement that all teachers must earn an SEI Endorsement in order to be prepared to teach ELs.

Policy Surrounding Arizona's Mandated SEI Endorsement

In 2000 Arizona voters passed Prop. 203, English for the School Children. The law replaced BLE and ESL models for ELs with SEI. The prescribed SEI model carried the mandate to prepare all teachers for teaching in SEI classrooms. Specifically, two pieces of policy, Arizona Board Rule R7-2-615 and Arizona Revised Statute 15-756.09 (A.R.S., 2008), outlined the mandate for and the creation of the SEI Endorsement.

As per Arizona Board Rule R7-2-615 (2006), educators receiving their teaching credentials after August 2006 are required to complete 90 hours of coursework in order to earn the SEI Endorsement. The 90 hours of coursework are broken into two courses: completion of the first course (45 hours) earns teachers an SEI Provisional Endorsement (valid for three years) and completion of the second course (45 hours) provides teachers with their Full SEI Endorsement. Stemming from this board rule, A.R.S. 15-756.09 describes that the State Board of Education:

- shall determine the content of the full and provisional SEI Endorsement curriculum;
- must approve the syllabi for all SEI Endorsement coursework to ensure that courses offered across the state are comparable in amount, scope and quality (including ensuring that teachers offering the courses are qualified to do so); and

- shall require all teacher training programs to include courses necessary for pre-service teachers to obtain a full SEI Endorsement as part of their preparation program.

Based on this, all institutes of higher learning (such as universities) offering teacher-certification coursework are required to insert six credit hours of SEI coursework into their teacher preparation programs (A.R.S. 15-756.09, 2008). Without these additional two courses, pre-service teachers graduating after August 2009 are unable to obtain their institutional recommendation from the university and ineligible to receive a teaching certificate (ADE, 2007). Additionally, before colleges of education may offer the SEI Endorsement courses, they must submit course syllabi to the ADE for approval. The ADE is responsible for approving courses based on compliance with the state mandated curriculum (a description of the curriculum follows later in this chapter). In this sense, the ADE has the final (only) say on the content teacher educators deliver in Arizona's courses for preparing teachers for ELs.

Before we discuss the limitations of the mandated SEI Endorsement curriculum, a review of the literature regarding preparing teachers for ELs provides the necessary context for understanding how Arizona's approach to preparing teachers for ELs is misaligned with the recommendations in the literature.

Qualities, knowledge and skills that all teachers need to effectively teach ELs

In their recent review of the literature, Lucas and Grinberg (2008) acknowledge the importance of preparing teachers for diversity, yet at the same time argue that preparing educators to teach ELs involves ascertaining whether those teachers have specific competencies and dispositions related to linguistically diverse learners. This vision is one in which linguistic diversity is separated out from the overarching ideas of diversity in general (such as culturally diverse, ethnically diverse or economically diverse), going beyond 'the nature of knowledge and skills that teachers must have in addition to what they acquire through their regular teacher preparation' (de Jong & Harper, 2005: 102). In order to identify the additional language-related understandings and qualities teachers need, Lucas and Grinberg (2008) reviewed the empirical literature addressing the preparation of all teachers for linguistically diverse learners.

In their review, they categorize these language-related understandings and qualities as experience, attitudes and beliefs, knowledge and skills (Lucas & Grinberg, 2008: 611). The difference between what we present here and the categories identified by Lucas and Grinberg (2008) is that we have chosen to separate the knowledge category into two categories. The first focuses on knowledge related to ELs (their backgrounds, experiences, cultural norms, etc.); the second relates to knowledge about second language acquisition (SLA).

Using this five-category framework, Figure 5.1 illustrates the interconnectedness across our understanding of the shared agreements in the literature concerning the work of preparing all teachers for ELs:

- experience with language diversity;
- a positive attitude towards linguistic diversity;
- knowledge related to ELs;
- SLA knowledge; and
- skills for simultaneously promoting content and language learning.

Based on our review of the literature and our experience with both teaching ELs and preparing teachers to teach ELs, we perceive these categories to be interrelated, each one affecting the other. Figure 5.1 represents the notion that teachers' dispositions towards, and experience with, language diversity are iterative, both informing and being informed by teachers' knowledge about, and skills for, teaching ELs. Furthermore, we assert that skills for teaching ELs must be situated on top of a foundational understanding of EL-related knowledge and SLA.

Experience with language diversity

Literature on preparing teachers for ELs speaks to the importance of teachers experiencing language diversity for themselves (Lucas & Grinberg, 2008; Mora, 2000; Walqui, 2008). Language experiences can range from taking a foreign language class, to traveling in countries where English is not the primary language, or interacting with ELs in classrooms. Through these experiences,

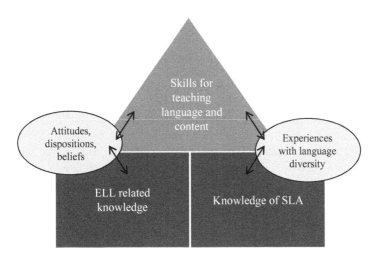

Figure 5.1 The interconnectedness of qualities, knowledge and skills related to preparing teachers for ELs

teachers have opportunities to experience language diversity, reflect on their experiences and create new understandings for future actions with ELs.

Lucas and Grinberg (2008) and Mora (2000) both speak to the importance of teachers taking a foreign language class, an experience which allows teachers a chance to experience what it is like to learn a language. While a teacher's experience of learning a foreign language does not directly correlate to the experience ELs have in mainstream classrooms, it does afford teachers the chance to experience learning a second language. Contact with people who speak a language other than English is also a beneficial experience for teachers of ELs. As a way to empathize with what ELs go through on a daily basis in schools, Lucas and Grinberg (2008) discuss how teachers should reflect on experiences wherein they had to struggle to communicate in order to get their ideas across.

Of all the experiences teachers could have in order to familiarize themselves with language diversity, the most preferable are field experiences in classrooms with ELs (Walqui, 2008). Field experiences allow developing teachers to integrate into a classroom with ELs, and an in-service teacher, giving them the chance to observe and work with language learners. If the in-service teacher is knowledgeable concerning EL instruction, developing teachers also have the chance to see successful instructional approaches for ELs in action. Field experiences can serve as a tool for reflecting on what works, or does not work, for ELs in classrooms and why (Walqui, 2008).

A positive attitude toward linguistic diversity

Tied to experiences with language diversity are teachers' attitudes and beliefs about language learners. Acknowledging that teachers' attitudes affect the way they teach and what they expect from students has significant importance in considerations of how to prepare teachers (Pajares, 1992; Richardson, 1996). To this end, teachers should have a positive attitude towards ELs and linguistic diversity (Lucas & Grinberg, 2008).

While a preparation program cannot change a teacher's attitude (only teachers themselves can change their attitudes), preparing teachers for ELs should include opportunities for teachers to examine and reflect on their attitudes and beliefs about ELs. This includes the necessity that teachers examine their attitudes about their perceived responsibility to teach ELs, bilingualism, the educability of ELs, their willingness to develop as a teacher of ELs, and the sociopolitical nature of teaching and learning. Ideally, teachers of ELs should have the following dispositions:

- a positive attitude about their responsibility to educate ELs;
- a willingness to consider the sociopolitical nature of school and the impact of political dimensions on teaching (Gándara & Maxwell-Jolly, 2000; Lucas & Grinberg, 2008);

- a view on language as both a resource and a right, as opposed to a problem (Ruiz, 1984);
- a view of ELs' cultural experiences and linguistic knowledge as funds of knowledge – a resource for both content knowledge and English learning (Moll *et al.*, 1992; Mora, 2000); and
- a willingness to collaborate with others to better the educational experiences of ELs (Merino, 2007).

As teacher education moves to prepare all teachers for ELs, we believe it is essential to include opportunities for developing teachers to examine their attitudes and beliefs about ELs. Teachers who choose to pursue a BLE or ESL Endorsement typically enter their preparation program with affirming attitudes towards ELs and linguistic diversity. But this is not necessarily the case when preparing the masses.

Teachers may come from backgrounds where they have had little experience in minority communities. Additionally, the increase of English-only models for teaching ELs means pre-service teachers often come to college with little to no personal experiences with bilingual or dual language programs (de Jong *et al.*, 2010). These experiences, combined with media-fueled stereotypes about language learners (Lucas *et al.*, 2008) make it likely that teachers might hold negative attitudes towards ELs (Merino, 2007). When preparing all teachers for language learners, it is essential that preparation coursework includes opportunities for teachers to examine their attitudes towards ELs and develop positive views about language minority students.

Along with experiencing language diversity and having opportunities to examine attitudes and develop positive dispositions about ELs, the work to prepare teachers necessitates effective knowledge about ELs and SLA. We argue that these two categories are the foundation for effectively using skills to teach language and content.

Knowledge related to ELs

The literature reports that teachers need specific knowledge related to ELs. EL-related knowledge includes understanding the interconnectedness between language, culture and identity, the experiences ELs bring to the classroom, how to build relationships with families of language learners, and how to create a comfortable learning environment for ELs. We view EL-related knowledge as part of the foundation for effectively teaching ELs in classrooms (see Figure 5.1). Without these understandings, any 'skills' teachers acquire for teaching ELs may be misused and, therefore, ineffective.

Connections between language, culture and identity

Before teachers can learn 'how' to teach ELs, they must first understand the powerful connections between language, culture and identity (Lucas &

Grinberg, 2008; Merino, 2007; Mora, 2000; Téllez & Waxman, 2005; Walker *et al.*, 2004). An understanding about the connectedness of language with culture and identity will afford teachers the ability to support students' English acquisition in ways that value and respect their native language (L1) and home culture. Additionally, an understanding of the connections between language and culture will offer teachers an awareness of the cultural and linguistic differences between ELs and the mainstream culture and language represented in schools (Walqui, 2008). This understanding can prevent misunderstandings about communication and classroom behaviors between teachers and their ELs (de Jong & Harper, 2005; Lucas & Grinberg, 2008). As classrooms increasingly focus on the acquisition and use of English, it becomes even more critical that teachers understand the connectedness between language, culture and identity. Teachers who work out of this understanding enable ELs to view themselves as part of the classroom experience, rather than outsiders to it.

Background, experiences and proficiencies

Given the powerful connections between language, culture and identity, we support the idea that teachers need an understanding about ELs' backgrounds, prior school experiences and their proficiencies in both their native language and English (Lucas & Grinberg, 2008; Lucas *et al.*, 2008; Merino, 2007; Téllez & Waxman, 2005; Walqui, 2008). With this knowledge, teachers can build relationships with students that will support both their human and academic development. By building on the strengths and experiences ELs bring to the classroom, teachers will be able to plan effective instruction. Without this knowledge, teachers will not be able to anticipate aspects of learning that may be too difficult, nor will they know how to build on prior knowledge and experience in order to support new learning (de Jong & Harper, 2005; Lucas *et al.*, 2008). Teachers must develop an understanding of their ELs and believe that the time and effort it takes to do so is essential for their students' success.

EL families and communities

Just as teachers must build relationships with students in order to adequately meet their needs, they must do the same with ELs' families and communities. This involves understanding the cultural and linguistic differences between mainstream families and families of ELs. Getting to know parents and community members makes it possible to effectively invite parents into the school or extend learning opportunities into the home (Merino, 2007). Being involved with EL families and communities leads teachers away from the misconception that language learners are 'blank slates' (Walqui, 2008: 107) and offers a backdrop for what ELs can do. These relationships constitute a valuable resource, which enables teachers to co-mediate with families a student's future academic and social goals (Mora, 2000).

Creating a comfortable learning environment for ELs

Teachers who are committed to knowing their students' backgrounds and their families, and to understanding how language relates to identity are better able to create a comfortable classroom environment for ELs. All students need a comfortable environment for learning; however, specific attention to creating an environment that is comfortable for ELs is essential because, as Lucas *et al.* (2008: 4) note, 'ELs have been found to feel stigmatized, anxious, unwelcomed and ignored in U.S. classrooms'. According to Krashen's (1982) affective filter theory, if ELs are anxious or fearful about speaking English, they are unable to process linguistic inputs or to produce language, which severely limits their learning about language and content. Not only can anxiety limit ELs' learning, it also stifles their social interactions in the classroom. Therefore, teachers must also be prepared to support students in upholding a safe and anxiety-free environment (Lucas & Grinberg, 2008; Lucas *et al.*, 2008; Pappamihiel, 2002). The classroom environment becomes the capstone of teachers' learning related to ELs; creating a safe environment is only possible when teachers spend time knowing their ELs' backgrounds, their families and their cultures.

In summary, if teachers are to effectively teach ELs, they must have knowledge related to ELs that includes: (a) an understanding of the connectedness between language, culture and identity; (b) ELs' backgrounds, experiences and proficiencies in the L1; (c) an understanding of ELs' families and communities; and (d) ways to create a comfortable learning environment for ELs. This knowledge is half of the foundation teachers need in order to understand how to use strategies for teaching content and language effectively; the other critical piece of the foundation is an understanding of how students acquire a second language.

SLA knowledge

Equally as important as a teacher's knowledge about ELs is the opportunity for them to develop knowledge related to the domain of language and SLA. Teachers can rely on their knowledge of SLA as the basis for future instructional and affective decisions concerning the education of ELs. We perceive teacher knowledge about second language development to include understandings about the differences and similarities between L1 and second (L2) acquisition and the role of a students' L1 in developing their L2. Knowledge about SLA also includes the various language mechanics, forms and uses surrounding language learners both within and beyond the walls of the classroom.

Differences and similarities between L1 and L2 acquisition

The beginning of an understanding of SLA requires an understanding of the similarities and differences between learning a first and second language. Without SLA knowledge, teachers are left to assume that learning a second language mirrors learning a first. While L2 development does in some ways mirror L1 development, without specific knowledge about SLA, teachers may rely too much on the similarities and 'overlook the impact of differences between L1 and L2 learning on effective oral language and literacy development and academic achievement for ELs' (de Jong & Harper, 2005: 103).

Additionally, teachers need to comprehend the complexities of learning a language and content simultaneously. Without such, they may misleadingly rely on their experiences of learning a foreign language as equal to an EL's experience of learning an L2 while simultaneously learning content. In order for teachers to understand SLA, they should have a foundational understanding of the main theories of SLA (behaviorist, nativist and interactionist) and how these theories influence classroom practices (Peregoy & Boyle, 2008).

Language mechanics and forms

Teachers also need an understanding of language forms (such as academic versus social) and mechanics (Lucas & Grinberg, 2008; Lucas et al., 2008; Mora, 2000; Téllez & Waxman, 2005; Walqui, 2008). There are two main forms of language that ELs need in order to be successful in school: academic and social/conversational language. Attention to these forms of language will prepare teachers to address the values and differences of these language forms, especially as they are used in school. Teachers need to be able to honor the social forms of language ELs bring to and use in the classroom, while also preparing them for academic success by explicitly teaching academic language (Lucas & Grinberg, 2008; Lucas et al., 2008; Schleppegrell, 2012; Walqui, 2008).

Along with language forms, teachers need to understand the different approaches for teaching the mechanics of language and know which to use with ELs and why. Unfortunately, there is not one 'right' way to teach language mechanics, and most ELs benefit from a combination of explicit (through direct instruction) and implicit (through communicative approaches) teaching methods. Additionally, teachers need to be able to recognize language forms in the content areas and discern the language mechanics instruction that will enable ELs to be successful in content areas (Lucas et al., 2008: 5). In this sense, teachers should not just look through language for content learning, but look at language in the content areas (de Jong & Harper, 2005). Understanding the forms of language, as well as how language mechanics relate to content topics, will further teachers' knowledge about SLA.

The role of L1 in developing L2

A final component of SLA knowledge that is critical for teachers is an understanding of how students' native language supports their English development. As policy and societal demands place increasing pressure on ELs to acquire English quickly, less attention is spent on the role of the L1 in developing an L2 (Mora, 2000). To move teachers beyond a limited focus of English-only, teacher preparation needs to include the importance of using a student's L1 to develop their abilities in English (such as accessing prior knowledge and making connections to previous learning processes). In addition, EL teachers need to understand the value of using students' first languages in content area instruction. Knowing how to use a student's L1 (in instructional tasks such as brainstorming, verbal clarification or writing first drafts) will prepare teachers for increasing that student's English acquisition by purposefully integrating their native language abilities. Finally, if teachers have an understanding of a student's first language, they are better prepared to assess typical EL mistakes in oral and written English production (de Jong & Harper, 2005).

When teachers have an understanding of SLA, combined with knowledge about their students on a personal level, they have a solid foundation for effectively using strategies for teaching ELs. Without this foundation, teachers may assume that 'just good teaching' is sufficient to meet ELs' needs. However, overlooking the linguistic and cultural needs of ELs renders 'good teaching' ineffective (de Jong & Harper, 2005).

Skills for simultaneously promoting content and language learning

Finally, building from a foundational understanding about ELs and SLA, all teachers must develop skills for integrating content and language instruction (de Jong & Harper, 2005; Gándara & Maxwell-Jolly, 2006; Lucas & Grinberg, 2008; Lucas et al., 2008; Merino, 2007; Mora, 2000; Téllez & Waxman, 2005; Walker et al., 2004; Walqui, 2008). Teachers of ELs must be able to simultaneously teach content and language, promoting language development and content knowledge at the same time. Therefore, effective EL teachers need skills in the following areas: developing lessons that integrate content and language, understanding and implementing appropriate assessments, and collaborating with colleagues.

Developing lessons that incorporate language and content

In order to meet the needs of ELs, all teachers need to be able to design lessons that incorporate content and language. To do so, teachers must first consider the language demands in a subject area, as well as the possibilities for developing language in the content areas (de Jong & Harper, 2005; Lucas & Grinberg, 2008; Merino, 2007; Téllez & Waxman, 2005). Once teachers are able to see how language connects to content, they need to be prepared to explicitly (through mini lessons) and implicitly (through natural communication in the lesson) draw attention to language. Along with recognizing the language demands in the content areas, there are certain pedagogical skills (Echevarria et al., 2008; Gándara & Maxwell-Jolly, 2006; Lucas & Grinberg,

2008) that are helpful for designing and implementing lessons that integrate content and language, such as:

- making connections between academic language and students' L1 (Lucas & Grinberg, 2008; Walqui, 2008);
- providing additional resources for students to access content information (such as L1 texts or books, visuals, multimedia, etc.) (Echevarria *et al.*, 2008);
- using interaction in lessons to promote the academic and conversational skills of ELs (Echevarria *et al.*, 2008; Lucas & Grinberg, 2008; Lucas *et al.*, 2008; Walqui, 2008); and
- creating language-rich lessons in which ELs have the opportunity to read, write, speak and listen (Echevarria *et al.*, 2008; Lucas & Grinberg, 2008).

The use of pedagogical strategies will help teachers in planning and implementing effective lessons for ELs. Along with planning and delivering lessons, teachers need skills for understanding and implementing assessments that inform their instruction and monitor student growth.

Understanding and implementing appropriate assessment

As teachers learn how to modify and adapt their instruction for ELs, so must they learn to do so for their assessment practices. Assessing ELs in the classroom involves assessing both students' content and language, as well utilizing a variety of assessment measures. Teachers need to be prepared to assess content and language effectively. In order to do so, they must first understand that typical content assessments rely heavily on language. Once they recognize that language may be a barrier for accurately gauging content understanding, teachers need skills for modifying content assessments accordingly (Echevarria *et al.*, 2008; Merino, 2007; Peregoy & Boyle, 2008). These could include modifications such as reading test questions to ELs, allowing students to share their answers verbally (as opposed to in writing), and looking beyond language mistakes (grammar, punctuation and spelling) to assess content understanding on written assessments.

In addition to modifying content assessments as necessary, teachers also need to be prepared to assess ELs' language development. Similar rules apply for assessing language in the content areas. Teachers need skills to decipher whether an assessment of students' language ability might be hindered by content area knowledge (Peregoy & Boyle, 2008). For example, in an attempt to gauge a student's oral proficiency, a teacher may ask a student to give five causes for the Civil War. If the student is unable to do so, the teacher may assume the student does not have the oral proficiency to answer, when in reality it may be that the student has the language skills but is lacking content knowledge. Teachers need skills for deciphering both, when language impedes accurate content assessment and when content impedes accurate language assessment.

Along with becoming more cognizant of what assessments intentionally and unintentionally assess, teachers need to be prepared to utilize a variety of assessments: formal, informal, whole group, individual, authentic assessments and portfolios (Echevarria *et al.*, 2008; Merino, 2007; Peregoy & Boyle, 2008; Walqui, 2008). Through a multidimensional approach to assessment, teachers will be better prepared to access students' abilities in both content and language in order to effectively monitor student progress and plan future instruction. When teachers are prepared with skills for promoting both language and content (through lesson planning, delivery and assessment), they are equipped with the actions necessary for putting their theoretical and foundational knowledge about ELs to use in the classroom.

Collaborating with colleagues

Finally, because preparing teachers for ELs does not stop once they complete a program or class, teachers need skills for future collaboration with colleagues as they continue to make sense of how to meet the needs of ELs (Merino, 2007; Walker *et al.*, 2004; Walqui, 2008). The pedagogical skills a teacher learns will need to be refined as they continue throughout their career. Therefore, teachers need skills for working effectively and collaboratively with others (peers and EL specialists) so that, as the needs of ELs change, so can teacher effectively change their practice (Walqui, 2008). Teachers also need skills for establishing small communities or partnerships with colleagues that allow for sharing ideas and supporting one another (Merino, 2007; Walker *et al.*, 2004). It is through collaboration that teachers can balance the responsibilities of meeting the needs of ELs.

In summary, the literature on preparing all teachers for ELs reports that preparation should address teacher qualities, knowledge and skills. Qualities relate to preparing teachers through experiences with language diversity and opportunities to examine their attitudes and beliefs about ELs. Knowledge relates to teachers understanding of ELs and SLA. Skills refer to the strategies teachers need to act on their knowledge about ELs and SLA in a way that allows for effective integration of content and language instruction. Effective teachers of ELs are those that have a balanced preparation addressing these qualities, knowledge and skills. Without such a balance, teachers are mis-prepared for their future work with ELs. It is on this note that we move to discuss the (mis)alignment between the literature on the preparation of teachers for ELs and the SEI Endorsement curriculum mandated in the state of Arizona.

Arizona's SEI Endorsement Curriculum

While it was the law that required that all teachers earn an SEI Endorsement, it was ADE that determined what the SEI Endorsement

Table 5.1 Curricular Frameworks for the two SEI Endorsement courses: Content objectives and hours

Course #1: Provisional SEI Endorsement (45 hours)		Course #2: Full SEI Endorsement (45 hours)	
Content objective	Hours	Content objective	Hours
EL proficiency standards	3 hours	EL proficiency standards	1 hour
		Data analysis and application	3 hours
Formal and informal assessment	3 hours	Formal and informal assessment	3 hours
Foundations of SEI	3 hours	Foundations of SEI	1 hour
SEI strategies	24 hours	SEI strategies	25 hours
		Parent/home/school scaffolding	3 hours
Flex hours*	12 hours	Flex hours*	9 hours

Notes: *ADE recommends that flex hours be put towards the SEI strategies content objective.

coursework would include. As developed by the ADE, the SEI Endorsement curriculum includes the following categories: EL proficiency standards, data analysis and application, formal and informal assessment, foundations of SEI, and SEI strategies. Along with outlining the curricular objectives, ADE also set hour requirements for each category. The categories of the state curriculum objectives and the minimum hours attached to each objective are listed in Table 5.1.

Both courses restrict pre-service teachers' access to knowledge regarding meeting the needs of ELs in K–12 classrooms. By narrowly focusing course content on Arizona's recently adopted SEI model, the courses limits pre-service teachers' exposure to English-only methods and approaches deemed appropriate within the current restrictive language environment. Overall, the 90 hours of the SEI Endorsement curriculum represents an unbalanced approach to developing the qualities, knowledge and skills all teachers need in order to be prepared to teach ELs.

The Misaligned Curriculum

While Arizona has outlined the requirements and curricular content for preparing teachers for ELs, the SEI Endorsement is misaligned with the literature on preparing teachers for ELs. The literature on preparing all teachers for ELs maintains that teachers need certain qualities, knowledge and skills in order to effectively teach ELs. To understand how teachers in Arizona are being (mis)prepared to teach ELs for each of these areas, we highlight the (mis)alignments between the literature and Arizona's approach to preparing teachers through the SEI Endorsement coursework.

Qualities: Attitude and experience

To effectively teach ELs, teachers need to have a positive attitude towards ELs and linguistic diversity. Arizona's mandated courses do not address teachers' attitudes and beliefs about ELs. Neither does it address whether teachers have past experiences with ELs, effectively ignoring strong conclusions from the literature (Lucas & Grinberg, 2008; Lucas et al., 2008; Merino, 2007; Mora, 2000; Téllez & Waxman, 2005; Walker et al., 2004). While Arizona mandates that all teachers must be prepared to teach ELs, they do not encourage teachers to examine their beliefs about ELs in the process. While it must be true that some teachers do examine their attitudes about ELs while taking the SEI coursework, this is a mere coincidence.

Furthermore, when completing their SEI coursework, teachers do not have to 'experience' anything. ADE does not require any outcome or output from teachers completing the coursework, other than they attend the class for the required hours. Pre-service teachers do not have the opportunity to intern in BLE and ESL programs while pursuing a BLE or ESL Endorsement because of the state's mandate that schools use the SEI/four-hour ELD model.

Knowledge: ELs and SLA

Along with not accounting for teacher qualities, the state curriculum scarcely includes time for foundational understandings related to ELs and SLA. Without generous attention to SLA principles and the impact of cultural considerations on classroom learning, future teachers are left with a misguided understanding of how to effectively teach ELs (de Jong & Harper, 2005).

Skills for promoting content and language

Furthermore, the curriculum overemphasizes skills (strategies) for teaching ELs to the detriment of foundational knowledge about linguistic and cultural diversity. With the suggestion that 70 of the 90 hours of coursework be devoted to SEI strategies, the coursework has the potential to promote an 'it's just good teaching' mentality among SEI-endorsed teachers.

Finally, although the curriculum for the SEI coursework emphasizes the skills teachers need, the strategies strongly emphasize English-only approaches. The literature emphasizes that students' L1 can and should be used for learning (content and language) (August & Hakuta, 1997; Echevarria et al., 2008; Lucas & Grinberg, 2008) as well as for promoting a comfortable learning environment (Lucas et al., 2008). Arizona's emphasis on English-only ignores these possibilities for supporting ELs through the use of their L1.

In conclusion, ADE's response to the mandate has effectively deregulated teacher preparation for ELs in Arizona. First, by narrowly defining what teachers need in order to complete their SEI coursework, ADE has created a checklist of items that are to be covered through clock hours, as opposed to thoughtful, reflective learning experiences. This creates the false assumption that teachers can be prepared merely by completing a set number of course-work hours. Second, the state's power to approve or deny syllabi dangerously restricts the preparation of teachers for ELs by limiting the content to that which aligns with the ADE curriculum. Third, ADE allows for a wide variety of institutions, organizations and school districts to offer the SEI coursework, thereby diminishing its consistency. Although ADE must approve any syllabus for content, methods of course delivery are not accounted for, resulting in great variations in delivery and effectiveness (Moore, 2008). In summary, with a narrow focus on English-only methods, an emphasis on skills over theory, and a lack of quality control across course delivery, we believe the state-mandated SEI courses mis-prepare teachers' for their future work with ELs.

In the final section of this chapter, we offer a call to teacher educators, addressing what needs to be done to make the most of the scripted, mis-aligned approach to preparing teachers in Arizona for their future work with ELs.

Teacher educators as agents of change

For now, it seems unlikely that Arizona will change its mandate that every teacher must earn an SEI Endorsement as part of the certification process. It is equally unlikely that the ADE will redesign the mandated curricular framework for the SEI teacher preparation courses. Knowing this, we suggest that it is not enough to *hope* for change; teacher educators must *make* change. As teacher educators in Arizona move forward with preparing future teachers to be effective instructors of ELs, there are a number of things they can do to make the most of the limited mandated curriculum through taking agency in the policy implementation process (Corson, 1999).

First, teacher educators must critique and expand Arizona's model for teacher preparation. This begins with dedication by teacher educators to remaining updated and knowledgeable about the literature and research regarding what we know about how best to instruct ELs, so that pre-service teachers can reconcile misalignments between the prescribed curriculum and the generally accepted research and theory in the field related to best practices for the instruction of ELs. Next, once misalignments have been identified, teacher educators must work to enact the mandated curriculum in a way that positions themselves within the confines of the policy/curriculum, while simultaneously teasing out state requirements in both a critical and a supportive manner. Through their selection of course resources, materials and learning experiences, teacher educators can find ways to expose pre-service teachers to models and approaches outside of Arizona's restrictive English-only model, ones that place a higher value on the linguistic and cultural resources ELs bring to school.

Finally, teacher educators must provide opportunities for pre-service teachers to examine their attitudes about diversity, policies related to language learners (i.e. instructional policies as well as policies related to immigration), and their responsibilities to teach ELs in K–12 classrooms. Pre-service teachers in Arizona are situated in a restrictive language policy environment and are required to take coursework that exemplifies those policies in practice. When teacher preparation programs simply implement the SEI Endorsement coursework, without addressing where the course curriculum and context originated or why pre-service teachers are required to complete the courses, pre-service teachers may falsely presume that SEI courses are required because they accurately reflect what teachers need in order to effectively teach ELs. Further, they might presume that through the completion of two courses, they are prepared to effectively teach ELs. In reality, however, there could be nothing further from the truth. It is the responsibility of teacher educators to be honest with future teachers about where the SEI coursework comes from and in what ways it supports *and falls short* of preparing teachers for ELs.

Teacher educators need to both prepare pre-service teachers based on familiarity with Arizona's SEI model, while also working to expose new teachers to models and approaches beyond the restriction-oriented context of Arizona. Pre-service teacher preparation should also reflect the resources ELs bring to school, and ways to honor ELs' educational rights. As teacher educators make critical and thoughtful changes and additions to SEI courses, it is important that these changes are explicit to their pre-service teacher students. When teacher educators critique and expand on the SEI curricular framework, therefore taking agency to enact the policy in thoughtful, local ways, future teachers are thus empowered to critique and expand on other prescribed curricula, including the state's model of ELD and the Discrete Skills Inventory, for educating ELs. While SEI mandates may be here to stay, it is essential that teacher educators continue to provide the required course curricula from a critical perspective.

References

ADE (2007) *Curricular Framework for SEI Endorsement*. Phoenix, AZ: Arizona Department of Education. See http://www.ade.state.az.us/oelas; http://www.azed.gov/english-language-learners/files/2011/10/sei-curricularframework-augmented-checklist.pdf; http://www.azed.gov/english-language-learners/files/2011/10/seicurricularframework-completion.pdf. Accessed May 28, 2010.
A.R.S. (2008) Arizona Revised Statute 15-756.09.

August, D. and Hakuta, K. (1997) *Improving Schooling for Language-minority Children: A Research Agenda*. Washington, DC: National Academy Press.

Batalova, J. and McHugh, M. (2010) *Number and Growth of Students in US Schools in Need of English Instruction*. Washington, DC: Migration Policy Institute.

Corson, D. (1999) *Language Policy in Schools: A Resource for Teachers and Administrators*. Mahwah, NJ: Lawrence Erlbaum Associates.

Crawford, J. (1992) *Hold Your Tongue: Bilingualism and the Politics of English Only*. Reading, MA: Addison Wesley.

Crawford, J. (2004) *No Child Left Behind: Misguided Approach to School Accountability for English Learners*. Philadelphia, PA: National Association for Bilingual Education.

de Jong, E.J. and Harper, C.A. (2005) Preparing mainstream teachers for English-language learners: Is being a good teacher good enough? *Teacher Education Quarterly* 32 (2), 101–124.

de Jong, E.J., Arias, M.B. and Sanchez, M.T. (2010) Undermining teacher competencies: Another look at the impact of restrictive language policies. In P. Gándara and M. Hopkins (eds) *Forbidden Language: English Learners and Restrictive Language Policies* (pp. 118–136). New York: Teachers College.

Echevarria, J., Vogt, M. and Short, D. (2008) *Making Content Comprehensible for English Learners: The SIOP Model*. Boston, MA: Pearson.

Gándara, P. and Maxwell-Jolly, J. (2000) Preparing teachers for diversity: A dilemma of quality and quantity. Santa Cruz, CA: Center for the Future of Teaching and Learning. See http://www.cftl.org/documents/Jolly_paper.pdf. Accessed March 22, 2014.

Gándara, P. and Maxwell-Jolly, J. (2006) Critical issues in developing the teacher corps for English learners. In K. Tellex and H. Waxman (eds) *Preparing Quality Educators for English Language Learners: Research, Policies, and Practices* (pp. 99–120). Mahwah, NJ: Lawrence Erlbaum.

Kindler, A.L. (2002) *Survey of the L.E.P. Students and Available Educational Programs and Services, 2000–2001 Survey Report*. Washington, DC: National Clearinghouse for English Language Acquisition and Language Instruction Educational Programs.

Krashen, S.D. (1982) *Principles and Practice in Second Language Acquisition*. New York: Pergamon Press.

Lucas, T. and Grinberg, J. (2008) Responding to the linguistic reality of mainstream classrooms: Preparing all teachers to teach English learners. In M. Cochran-Smith, S. Fieman-Nemser and D.J. McIntyre (eds) *Handbook of Research on Teacher Education* (3rd edn) (pp. 606–636). New York: Routledge.

Lucas, T., Villegas, A.M. and Freedson-Gonzales, M. (2008) Linguistically responsive teacher education: Preparing classroom teachers to teach English learners. *Journal of Teacher Education* 59 (4), 361–373.

Menken, K. (2008) *English Learners Left Behind: Standardized Testing as Language Policy*. Clevedon: Multilingual Matters.

Merino, B. (2007) Identifying cultural competencies for teachers of English learners. *UCLMRI Newsletter* 16 (4), 1–8.

Milk, R., Mercado, C. and Sapiens, A. (1992) Re-thinking the education of teachers of language minority children: Developing reflective teachers for changing schools. *NCBE Focus* 6 (Summer).

Moll, L.C., Amanti, C., Neff, D. and Gonzalez, N. (1992) Funds of knowledge for teaching: Using a qualitative approach to connect homes and classrooms. *Theory Into Practice* 31 (2), 132–141.

Moore, S.C.K. (2008) Language policy implementation: Arizona's SEI training. Unpublished doctoral dissertation, Arizona State University.

Mora, J.K. (2000) Staying the course in times of change: Preparing teachers for language minority education. *Journal of Teacher Education* 51 (5), 345–357.

Pajares, M.F. (1992) Teachers' beliefs and educational research: Cleaning up a messy construct. *Review of Educational Research* 62 (3), 307–332.

Pappamihiel, N.E. (2002) English as a second language students and English language anxiety: Issues in the mainstream classroom. *Research in the Teaching of English* 36 (3), 327–355.

Peregoy, S.F. and Boyle, O. (2008) *Reading, Writing and Learning in ESL: A Resource Book for Teaching K-12 English Learners*. Boston, MA: Allyn and Bacon.

Richardson, V. (1996) The role of attitudes and beliefs in learning to teach. In J. Sikula (ed.) *Handbook of Research on Teacher Education*, 2nd edn (pp. 102–119). New York: Association of Teacher Educators.

Ruiz, R. (1984) Orientations in language planning. *NABE: The Journal for the National Association for Bilingual Education* 8 (2), 15–34.

Rumberger, R. and Gándara, P. (2004) Seeking equity in the education of California's English learners. *Teachers College Record* 106, 2031–2055.

Schleppegrell, M. (2012) Academic language in teaching and learning: Introduction to the special issue. *Elementary School Journal* 112 (3), 409–418.

Téllez, K. and Waxman, H. (2005) *Quality Teachers for English Learners*. Philadelphia, PA: Laboratory for Student Success, Temple University Center for Research in Human Development and Education. See http://files.eric.ed.gov/fulltext/ED508447.pdf Accessed March 22, 2014.

Walker, A., Shafer, J. and Liams, M. (2004) 'Not in my classroom': Teacher attitudes towards English learners in the mainstream classroom. *NABE Journal of Research and Practice* 2 (1), 130–159.

Walqui, A. (2008) The development of teacher expertise to work with adolescent English learners: A model and a few priorities. In L.S. Verplaetse and N. Migliacci (eds) *Inclusive Pedagogy for English Learners: A Handbook of Research and Informed Practices* (pp. 103–125). New York: Lawrence Erlbaum.

Wilde, J. (2010) Comparing results of the NAEP long-term trend assessment: ELLs, former ELLs, and English-proficient students. Paper presented at the Annual Meeting of the American Educational Research Association, Denver, CO.

Wright, W.E. and Choi, D. (2006) The impact of language and high-stakes testing policies on elementary school English language learners in Arizona. *Education Policy Analysis Archives* 14 (13), 1–56.

6 Exploring Principals' Concerns Regarding the Implementation of Arizona's Mandated SEI Model

Giovanna Grijalva and Margarita Jimenez-Silva

This chapter tracks the implementation of Structured/Sheltered English Immersion (SEI) in Arizona schools from principals' perspectives. Eight participating principals were interviewed regarding their impressions of, and experiences with, SEI implementation, including the mandated four-hour English language development (ELD) block. The Concerns Based Adoption Model (CBAM) (Hall & Hord, 1987) provides a framework for situating participants' understanding of Arizona's language policy and was used to identify and document principals' levels of concern regarding the implementation of the policy.

Legal Context Affecting ELs in Arizona

As is documented in previous chapters, the context of educating English learners (ELs) in Arizona has changed significantly in recent years. Beginning with *Flores v. Arizona* (1992), the impact of shifts in educational language policy continues as part of the legal backdrop in Arizona schools serving ELs (see Appendix A). The effects in schools include programs of instruction, the identification and placement of ELs, funding, and teacher preparation and education, to name a few (Jimenez-Silva & Nguyen, 2012). Ultimately, principals and teachers in schools working with ELs are left to make sense of what new laws and mandates mean and grapple with the day-to-day implications. Most of the issues raised by the principals interviewed as part of the research discussed in this chapter stem directly from the passage of House Bill 2064 (HB, 2006) (see Appendix B), which generated Arizona's SEI model. The model consists of a four-hour block of instruction for ELs. It is important to understand that HB 2064 grew out of preceding legislation in Arizona. Others have argued that HB 2064 and its related preceding legislation highlight patterns in language ideology represented by both Arizona's policymakers and its constituents (Mahoney *et al.*, 2010; Wright, 2012).

English Language Learners Task Force

In the spring of 2006, the Arizona Revised Statutes (A.R.S. 15-756.01) established an English Language Learners Task Force (2007), which consisted of a nine-member committee comprised of three members appointed by the Superintendent of Public Instruction, two members by the Governor, two members by the President of the State Senate, and two members by the Speaker of the House of Representatives. Members of the Task Force served a four-year term. At its inception, seven of the original Task Force members were appointed by conservative office holders; two were appointed by the Arizona Democratic governor, Janet Napolitano. This first Task Force was charged with developing and adopting a research-based model of SEI programs for use by school districts and charter schools mandated to implement SEI as the primary program model for the instruction of EL students. Furthermore, the Task Force was mandated, as stated in §ARS 15-756.01, to create an SEI model(s) that included a minimum of four hours per day of ELD for students classified as ELs in their first year of instruction. A second Task Force served a four-year term and its focus included the continued monitoring of the implementation of the SEI model. Currently, there is no Task Force and the responsibilities previously assigned to it have been transferred to the Arizona Board of Education.

Policy and the SEI model

Students in Arizona are formally identified as ELs based on scores on a single statewide assessment, the Arizona English Language Learner Assessment (AZELLA). The proficiency levels identified as part of test score reporting for the AZELLA include Pre-Emergent, Emergent, Basic, Intermediate and Proficient. Once identified, students identified as ELs are placed in a transitional SEI program until they attain proficiency in the English language, which according to Proposition 203 (Arizona Voter Initiative, 2000) should not normally exceed one year. In compliance with federal legislation, school districts conduct annual language proficiency assessments for all students identified as ELs. Scores from annual assessments are used for EL student placement in instructional programs in the following school year.

In 2006, the Task Force adopted a model of SEI. Schools had previously adopted SEI as the model of instruction for ELs in English-only settings, as required by the passage of Prop. 203. The new, further explicated version of SEI specifies how school principals are to allocate and design four hours of ELD instruction for EL students. The model also outlines guidance for principals' placement of ELs in programs of instruction. Based on the model of SEI mandated by the 2006 Task Force, the impact of students' AZELLA scores is weighty because scores predict student grouping. Students are to be grouped for instruction according to AZELLA scores, and once students score as Proficient on the AZELLA, they are to be transferred into mainstream classrooms.

According to the ADE (2008), the SEI model provides a clear direction for teachers, achievable targets for students, and student progression to proficiency in English. It claims that the four key principles of the model are: (a) English is fundamental to content area mastery; (b) language ability-based grouping facilitates rapid language learning; (c) time on task increases academic learning; and (d) a discrete language skills approach facilitates English language learning. The structure of the model is based on aligning classroom instruction with English Language Proficiency (ELP) standards and the Discrete Skills Inventory (DSI), a publication from ADE (n.d.) (see Lillie & Markos, Chapter 8, this volume). ELs are to receive four hours of ELD in the areas of reading, vocabulary, writing, grammar and oral English as outlined in the ELP Standards (ADE, 2008). Specific times (ranging from 15 to 60 minutes) are allocated for each area based on AZELLA proficiency levels (Table 6.1). Implementation is mandated and school principals are required to comply with ELD and DSI time allocations, as well as student grouping structures.

Critiques of SEI

In developing the four-hour SEI model, the Task Force rightly recognized that ELs need to acquire English language skills in order to benefit from English-only content area instruction. Most scholars in language education and acquisition agree that learning a new language is a process that occurs

Table 6.1 Time allocations for ELD by AZELLA level

Students testing at AZELLA Pre-emergent and Emergent

Conversation	Grammar	Reading	Vocabulary	Pre-writing
45 min.	60 min.	60 min.	60 min.	15 min.

Students testing at AZELLA Basic

Conversation	Grammar	Reading	Vocabulary	Pre-writing
30 min.	60 min.	60 min.	60 min.	30 min.

Students testing at AZELLA Intermediate

Conversation	Grammar	Reading	Vocabulary	Writing
15 min.	60 min.	60 min.	60 min.	45 min.

over many years, and that it is nearly impossible to become academically proficient in a new language within one year (Hakuta *et al.*, 2000; Lightbown & Spada, 2006; Ovando *et al.*, 2006).

Numerous studies have demonstrated the effectiveness of utilizing ELs' native languages for both content learning and the development of English language and literacy proficiency (August & Shanahan, 2006; Cummins, 2000; Krashen, 1996). However, educational language policies in Arizona have effectively dismantled instruction for bilingual speakers using any language other than English. The discrepancy between evidence supporting native language instruction and policies requiring English-only instruction elicit an overarching question guiding our research: how do educators reconcile their understanding of research with the practical demands of mandated programs and policies in their school communities?

Many educators and EL experts across the nation are skeptical and concerned about the educational language policies adopted in Arizona. Focusing on four hours a day of intensive English conversation, vocabulary, grammar, reading and writing only is an instructional innovation that has not been scientifically proven (August *et al.*, 2010; Blanchard *et al.*, in press; Martinez-Wenzl *et al.*, 2010). Early critics of Arizona's policies (Krashen *et al.*, 2007) published concerns regarding the new SEI model and its lack of alignment with scientific evidence for educating EL students.

Understanding and Implementing Language Policy

The findings presented in this chapter explore school principals' interpretation of the mandates regarding ELD and DSI implementation for the instruction of ELs in Arizona. The context of the study includes the ADE's emphasis on school leaders' faithful implementation of the SEI model, including the four-hour block. One example of its oversight is the establishment of mechanisms that monitor school principals through investigating EL English proficiency achievement rates. Researchers have investigated the implementation of English-only language policies and the responsibilities of school principals and teachers to make sense of their short- and long-term effects and the challenge inherent in interpreting policies (Gándara *et al.*, 2003; Wright & Choi, 2006). The debate continues over the effectiveness of English-only language policies and whether policymakers are mandating appropriate educational approaches for ELs across the country (Krashen *et al.*, 2007; Mahoney *et al.*, 2010).

Under these state policies and mandates, school principals are grappling with reconciling the gap between what the law requires and what educators and researchers understand to be effective. For example, many questions have surfaced regarding the theoretical basis underlying ability grouping for the instruction of English language prior to academic content. Mora (2009) identified educators' concerns about guiding instruction based on English language standards first, and then transitioning students into mainstream, content-based instructional classes (with peers who have been receiving grade-level content instruction from the outset). Flores (2010) and Garcia *et al.* (2010) have specifically questioned the validity of using AZELLA for grouping purposes. While school principals generally would likely agree that time, resources and staff development are necessary components of effective implementation, meeting the academic and language needs of ELs remains a key priority.

The passage of statutes such as those resulting from HB 2064, with its accompanying rules and regulations, does not ensure immediate policy implementation in practice. Educational policies are implemented at the grassroots level – by district administrators, principals and classroom teachers. We know, based on research from the field (Fowler, 2004) and our own experiences in schools, that educators are not typically enthusiastic about top-down policies regardless of whether mandates are federal or state-based. Therefore, the success of programs depends largely on both motivating school principals to implement policies, and on the provision of resources for effective implementation. With the desire to find out how school principals understand and implement challenging and sometimes conflicting language policies, we sought out the research outlined in this chapter.

Exploring Principals' Concerns

What follows is our attempt at understanding how language policy in Arizona affects school principals and their concerns about implementing such policy. Specifically, we are interested in addressing the following questions:

(1)   How do Arizona Department of Education (ADE) educational language policies affect school principals and the educational environments in which they work?
(2)   What are the concerns of eight school principals regarding their capacity to meet the language needs of ELs?

Purpose of the study

Educational language policies can be complex and unwieldy. As such, they are often subject to varied interpretations by educators. However, all school leaders and teachers are required to work within the confines of educational language policies. Currently in Arizona, school principals continue to grapple with how to best implement the new SEI model as mandated by HB 2064. It is imperative that policymakers support the principal practitioners regarding required program implementation, which also involves developing an understanding of the policies themselves. Particularly given the increasing population of ELs in today's schools, state and federal policies must provide clear and precise direction, support and resources for the principal practitioners being held accountable for educational language policy implementation.

This study explores issues related to how language policy is put into practice. The findings illustrate how school principals are coping with top-down policy mandates regarding ELs in Arizona's schools. In the following sections, we outline the story of how school principals have reacted to meeting the needs of their EL and larger student populations in the face of the SEI, ELD and DSI educational language policies that have been mandated in the state, including reactions to their responsibility for the implementation of the SEI-based curricula and instruction.

Theoretical Overview

To examine principals' discursive practices and actions within a theoretical framework, we used the lens of Hall and Hord's (1987, 2001) Stages of Concern (SoC). SoC, a modified portion of the larger CBAM, served as our overarching framework for identifying concerns around principals' implementation of the four-hour language block for our study. Although all school principals are required to execute state SEI mandates, individual principals likely perceive implementation issues differently, and therefore each may have different kinds of concerns, depending upon their own knowledge and experience (Hall & Hord, 1987).

Concerns Based Adoption Model

According to the CBAM (Hall & Hord, 1987, 2001), individual principals are likely to navigate various stages of concern as they learn more about implementing the SEI four-hour language model. As principals move through these stages, they may respond to change in their schools and in their community environment in different ways. Hall and Rutherford (1983) note how principals involved with the implementation of a new innovation might be viewed as change agents, whose responses to change may vary depending on their setting and the amount of support they receive to facilitate implementation of a new innovation. In this way, certain principals may be more or less likely to function as change agents amid a new innovation.

Change, in this case related to the implementation of new innovation(s), is complicated, and principals today are placed in complex situations when they are responsible for implementing new policies. The CBAM approach was originally proposed with an important precondition: that the effective change facilitator understood the clients (e.g. students or teachers) and made adjustments according to their needs (Hall & Hord, 1987). This method is an approach that stemmed from concerns theory (Hall & Hord, 1987) and has been incorporated into CBAM through the SoC. The SoC, as one part of the larger CBAM framework, is used as a tool to explain the 'human' aspect of change.

The CBAM's SoC provided a method for us to compare principals' concerns, perspectives and interpretation of the process of implementation for the SEI model. This framework further revealed the meaning of and the concerns around the SEI policy, including the four-hour language block, adopted by Arizona's English Language Learners Task Force.

Methods

The participants: Eight school principals

The primary source of data for research was information from conversations with eight school principals who were interviewed regarding their understanding of and concerns related to meeting the needs of ELs within the context of Arizona's SEI mandates (Table 6.2). Findings from interviews therefore became the foundation for telling the story of how school principals understood, interpreted and implemented the SEI model in their schools, with their teachers, and for their students.

Data sources and analysis

The primary data source was semi-structured, open-ended interviews. We began each interview with open-ended structured questions such as, 'Are you aware of the innovation, and how do you feel about it?' We then probed to clarify, for example, 'How are you concerned with the four-hour ELD

Table 6.2 Participant demographics

Pseudonym	Gender	Race	Total no. students	EL %	Setting	Years as principal, current site
1. Bryan	M	White	740	34	Elementary	18 years
2. Jeff	M	White	1017	39	Elementary	4 years
3. Susana	F	Hisp.	524	30	Elementary	10 years
4. Debra	F	Hisp.	608	58	Elementary	3 years
5. Martha	F	Hisp.	320	15	Secondary	5 years
6. Daniel	M	Hisp.	271	8	Secondary	3 years
7. Michael	M	White	2217	4	Secondary	3 years
8. Anthony	M	Hisp.	2201	21	Secondary	8 years

Table 6.3 Stages of concern

Stage of concern	Description of the school leader's attitude and approach toward the innovation
6	REFOCUSING: A school leader has definite ideas about alternatives to the existing innovation.
5	COLLABORATION: The focus is on coordination/cooperation with others regarding the use of the innovation.
4	CONSEQUENCE: Attention focuses on the impact of the innovation and the relevance of the innovation for students and changes to increase student outcomes.
3	MANAGEMENT: Attention is focused on the task of using the innovation and the best use of information and resources.
2	PERSONAL: School leader is uncertain about the demands of the innovation and his/her role with the innovation.
1	INFORMATIONAL: A general awareness of the innovation.
0	AWARENESS: Little concern about the innovation.

implementation?' The interview responses were to identify the levels of concern. Each participant was interviewed for approximately one to two hours total using the modified 'three interview series' (Seidman, 2006).

Analysis of the data gathered through interviews was conducted to identify principals' impressions of the intent behind Arizona's educational language policies. We analyzed how each of the eight principals approached the work of being a change facilitator through one section of the CBAM (Hall & Hord, 1987), the SoC. The seven stages in the SoC (Table 6.3) describe and measure the levels of concern around an 'innovation' such as the mandated four-hour language block in Arizona.

We analyzed interview data for salient themes reflecting principals' SoC. As we familiarized ourselves with the data, we created note cards to generate categories and themes, we analyzed recurring words or phrases to identify the levels of concern, and we coded the data accordingly (Maxwell, 2005). We then 'chunked' the data as suggested by Rossman and Rallis (2003). The themes that emerged served as a primary foundation for describing how school principals are concerned with meeting the needs of ELs through the new 'phenomenon' of the four-hour block language policy.

Findings

After coding and analyzing the data, we found that no principal's stage of concern was within the 0 category. This was due to the fact that all eight principals were aware of the mandates regarding the education of ELs.

Table 6.4 Principals' levels of concern

6	REFOCUSING	Anthony
5	COLLABORATION	Jeff
4	CONSEQUENCE	Debra, Martha, Susana
3	MANAGEMENT	Bryan
2	PERSONAL	Daniel
1	INFORMATIONAL	Michael
0	AWARENESS	

Table 6.4 shows the range of levels of concern identified for each of the eight participating principals.

In the following sections, we will generally describe principals' concerns in order based on the level in which respective concerns most resonated, ranging from 1–6.

Michael's concerns about SEI implementation classified in Stage 1, since his focus seemed mostly on the general awareness of the policy.

> I have not had any issue with the ELD model. In fact, my English Department has 24 teachers and I had a handful of teachers that were interested in teaching the ELD component. It's interesting because the legal perspective research was presented from the Department of Education, which I understood. Then, they provided a listing of what research was put together to justify the model recently created; it also made sense. I just thought kids must improve if previously, ELs were getting anywhere from 30 to 60 minutes a day in language instruction, learning English, now up to four hours. From a math perspective, it seems to make sense. You're getting anywhere from four to eight times as much instruction; it has to in my estimation translate into some kind of improvement in the kids learning English. So, up until very recently I've had absolutely no problem with it whatsoever. Now, because I am taking a class in the doctorate program, I'm suddenly going to be exposed to research refuting the state's research; I am anxious to hear that conversation.

Daniel, a good example of a principal in Stage 2, approached the SEI model from his personal belief system:

> Yeah, I mean, with the lack of research and lack of things that are being developed, I mean, to me it's all political, and not an educational policy. Nobody thought it was a good idea. For me it's just another piece of national anti-immigration legislation, it's all political. This policy doesn't make any sense, for anybody who knows anything about language acquisition, and anybody that knows anything about how students grow, or how they learn, and knows that acquisition is not gained by

hours of being immersed learning the English grammar with no English models. Being a doctoral student, the first thing you look at is, what research backs up this ideology of this method that Arizona is using? This principle of 'time on task' is absolutely ridiculous. I disagree, and even people who are not language acquisition specialists know that the time on task [approach] is not the most respected way of teaching anything. It's effective instruction or differentiated instruction, the type of instruction really makes an impact on kids, not so much how much time you spend on doing something. My biggest concern it is much directed towards immigrants and things like that, it's racist.

Bryan's statements focused on logistical issues related to his implementation of the ELD model and therefore place him in Stage 3 (Management) of CBAM:

Well, we didn't follow that model as effectively as we probably should have, because we found it to be isolationist, and we wouldn't do that. Logistically, how do you do it on a campus that has 80% Hispanic kids? It's impossible. You'd end up with – well, you just couldn't do it. You would end up with loads of 30 students in your mainstream classes and 10 in your SEI class. Then you have that dichotomy, and it creates problems, and plus it just isn't good for kids. We made it work, and it worked okay.

School principals in this study tended to have a stronger focus on increasing the effective use of the innovation – these participants had resolved Self and Task-level concerns. The remaining teachers' responses resonated with SoC Stages 4–6 (Impact). Debra, Susana, Martha, Jeff and Anthony were all categorized as sharing Impact level concerns due to their desire to improve the new innovation.

Debra's stage of concern focuses on the consequences (Stage 4) of the SEI model on her ELs:

As we try to follow the four-hour model, but it does not fall exactly, I am concerned because I'm completely philosophically against it. I think there's so many other better ways that you could teach children English, and I'm not saying just dual language. But just in general, there are so many other things that we could put in place that would be so much better. It's a civil rights issue because of two things. One is not that I have that many Anglo kids, but I'm physically separating them during the day. Secondly, the state is asking me to give them a totally different curriculum. Truly, the number one indicator of student success is the quality of education, the quality of teaching that's going on in the classroom. That is the number one indicator, and I don't care what research the state has to say. That is what we need to focus on, the quality of instruction which in essence will provide many opportunities for students to comprehend and learn.

Another principal in Stage 4, Susana, was concerned about the lack of math and reading content students would receive under the four-hour language block, so she decided to create 12 different lunch schedules in order to accommodate students' needs:

> It's ridiculous, but it works out. [ELs] stay with their ELD teacher in the early years. In second grade they go to their ELD teacher. Third grade is similar to second grade, then [in] fourth and fifth grade, the ELD students go to this one resource teacher. All the fourth and fifth graders go to an ELD teacher, so it doesn't affect the instruction of the other kids or the schedule of fourth and fifth grade.

A third principal, Martha, also expressed concerns that place her in Stage 4; she was most preoccupied with the impact of the four-hour SEI model on student learning outcomes:

> Now I am really worried about how we are going to put together a four-year plan for ELLs [English language learners], because in these ELD classes, they are not state required credit courses for graduation, and how can you comply with 20 required credit courses if you end up two, three, years with students in these programs, because let me tell you something, I have students who have taken the AZELLA for four years in a row who have not passed it. But I think even more important that there needs to be an acceptance of the fact that language is an asset at schools and that it can be utilized to move students forward in the academic areas before they become proficient in English. I have a lot of students who are not yet proficient in English and yet go to college and pass the math test, and I am not able to place them into the math because they haven't passed the language portion of it. And yet, they could qualify for Math 180, but because they haven't passed the language requirements, they are kept from doing other areas that they could be doing.

Jeff was concerned about how his teachers can be more effective in providing an equal opportunity for students to become academically successful and has focused on Collaboration (Stage 5) concerns in order to meet the needs of ELs. Collaborating with teachers, he has implemented professional learning communities (PLCs) to assist teachers with staff development in second language acquisition (SLA):

> During PLC meetings, we would talk and discuss what to expect in the classroom; for example, the usage of different learning strategies and posting objectives. To this day, I model everything; I posted content and language objectives during the meetings with faculty. In addition,

ELL teachers, ELL testers, and the leadership team, we all got together during the summer for three days and talked about the discrete skills inventory (DSI), talked about different strategies to incorporate throughout grade levels, and how to manage and group ELLs into designated ELD classes. We also discussed techniques and strategies to use when students in sixth grade are functioning at a second grade level, because that was the majority of last year: dealing with teachers that struggled with accommodating and teaching ELLs. This year we want all students to succeed.

Anthony is a school principal who displayed strong Impact concerns (Stage 6) for meeting the needs of his school's ELs. He has encouraged and supported his teachers by 'refocusing' the school into a community atmosphere, and he has stated the importance:

Frontloading with teacher training has been real important. I have awesome teachers here, and they are compelled to problem solve with students. In addition, I know that the best way to teach second language learners is by cooperative learning. Therefore students are allowed to work cooperatively which permits to feel comfortable allowing ELLs do better academically.

Anthony has located additional sources of funding for programs that help students envision graduating from high school and continuing with a university degree, regardless of the educational restrictions that have impeded their progress based on their second language proficiency:

I've been able to secure extra funding from private sources, so we can run a Saturday school. We run a summer program especially for ELL Pre-Emergent [AZELLA proficiency level] students. 80% of our families [have] PHLOTEs, so when [students] go home, they're not speaking English, they're speaking Spanish to their parents or grandparents or whoever they're living with. So, with those types of numbers, we have to try and keep them here as much as we can, and that's why we run Saturday school, summer school and after school activities. We had to go out and find extra dollars from private sectors, because we couldn't pull it out of our budget. People have been very supportive; people have donated millions of dollars over the years to run the programs.

By analyzing principals' discourse using the SoC, it is evident that school principals are concerned at different levels about the language policy in Arizona, especially with implementing the prescribed hours associated with the DSI instruction in ELD pull-out settings. As school principals continue to implement the model, many different challenges have been exposed, although all school principals find solutions to continue to carry out the mandate.

Discussion

The framework outlining a range of SoC identified principals' levels of concern regarding their role in implementing the SEI policy, including the four-hour ELD block. Findings from the analysis provide a glimpse into principals' understanding of their own implementation of Arizona's educational language policy and addressed the research questions guiding this work: (1) How do ADE educational language policies affect school principals and the educational environments in which they work? (2) What are the concerns of eight school principals regarding their capacity to meet the language needs of ELs?

Interpreting language policy implementation

The school principal participants showed a degree of understanding of the legislative document outlining the SEI model (A.R.S. 15-751-756.01), and articulated how the ADE has provided monitoring mechanisms for its required SEI programs. All school principals showed awareness of the requirement to implement a four-hour language block for ELs under the SEI model. Although the principals supported teaching the five required ELD areas of conversation, grammar, reading, vocabulary and writing, the principals we interviewed did not consistently follow the prescribed minutes for each area as outlined in SEI model documents published by the ADE.

To ensure SEI implementation in Arizona, the ADE adopted a range of strategies to assist schools in tracking and managing accountability within the new SEI mandates. One example of these strategies involved outreach. In fact, the ADE facilitated monthly Practitioners of English Language Learners (PELL) meetings to support schools with additional updates and clarification on instruction for SEI model implementation, assessment (AZELLA), and technical support for tracking ELP AZELLA scores (a process involving receiving student scores from the test publisher and entering them into the state database system). At the time of this publication, all documents related to the SEI model implementation, including placement and assessment forms, were posted on the ADE website (http://www.azed.gov/english-language-learners/) to ensure accessibility and wide dissemination. Of these, perhaps the most important under the SEI model is the Primary Home Language Other Than English (PHLOTE) form, which is used to identify students who are required to take the AZELLA to determine classification as an 'EL' or as an 'Initially Proficient' English speaker.

The principals interviewed for this study all complied with the official procedures for identifying and placing ELs in SEI settings through the above process, as reflected in CBAM placements of minimally Stage 1. Dissemination of the procedures outlined above cycled from district-level administrations to school-based principals for legal compliance with the SEI model. Many principals interpreted the law according to what best fit their school population, but overall, school principals in this study met the legislative requirements of identifying ELs through the use of the PHLOTE form, placing them according to their results on the AZELLA, and then placing them in instructional settings aligned with the four-hour language block according to the SEI model.

However, despite their consistent implementation of the identification and placement requirements, all but one of the school principals interviewed in this study remained baffled by the ambiguous nature of other parts of the policy, resulting in various interpretations of how to schedule and train teachers for the four-hour language block. The prescribed SEI model conflicted with the previous school structures and processes for scheduling, instruction and staff development. For example, all eight principals encountered challenges in grouping students by their English proficiency levels due to the logistics of scheduling and its relationship to grade level assignment. For example, a fourth grade student who tests at Level 1 ELP may have a different daily schedule from a Kindergartener who also tested as Level 1 ELP. Also, meeting the four-hour time requirement limited the time available for scheduling other mandatory classes, as well as PE and specials (e.g. Art), while forcing teachers to take on classes that they would not normally instruct. Many principals, crippled with compliance requirements and real-world implementation challenges, had to become creative and explore entirely new ideas in collaboration with district personnel or leadership teams to make implementation of the SEI model achievable.

All principals interviewed articulated the dilemma of teaching English language skills in isolation rather than teaching them through and with the content areas, since the mastery of content knowledge is essential for ELs' academic success. When ELs are separated into a discrete four-hour block of language skills, they miss exposure to the content area knowledge, skills and instruction their mainstream peers encounter on a daily basis. Principals' foci on consequence, collaboration and refocusing placed the majority of the principals in Stages 4–6 of CBAM's levels of concern.

Implementation: Concerns for Arizona's ELs

After analyzing principal interview transcripts through CBAM's SoC, we concluded that school principals are 'concerned' about their implementation of the four-hour model and how it directly affects ELs. Salient themes that emerged across participants related to segregation, funding, the fear of being perceived as incompetent and access to the curriculum.

Segregation

Many school principals in this study felt that the four-hour SEI model violated current laws against segregation. For instance, Susana articulated the challenges of segregation:

> I have classrooms with ELs only that are focusing on English Language Development ... So in Kinder and first grade, I have two classrooms full of ELs separated from the two classrooms that had completely English-dominant students all day long.

Another principal, Martha, expressed outright confusion related to the segregation of EL students, noting that it inhibits equal access to all students by not providing full access to the curriculum:

> But right now the state has kind of undone our program with their new requirements. Now I have to segregate out all my English language learners and I am just going to straight out and say it: I have no idea where the state is getting their research for the model that they are forcing schools to implement. They are requiring that I segregate English language learners into four hours a day, *que locura* (what craziness).

Most of the principals expressed their concerns about the SEI model; however, as public servants, some felt it was necessary to align the policy as best as they could to the school curriculum and community. Jeff explained his decision to implement the model with as much fidelity as possible despite his uncertainties:

> I decided to do the four hour ELD model as close[ly] as possible. If I am going to have half my school doing it, we are doing it right. Right or wrong, we are doing it right. The four hour model has a lot of holes in it. I have taken the law and made it the best for my reality. Will I see some rewards? Sure. But overall, the ELD model has a lot of flaws and that is the philosophy of those battles I deal with every day because I am going against a lot of things that I believe in, because I have to comply with the law. I didn't need to do it but I figured I am going to try it and see what it is like. It is totally segregating kids.

Mendez v. Westminster (1946) struck down the segregation of Mexican and Mexican American students in California school districts, because it violates the equal protection clauses of the US Constitution's 14th Amendment by segregating students with a deficiency in English. *Brown v. Board of Education* (1954) was one of the first cases to strike down racial segregation, allowing all students, regardless of race, to be integrated in a classroom, also based on the 14th Amendment. *Lau v. Nichols* (1974) struck down a school district's policy of segregation on the basis of language ability; under *Lau*, the US Supreme Court ruled that schools offering no instructional modification to support the education of language minority students are in violation of the Civil Rights Act of 1964. Similar to these cases, the principals interviewed for this study argued that the SEI four-hour model misinterprets *Castañeda v. Pickard* (1981), which clarified the provision of the Equal Educational Opportunities Act (EEOA, 1974). In *Castañeda*, a three-pronged test was put into place to evaluate whether educational officials have violated the rights of limited English proficient students. The first prong probes whether officials are pursuing a program informed by educational theory that is recognized by experts as sound. The second examines the steps that officials are taking to implement the approach, including whether they are providing the resources necessary to implement it effectively. The third question concerns whether, after a reasonable period, officials have evaluated the program and modified it as necessary. Gándara and Orfield (2010) examined the impact of segregation on Latino and EL students based in part on empirical research conducted in Arizona and concluded that the excessive segregation of Arizona's Latino and EL students is detrimental to the students' academic achievement, as well as to their social and emotional development.

Lack of funding

Most of the principals in this sample cited lack of resources and materials from the ADE as a basic flaw in the mandated policy, including the limited amount of funding that is available to offer an adequate education to ELs. Daniel describes the ADE's process of developing the model as impulsive and therefore far too subject to individual interpretation, particularly during this initial implementation:

> Our superintendent is mandating that we implement this policy and make it work. We're afraid the state could remove our funding, although in order to make this work we need more resources and time and there's not enough financial support to provide an equal education.

Some principals reported that they believed that the four hours of intense English would be beneficial to ELs, since it also means a more focused emphasis on educating ELs. However, many also acknowledged that the theoretical principles underlying the new SEI model are inconsistent with established research regarding effective instructional practices for EL students. The majority of principals interviewed believed that postponing ELs' exposure to subject area content while separating them from native English-speakers for four hours per day would have a deleterious effect on ELs.

Fear of ramifications

Although they felt compelled to implement the new SEI model due to both their roles as school leaders and their obligations to follow the legal mandate, interview discourse also demonstrates principals' belief that the four-hour SEI policy is fundamentally inappropriate, and potentially harmful, for language minority students. As Jeff mentioned:

> I think that we [Arizonans] are crazy; did educators even get involved in creating this model? It was a negative thing; it is horrible, I can't believe we are doing this. So I think it was about March or April, our leadership comes to us and says, 'Here is what is coming down the chute. [We] want you to mull over it for a while, but before you go home for the summer, you principals need to have a plan in place on how you are going to address your ELL population. Here is how many ELL kids you have according to today. Obviously it is not what you are going to have next year, but have a plan on what you are going to do with that'. The principals are sitting there going, 'How can we do that? You want us to make schedules? You want us to block kids? We don't know if they are Beginning or Intermediate, but you want us to put a plan?' 'Just put it in place' was the directive. If not, start looking for a job tomorrow.

Nonetheless, regardless of the how school principals perceived, conceptualized and viewed the policy, they explained how they are making it work and are adjusting the policy to best fit their school and community, tailoring it to the needs of their ELs. With the influx of accountability mandates accompanying the SEI Language policy, fear of losing their jobs due to insubordination was on the forefront of the school principals' minds.

Access to the curriculum

All principals interviewed mentioned the dilemma of teaching English language skills in isolation, as opposed to through and with the content areas, since the mastery of content knowledge is essential for academic success. When ELs are isolated from fully English proficient peers, into a separate four-hour block of language skills, they miss exposure to the content area knowledge and skills their mainstream peers receive on a daily basis. As Debra mentioned:

> Students are grouped based on the AZELLA scores. I have to take all of those students who have not posted a proficient score and I have to give them 1 hour of English writing, 1 hour of English reading, 1 hour of language arts, and the Basic [proficiency level] students need an additional hour of language speaking. So that is four hours in [which] they cannot take required courses. They cannot take their math courses, their English courses; because we only come to school 7 hours and 4 of those hours are being used to teach English only. What the state doesn't understand is that the Intermediate [AZELLA proficiency level] kids are ready for content area English.

Under *Lau v. Nichols* Supreme Court findings and subsequent *Lau Remedies*, principals voiced concerns regarding whether the SEI model meets the criteria for provision of proper accommodations for language minority students.

Grappling with Educational Equity

We have provided perspectives on how school principals implement educational language policies, incorporate directives from legislation, and struggle to meet the needs of ELs. After analyzing principal interviews, and the SoC, two overarching issues emerged: (1) tolerance of the language policy upholds hegemony, and (2) language policies perpetuating social inequalities for language minority students.

School principals in this study perceived the new SEI educational language policy and related model as inappropriate at best. They were highly concerned about meeting the social and academic needs of their language minority students. The language policy in Arizona discriminates against language minority students through a systematic, prescribed model allowing practices that disadvantage ELs because schools are failing to provide them with equal access to the core curriculum (Wiley, 2008).

However, school principals have promoted equity within the confines of the SEI model by implementing practices that utilize opportunities for meaningful interaction within their toleration of the SEI model. According to Rallis *et al.* (2008), tolerability is the equitable reallocation of resources. Each of the principals interviewed in this study was dedicated to redesigning the SEI model as an educational language policy and reconstructing it in such a way that it might benefit the students and community they serve (Rallis *et al.*, 2008). Homogeneity holds society together, and tolerance in the educational system will continue until a change is made in how minority students are viewed and educated (Kozol, 2005).

As frontline supporters of student learning, principals need to be cognizant of educational equity and strive to uphold the civil rights of every student by prohibiting discrimination on the basis of race, ethnicity or national origin. Thus, the Civil Rights Act of 1964 has played an important role in protecting the educational rights of language minority students in the United States. Equal educational access and protection for students whose first language is not English was adjudicated in the landmark 1974 case of *Lau v. Nichols* (Varghese, 2004). In *Lau*, the Supreme Court guaranteed children an opportunity to a 'meaningful education' regardless of their language background, ruling that 'there is no equality of treatment merely by providing students with the same facilities, textbooks, teachers and curriculum; for students who do not understand English are effectively foreclosed from any meaningful education' (*Lau v. Nichols*, 1974). Overwhelmingly, the principals we spoke with questioned Arizona's English-only policies. We also doubt whether the educational language policies that have resulted in the implementation of SEI models, ELD segregation and DSI instruction in Arizona would hold up to the equal educational opportunities provisions further codified in *Lau* (1974) and *Castañeda* (1981).

Critical Lens for the Future: The Dichotomy of Policy

The passage of a statute does not result in its immediate and smooth realization. The implementation and application of education policies are executed at grassroots levels by district administrators, principals and classroom teachers. Educators, who are not always accepting of new top-down laws and guidance (Fowler, 2004) must exercise stronger voices and actions to truly advocate for the equity of all students.

There is a central need for educators to be mindful of new policies and their impact on teachers, students and communities. We found that SEI is implemented by school principals and within respective educational environments in two distinct ways: first, through a 'policy of choice and action' approach, and second, through an informal 'policy of blind leap of faith'. The SEI model originated in legislation delivered as a policy directive to school principals. However, a nexus of conflict between the SEI policy and principals' personal beliefs was evident in each administrator's implementation of SEI.

Policy of choice and action

A 'policy of choice and action' describes the approach taken by six of the eight interviewed administrators, who challenged the law by finding their own ways to incorporate parts of the SEI model while doing what they believed to be best for their students and for their school community. These six principals had specific concerns about the language policy in the following areas: (a) the lack of research to support its theoretical foundations; (b) the ideological principles underlying the policy; (c) a potential drop in graduation rates; and (d) the civil rights of every student in a system of segregated instruction.

Policy of blind leap of faith

Two principals' approach to SEI implementation followed a blind leap of faith oriented pathway. Arizona's four-hour block of ELD is the first curriculum design of its kind both within the state and external to it. Although experts in the field of language minority schooling refute these claims, according to ADE, the principles underlying Arizona's version of SEI are research based. Principals who are fully compliant with SEI implementation are operating in conflict with what most researchers and scholars have argued regarding not only best practices for EL instruction and language learning, but also the promotion of equal educational access. In essence, principals implementing SEI without dispute are blindly trusting the state's decision to justify and mandate a four-hour language block that also involves segregation and discrete instruction. One of the participating principals, although philosophically against SEI, executed its implementation as closely as possible to comply with mandates from district administration. The second whose approach we characterize as 'blind leap of faith' agreed with the foundation of SEI and the four-hour block and believed that ELs would be better educated because of it.

Ultimately, all the principals in Arizona's schools were faced with a decision regarding SEI implementation. The reality of the situation is that navigating between legal requirements and personal convictions is complex, multifaceted and a challenge. We argue that, despite these challenges and conflicting messages, school administrators should be unyielding advocates for their students, especially with regard to actions that might be potentially harmful to students. Beyond the responsibilities of administrators, stakeholders in the field of education and beyond must also be willing to stand with on-the-ground practitioners during these times of conflict and uncertainty.

Social Inequalities: Equity and Justice for All Students

Injustice is perpetuated through public school funding and inequitable access to resources. The SEI model created by Arizona's English Language Learners Task Force embodies such injustice. After its charge to implement the requirements of English for the Children and HB 2064, this new educational language policy of rapid acquisition through strict English immersion in a segregated setting promotes a philosophy that is not only controversial, but also defies research findings and longstanding theoretical principles underlying approaches to the instruction of language minority students. Researchers agree that the process of SLA may take as little as three or as many as 10 years (Hakuta *et al.*, 2000). The model outlined by the English Language Learners Task Force and its embedded expectation that students are able to acquire English in just one academic year is both unrealistic and damaging (Baker, 2011).

Moreover, Thomas and Collier (2002) have proven through extensive research that ELs should not be segregated when learning academic content or ELD and that the best way to close the achievement gap between ELs and native English speakers is to provide the bulk of academic instruction in the students' native language. Given that Arizona's educational language policy requiring SEI models limits opportunities to provide instruction in the native language and requires that schools provide intensive ELD for four hours a day, principals' hands are, in many ways, inexorably tied as they strive to support teachers and ELs and uphold Arizona's legal instructional mandates.

In conclusion, this study was important to further investigate what principals think and feel about the implementation of language policy because the more principals understand the innovation the more change actually occurs. ELs are critical members of society and an asset to the education system in the United States. Educators must take a stance and do everything to provide language minority students with the opportunity to learn and become educated in all content areas (Faltis & Coulter, 2008). In particular, it is important for educators who have ELs in their classrooms to remember that ELs experience injustices every day in the classroom because of the bias in testing and achievement. Furthermore, the greatest challenge may be reconciling what we know to be effective education practices for ELs with mandated policies that provide inequality to students.

References

ADE (n.d.) *Discrete Skills Inventory (DSI)*. Phoenix, AZ: Arizona Department of Education. See http://www.azed.gov/english-language-learners/files/2013/02/dsialllevels.pdf Accessed March 21, 2014.

ADE (2008) Nuts and Bolts [Power Point slides].Phoenix, AZ: Arizona Department of Education. See http://www.azed.gov/english-language-learners/files/2013/02/administratorsmodelimplementationtraining.pdf. Accessed March 23, 2014.

Arizona Revised Statutes §§15-751 to 15-756.

Arizona Voter Initiative (2000) Proposition 203, *English for the Children*.

Arizona English Language Learners Task Force (2007) Research summary and bibliography for structured English immersion programs. Phoenix, AZ: Arizona English Language Learners Task Force. See http://www.azed.gov/wp-content/uploads/PDF/modelcomponentresearch.pdf. Accessed March 23, 2014.

August, D. and Shanahan, T. (eds) (2006) *Developing Literacy in Second Language Learners: Report of the National Literacy Panel on Language-minority Children and Youth*. Mahwah, NJ: Lawrence Erlbaum.

August, D., Goldenberg, C. and Rueda, R. (2010) Restrictive state language policies: Are they scientifically based? In P. Gándara and M. Hopkins (eds) *Forbidden Languages: English Learners and Restrictive Language Policies* (pp. 139–158). New York: Teachers College Press.

Baker, C. (2011) *Foundations of Bilingual Education and Bilingualism* (5th edn). Bristol: Multilingual Matters.

Blanchard, J., Atwill, K., Jimenez-Silva, M. and Jimenez-Castellaño. O. (in press) Beginning English literacy development among Spanish-speaking children in Arizona's English-only classrooms: A four-year successive cohort study. *International Multilingual Research Journal*.

Brown v. Board of Education of Topeka (1954) 347 U.S 483.

Castañeda v. Pickard (1981) 648 F.2d 989 (U.S. Ct. App. 1981).

Civil Rights Act (1964) Pub.L. 88-352, 78 Stat. 241, enacted 2 July.

Cummins, J. (2000) *Language, Power and Pedagogy: Bilingual Children in the Crossfire.* Clevedon: Multilingual Matters.

EEOA (1974) Equal Educational Opportunities Act. 20 U.S.C. §1701.

Faltis, C.J. and Coulter, C.A. (2008) *Teaching English Learners and Immigrant Students in Secondary School.* Upper Saddle River, NJ: Pearson Education.

Flores, I.R. (2010) *Do the AZELLA Cut Scores Meet the Standards? A Validation Review of the Arizona English Language Learner Assessment.* Los Angeles, CA: Civil Rights Project/Proyecto Derechos Civiles at UCLA. See http://civilrightsproject.ucla.edu/ research/k-12-education/language-minority-students/is-arizonas-approach-to-educat-ing-its-els-superior-to-other-forms-of-instruction. Accessed March 24, 2014.

Flores v. Arizona (1992) No. CV 92-596.

Flores v. Arizona (2000) Consent Order. CIV 92-596. (D. Ariz. 2000).

Fowler, F.C. (2004) *Policy Studies for Education Leaders: An Introduction* (2nd edn). Upper Saddle River, NJ: Pearson Education.

Gándara, P. and Orfield, G. (2010) A Return to the *'Mexican Room': The Segregation of Arizona's English Learners.* Los Angeles, CA: Civil Rights Project/Proyecto Derechos Civiles at UCLA. See http://civilrightsproject.ucla.edu/research/k-12-education/ language-minority-students/a-return-to-the-mexican-room-the-segregation-of-ari-zonas-english-learners-1. Accessed March 24, 2014.

Gándara, P., Rumberger, R., Maxwell-Jolly, J. and Callahan, R. (2003) English learners in California schools: Unequal resources, unequal outcomes. *Education Policy Analysis Archives* 11 (36). See http://epaa.asu.edu/epaa/v11n36/. Accessed March 24, 2014.

Garcia, E., Lawton, K. and Diniz de Figueiredo, E.H. (2010) *Assessment of Young English Language Learners in Arizona: Questioning the Validity of the State Measure of English Proficiency.* Los Angeles, CA: Civil Rights Project/Proyecto Derechos Civiles at UCLA. See http://civilrightsproject.ucla.edu/research/k-12-education/language-minority-students/assessment-of-young-english-language-learners-in-arizona-questioning-the-validity-of-the-state-measure-of-english-proficiency/. Accessed March 24, 2014.

Hakuta, K., Butler, Y.G. and Witt, D. (2000) How long does it take English learners to attain proficiency? Policy Report 2000-1. Santa Barbara, CA: University of California Linguistic Minority Research Institute.

Hall, G.E. and Hord, S.M. (1987) *Change in Schools: Facilitating the Process.* Albany, NY: State University of New York Press.

Hall, G.E. and Hord, S.M. (2001) *Implementing Change: Patterns, Principles, and Potholes.* Boston, MA: Allyn & Bacon.

Hall, G.E. and Rutherford, W.L. (1983) Three change facilitator styles: How principals affect improvement efforts. Report No. 3155. Austin, TX: University of Texas at Austin, Research and Development Center for Teacher Education.

HB (2006) House Bill 2064, 7 A.R.S. §§15-756.01-.11.

Jimenez-Silva, M. and Nguyen, T.R. (2012) Professional development reflected in English language learner (ELL) classrooms: Final report. Paper presented at American Education Research Association, April, Vancouver, B.C.

Kozol, J. (2005) *The Shame of the Nation: The Restoration of Apartheid Schooling in America.* New York: Three Rivers Press.

Krashen, S. (1996) *Under Attack: The Case Against Bilingual Education.* Culver City, CA: Language Education Associates.

Krashen, S., Rolstad, K. and MacSwan, J. (2007) Review of 'Research summary and bibli-ography for structured English immersion programs' of the Arizona English language learners task force. See http://www.google.com/url?sa=t&rct=j&q=&esrc=s&sour ce=web&cd=1&ved=0CCoQFjAA&url=http%3A%2F%2Fwww.asu.edu%2Feduc% 2Fsceed%2Fazell%2Freview.doc&ei=diEtU5SKA4fsqAGumYGABg&usg=AFQjCNGc Pdr-XhIQerWVilayzuAt7O3XOQ&sig2=QIeoh3YHJoJHbOnCFPnJgQ&bvm=bv.629 22401,d.aWM Accessed March 23, 2014.

Lau v. Nichols (1974) 414 U.S. 563.

Lightbown, P. and Spada, N. (2006) *How Languages Are Learned* (3rd edn). Oxford: Oxford University Press.

Mahoney, K., MacSwan, J., Haladyna, T. and García, D. (2010) *Castañeda's* third prong: Evaluating the achievement of Arizona's English learners under restrictive language policy. In P. Gándara and M. Hopkins (eds) *Forbidden Languages: English Learners and Restrictive Language Policies* (pp. 50–64). New York: Teachers College Press.

Martinez-Wenzl, M., Perez, K. and Gándara, P. (2010) *Is Arizona's Approach to Educating its ELs Superior to Other Forms of Instruction?* Los Angeles, CA: Civil Rights Project/ Proyecto Derechos Civiles at UCLA. See www.civilrightsproject.ucla.edu.http:// civilrightsproject.ucla.edu/research/k-12-education/language-minority-students/ is-arizonas-approach-to-educating-its-els-superior-to-other-forms-of-instruction. (Accessed March 23, 2014)

Maxwell, J. (2005) *Qualitative Research Design: An Interactive Approach.* Thousand Oaks, CA: Sage Publications.

Mendez v. Westminster School District (1946) 64 F.Supp. 544 (C.D. Cal. 1946), aff'd, 161 F.2d 774 (9th Cir. 1947) (en banc).

Mora, J.K. (2009) From the ballot box to the classroom. *Association for Supervision and Curriculum Development* 66, 14–19.

Ovando, C., Collier, V. and Combs, V. (2006) *Bilingual and ESL Classrooms: Teaching in Multicultural Contexts* (4th edn). New York: McGraw-Hill.

Rallis, S.F., Rossman, G.B., Cobb, C.D., Reagan, T.G. and Kuntz, A. (2008) *Leading Dynamic Schools: How to Create and Implement Ethical Policies.* Thousand Oaks, CA: Corwin Press.

Rossman, G.B. and Rallis, S.F. (2003) *Learning in the Field: An Introduction to Qualitative Research* (2nd edn). Thousand Oaks, CA: Sage Publications.

Seidman, I. (2006) *Interviewing as Qualitative Research: A Guide for Researchers in Education and the Social Sciences,* 3rd edn. New York: Teachers College Press.

Thomas, W. and Collier, V. (2002) *A National Study of School Effectiveness for Language Minority Students' Long-term Academic Achievement.* Santa Cruz, CA: Center for Research on Education, Diversity and Excellence, University of California, Santa Cruz.

Varghese, M.M. (2004) An introduction to meeting the needs of English Language Learners. *New Horizons for Learning,* September. See http://education.jhu.edu/PD/ newhorizons/strategies/topics/English%20Language%20Learners/Articles/An%20 Introduction%20to%20Meeting%20the%20Needs%20of%20English%20Language%20 Learners/. Accessed March 2, 2014.

Wiley, T.G. (2008) Language policy and teacher education. In S. May and N. Hornberger (eds) *Language Policy and Political Issues in Education* (pp. 229–242). New York: Springer.

Wright, W. (2012) Sheltered English immersion: From politics to effective practice. Presentation at ACCESS 5th Annual Institute, March. Arizona State University, Tempe, AZ.

Wright, W.E. and Choi, D. (2006) The impact of language and high-stakes testing policies on elementary school English language learners in Arizona. *Education Policy Analysis Archives* 14 (13), 1–56.

Appendix 6A: Legal Context in Arizona

Date	Law	Description	Implications
1992	Flores v. Arizona	A federal lawsuit filed claiming that Arizona failed to provide a program of instruction, funding and other resources to limited English proficient students.	Stating all public schools should provide an adequate program for ELLs. Including a program of instruction designed to assist ELLs in English and receive equal access to the curriculum.
January 2000	Flores v. Arizona District Court Judgment	The court ruled a violation of the federal Equal Educational Opportunities Act (EEOA) because the state of Arizona did not adequately educate or finance programs for ELLs.	There were deficiencies with the existing program as a result of inadequate funding. Some of the rulings included too many students in a classroom, not enough qualified teachers and insufficient teaching materials.
August 2000	Flores Consent Order	A consent decree resolved the issue of program adequacy and monitoring. The State Board of Education and the ADE adopted official rules and policies.	Set guidelines for instructing ELLs including individual education plans, state monitoring, determination of criteria and performance standards.
November 2000	Arizona Proposition 203, English for the Children (§A.R.S. 15-752-15-756)	All children in Arizona public schools shall be taught English. Students who are ELLs shall be educated through sheltered English immersion during a temporary transition period not normally intended to exceed one year.	Educators are required to integrate in the same classroom ELLs from different native-language groups but with the same degree of English fluency.

(Continued)

Date	Law	Description	Implications
September 2006	HB 2064 (adding sections §15-756 and 15-756.01 through 15-756.13)	This law added a section to revise §A.R.S 15-756 including subsections which identified ELLs and indicated specific requirements that included establishing a task force, and developing and adopting research-based SEI models.	Arizona English Language Task Force adopted SEI models. Main points included four hours daily of ELD, entry/exit and classification into an SEI program only through AZELLA and student grouping determined by proficiency level.

Appendix 6B: HB 2064 Subsection §15-756.01 Through 15-756.13

15-756.01	Arizona English Language Learners Task Force; research-based models of structured English immersion for ELLs; budget requests;
15-756.02	School districts and charter schools; ELL models; adoption and implementation
15-756.03	Structured English immersion; budget request
15-756.04	Arizona structured English immersion fund
15-756.05	Re-assessment and reclassification of ELLs
15-756.06	Re-evaluation of former ELLs
15-756.07	Office of English Language Acquisition Services; duties
15-756.08	Monitoring; corrective action plan
15-756.09	Teacher training
15-756-10	Reporting
15-756-11	Statewide compensatory instruction fund; reporting; definition
15-756-12	Auditor General; duties
15-756-13	School district and charter schools; responsibility to comply with state and federal law

7 The Four-hour Block: SEI in Classrooms

Karen E. Lillie and Amy Markos

Over a decade of research has examined the implications and influence English-only laws and policies have had on Arizona school systems since the passage of Proposition 203 in 2000. Much of the literature revolves around teacher preparation (de Jong *et al.*, 2010; Faltis & Arias, 2007; Mora, 2000; Murri *et al.*, 2012), the effectiveness debate surrounding bilingual or English-only instruction for English learners (ELs) (August & Hakuta, 1997; Krashen *et al.*, 2007; Mahoney *et al.*, 2004; Rolstad *et al.*, 2005; Ramirez *et al.*, 1991; Wiley, 2007; Wright, 2005), and the reliability of language assessment instruments used in Arizona K–12 schools (Florez, 2012; Mahoney *et al.*, 2010). While these studies and others have been influential in demonstrating the various effects of Prop. 203 on language learners, educators and schools, the study discussed in this chapter is the first to look specifically at the *implementation* of the policies within K–12 classrooms.

The implementation of Arizona's unique language policy can be traced through a convergence of language and education policies, legislation and judicial mandates dating back 20 years (Lillie *et al.*, 2012). In 1992 the court case *Flores v. Arizona* highlighted the struggle for adequate funding for EL programs. The focus of *Flores* has since shifted to whether or not ELs are receiving an education equal to that of their native-English-speaking peers (Hogan, 2008). Eight years after the initial *Flores* case was brought to court, the *Flores* Consent Order was issued by Federal District Judge Marquez in 2000. This Consent Order, in conjunction with Arizona's English-only voter initiative, Prop. 203, complicated matters in Arizona classrooms. The Consent Order required a defined language program for ELs with adequate funding, but it did not address the type of program to be used with ELs (e.g. bilingual, English as a second language). Despite the Consent Order's neglect regarding this matter, however, Prop. 203 was almost concurrently enacted, thus mandating English-only instruction in the state.

In response to the Consent Order, House Bill (HB) 2064 was passed by the Arizona state legislature in 2006. HB 2064, in a presumed attempt to require compliance with both Prop. 203, as well as the *Flores* Consent Order, stipulated that a *statewide* 'structured English immersion program' be defined and used with EL students in the state (HB 2064: 7, line 26[1]). HB 2064 also set parameters for what was now to be the primary instructional model for ELs, which incorporated and required: (1) four hours of English-only instruction[2]; (2) cost-effectiveness; (3) research-based approaches; and (4) a one-year goal for reaching English proficiency. These parameters put in motion Arizona's current version of *structured English immersion* (SEI). Starting in August 2008, all schools were required to place ELs in class-rooms wherein students are immersed in four hours of English language development (ELD) study *per day*. Other components of the state's interpre-tation of HB 2064 also included required teacher professional development, and a new teacher certification system for EL instruction (see Moore, Chapter 4 and Markos & Arias, Chapter 5, this volume) and a Discrete Skills Inventory (DSI) on which the ELD four-hour block was based (see Lillie & Moore, Chapter 1 and Grijalva & Jimenez-Silva, Chapter 6, this volume; also Combs, 2012).

In this chapter, findings from a previous study are presented which was conducted during the spring of 2010 (Lillie *et al.*, 2010), one year after the SEI model was put in place statewide. The study aimed to answer the question, 'What are the characteristics of the four-hour SEI model in practice?' In this chapter, the discussion is focused on findings from the study as they relate to three specific areas of Arizona's policy: (1) the grouping of ELs in ELD classrooms; (2) the content of ELD classrooms; and (3) promotion and gradu-ation practices surrounding ELs in ELD classrooms.

SEI Policy

To contextualize the findings presented in this chapter, we begin with a look at the policies and mandates surrounding the four-hour SEI model[3] cur-rently in place today. While there are many guidelines surrounding the entire model,[4] some pertain specifically to the classrooms and are consequently more relevant to the findings presented here. These mandates and policies are not only state statutes (Arizona Revised Statutes, A.R.S.) but also school board rules (S.B.R.). Together, these encompass the delivery of what Arizona delineates as the SEI program model to any child identified as an EL. In real-world practice, however, the SEI policy regarding ELs' instruction is multi-leveled and multi-faceted.

The policies leading up to and including HB 2064 have been driven top-down through a range of stakeholders and policymakers and have been codi-fied by written law. As a result, various interpretations and perceptions of Arizona's educational language policy culminating in this SEI model have been shaped by a variety of people, particularly those at the Arizona Department of Education (ADE). The complex and widespread nature of

Arizona's SEI policy resulted in the ADE playing a significant role in its interpretation and dissemination. Since the new instructional model of SEI was required for all ELs in the state and given the haste with which its implementation was expected, information was disseminated by the ADE in numerous formats, including PowerPoint training presentations, an observation protocol used by ADE to monitor SEI in classrooms, and other types of documents and forms such as the home language survey and parent notification forms. Ultimately, the information about and understanding of Arizona's new SEI instructional model and associated policy components was intended to reach classroom teachers, themselves responsible for on-the-ground implementation.

We believe that, in order to understand the influence of policy on practice for ELs in Arizona schools, consideration must be placed on 'policy' and 'policymaking' at all levels. Our study, therefore, defined three components of Arizona's SEI policy: (1) the grouping of ELs into classrooms which focus on ELD; (2) the content to be delivered to ELs; and (3) the promotion and graduation of ELs compared with their mainstream peers.

Model design and grouping

An English Language Learner Task Force was established in response to HB 2064 and was responsible for creating the delineation of preferred student grouping procedures, class size, teacher training and the rules for daily instruction (ADE, 2008). What resulted is the four-hour SEI model with distinct components of English instruction. All elementary-level ELs (K–5) get the following courses: oral English/conversation and writing; grammar; reading; and vocabulary. The middle (6th–8th) and high school (9th–12th) ELs get classes based on their AZELLA[5] scores and associated language proficiency determination (see Table 7.1). While the four hours need not be

Table 7.1 Four-hour courses required per proficiency level for middle and high school ELs

	Conversational English/academic vocabulary	English reading	English writing	English grammar	English language arts[a]	Academic English reading	Academic English writing & grammar
Pre-emergent (PE)	x	x	x	x			
Emergent (E)	x	x	x	x			
Basic (B)	x	x	x	x			
Intermediate (I)					x	x	x

Notes: [a]The ELA block is for two hours, while all other courses are 60-minute intervals. Students who are designated as Intermediate may not have to take the academic reading or academic writing/grammar hours pending their performance on the AZELLA test.

Table 7.2 ADE preferred classroom groupings

Preferred order	Proficiency levels in ELD classroom	Grade levels in ELD classroom
First	All Basic	All 9th graders
Second	Basic & Intermediate	All 9th graders
Third	Basic & Intermediate	9th–12th graders

consecutive, they must be included in a day's schedule for a minimum of 20 hours a week (ADE, 2008).

ELs are grouped together[6] for ELD instruction by grade levels and/or proficiency levels as determined by the AZELLA (see Table 7.2). This means that within classrooms, students are to be grouped preferably first into proficiency determinations within same-grade levels. If there are not enough ELs within the same proficiency designation, they may be grouped across proficiency bands (e.g. basic with intermediate) within the same grade. If there are not enough similar EL proficiency-level determinations to make up one class in one grade level, the ELs may be mixed into one classroom across both proficiency determinations and grade-level bands[7] (cf. ADE, 2008: 4). To clarify, grade-level bands are those wherein multiple grades are in one classroom, such as an elementary ELD class which includes students in grades 1 through 3.

Kindergarten is the one exception where EL children are to remain separate from other grades. The concern with this model design is that it creates an environment where ELs are segregated from their native-English-speaking peers for much of the school day, and that the linguistic input ELs receive will be restricted to their fellow EL classmates and ELD teacher.

Curriculum and content

The SEI model requires ELs to be in classrooms that follow an ELD curriculum[8] and immerses students in an English-only setting.[9] Interestingly, the law states that 'although teachers may use a minimal amount of the child's native language when necessary' (A.R.S. §15-751, Definitions, 5), this has been interpreted by many educators to mean English-only (see, for example, Lillie *et al.*, 2010; Mahoney *et al.*, 2010). This may be due to the training presentations provided by ADE in which they are explicit in that English skills alone are the key, stating: 'ELD is not a math, science or social studies lesson. Content from academic subjects are the vehicles to help achieve the goal of developing English language' (cf. ADE, 2007). This means that math, science and social studies are to be excluded from instruction unless ELD teachers are using those content areas as themes through which they teach English. Furthermore, any materials presented in an ELD classroom must be in English.[10]

Seemingly contradictory, the rules and stipulations around instruction for ELs further require that EL students receive a curriculum which is comparable in *amount, scope and quality*[11] to that of their English-proficient peers. The emphasis of the curriculum in ELD classrooms, however, is the English language, which the ADE defines as 'phonology... morphology... syntax... lexicon... and semantics' (ADE, 2008: 1). Consequently, the ELD classrooms are comprised of lessons which focus only on the English Language Proficiency (ELP) standards, as well as the DSI.[12] Mainstream classrooms do not focus on the discrete skills of the English language, but rather on grade-specific content area standards, so there is a question of the comparability of the curriculum with regard to amount, scope and quality. Therefore, not only are ELs segregated from their peers via the model design but they are also limited in their access to an equal education compared to that of their mainstream peers.

Promoting and graduating English learners

There are very few areas of Arizona's SEI policy that involve the promotion and graduation of ELs. Two key points are embedded within the multi-leveled policy and resulting implementation, however. The first is that the statutes mandate a timeline for ELs to remain in an ELD classroom. The second is that policy, as expressed to parents, states that ELs will be promoted to subsequent grades and remain on track to graduate with their peers. The overall goal of the SEI model is that all ELs shall become proficient in English and thus exit the program within one year.[13] This is significant because it implies that students should be able to be exited from the SEI program quickly and enter (or re-enter[14]) the mainstream. Under this assumption, students are believed to enter the SEI model at the beginning of the academic year, receive four hours of English instruction per day, and test out of the program as proficient English speakers via the AZELLA in April or May of that same academic year (for more information on the AZELLA, see Wright, Chapter 3, this volume; also Florez, 2012). When ELs do leave the program after successfully passing the AZELLA as proficient, they are monitored for two consecutive years and labeled as *reclassified fluent English proficient* (RFEP, or more commonly as RC). During this two-year monitoring period, ELs are tested annually using the AZELLA to reassess their English proficiency. Should a student not pass the AZELLA at any time during the two-year timeframe, s/he is re-immersed in the ELD classrooms and designated as an *English language learner after reclassification* (ELLAR).

Arizona's policies associated with SEI do not outline explicit stipulations about retaining students due to their designation as an EL. On the contrary, the mandates and school board rules imply that promotion between grades, as well as high school graduation within four years, is possible for ELs placed in ELD classrooms. The following Parental Notification letter, for example, as published by the ADE, states that the SEI model helps ELs meet age appropriate academic standards [as] based upon scientific research. The expectations for the ELL students are to fully transition into mainstream classes, meet appropriate academic achievement standards for grade promotion, and to graduate from high school at the same rate as mainstream students. (ADE, 2011: 2)

These policies also clarify that if an EL or RC student is not progressing satisfactorily in comparison to his/her mainstream peers, schools are required to provide 'compensatory instruction' to support EL students' academic achievement.[15] Some compensatory instruction is delivered as tutoring, while most is designed as summer school or after-school programs.[16] Therefore, while promotion may occur, the woefully inadequate access to core content instruction within the ELD classroom, in addition to limited resources to support students once they exit from the model (such as tutors, summer school opportunities or materials to support the continued language development of RC students in mainstream classrooms) have drastic implications for ELs and RC students. These voids ultimately hinder EL and RC students' ability to remain on a par with their native-English-speaking peers. Further, language acquisition experts lament the idea of learning English within one year, noting that it takes an average of five to eight years to learn a language well enough to succeed in academic arenas (August & Hakuta, 1997; August et al., 2010; Hakuta et al., 2000; TESOL, 2006; Wright, 2010).

Revisiting Policy in Practice

Methodology and participants

The purpose of the initial study (see, e.g. Lillie et al., 2010) was to document and describe the characteristics of the four-hour SEI policy in practice. Over a seven-week period during the spring semester of the 2009/2010 school year, researchers utilized qualitative ethnographic methods to document the four-hour SEI model implementation and instruction of ELs in Arizona. Eighteen ELD classrooms (10 at the high school level and eight at the K-8 level) in nine schools, within five districts across the state were included in the study. The five districts represent various types of Arizona schools including those with both high and low percentages of ELs and locations in both rural and urban areas. In this way, participating schools offered a diverse picture of EL population representation, locale, and number of economically disadvantaged students (e.g. of the observed districts, 60–80% of the student population were on free/reduced lunches). Table 7.3 illustrates information related to each ELD classroom included in the study. All classrooms observed included ELs at multiple proficiency levels (e.g. Pre-Emergent/Emergent, Basic/Intermediate or all four levels in one class).

Table 7.3 Grade-level bands and certifications of ELD teachers as observed

	Elementary (K-8th)	High school (9th–12th)
Grade-level/band		
	Kindergarten (3)[a]	9th–12th (10)
	2nd–3rd (1)	
	3rd grade (1)	
	3rd–6th grades (1)	
	7th/8th grades (2)	
Teacher endorsements		
SEI Provisional	3	2
SEI Full	2	1
ESL Endorsement	1	6
BLE Endorsement	2	1

Notes: [a]The number in parenthesis represents the total number of classrooms observed at that level.

A team of seven researchers collected and analyzed data for the study. Researchers interviewed each of the 18 participating ELD teachers, as well as EL coaches/coordinators, and some principals. In addition to interviews, researchers conducted a total of more than 264 observation hours in ELD classrooms. Observations were scheduled to ensure reflection of typical classroom practices. For example, researchers avoided observation on days involving test preparation or school assemblies. Classroom artifacts were also collected, including teacher certification information, lesson plans, copies of classroom instructional materials, and classroom rosters showing class size and proficiency levels of students. Archival data were accessed from information provided online by the ADE to the public (cf. https://www.azed.gov/english-language-learners/). This encompassed specific policies, laws, instructional suggestions as per the SEI training to teachers and administrators, and other SEI model implementation PowerPoints created by the ADE.

Data were analyzed using Erickson's (1986) method of modified analytic induction. Each researcher simultaneously collected and analyzed data on specific ELD classrooms, independently read over the data, and took notes along the way to make sense of the data as a whole. Throughout the seven-week period of data collection, researchers attended weekly meetings to discuss emerging themes across independent data sets. In the final weeks of data collection, researchers came to a consensus on a list of themes representing preliminary observation findings across all classroom settings. After all data were collected, researchers convened for four days, spending more than 30 hours on the final stages of analysis. Researchers ended up with a set of 13 major assertions to describe characteristics of the four-hour policy as practice in K–12 classrooms.

Findings from the Field

For the purposes of this chapter, the authors revisited findings from the *Policy in Practice* study (Lillie *et al.*, 2010). Using a constant comparison analysis (Miles & Huberman, 1994), the authors coded previous findings descriptively based on three areas of policy. What follows is a discussion of the findings as relevant to the three specific areas of (1) ELD model design and student grouping; (2) content of the ELD classroom; and (3) promotion and graduation practices surrounding ELs in ELD classrooms. Findings are presented as two separate cases: Case I includes the elementary district findings, K-8; and, Case II reports on the secondary districts, grades 9–12.

Case I: Elementary districts' findings as related to policy

There were eight elementary classrooms included in the study, representing two urban districts in the greater Phoenix metropolitan area. Of the eight elementary ELD teachers included in the study, three held a bilingual or ESL Endorsement, and the majority (five teachers) had participated in the state-mandated training/coursework required for their SEI Endorsement (see Markos & Arias, Chapter 5, this volume). Half of the participating classrooms were *grade-band* rooms, meaning more than one grade level of students were grouped together in the classroom.

Student grouping

Nowhere in the policy on SEI programs does the state call for *segregating* ELs. However, several factors combine to equate a degree of segregation. Together, the ELD classroom grouping policy, scheduling characteristics of the elementary school day and the tendency for students to socialize with those with whom they are most familiar all function as facilitating the separation of elementary-aged ELs from their English-speaking peers for the entire school day.

Although Arizona's SEI policy states that ELs are to be placed in ELD classrooms for four hours and then integrated into mainstream classrooms for the remainder of the school day, this is not what was observed. In the eight elementary classrooms included in our study, ELs remained in their ELD classroom with their ELD teacher and other ELs for the entire school day. Elementary ELD teachers and EL coaches reported that, because of scheduling for specials, lunch, recess and the four hours of mandated ELD instruction, it was unrealistic to integrate ELs into mainstream classrooms for any portion of the school day. When ELs did leave their ELD classroom for specials (art, music, physical education, library) they remained grouped with fellow EL-designated peers. Overall, if an elementary student was assigned to an ELD classroom he/she had very little opportunity to interact with English-proficient students during the instructional day.

There were two exceptions to this norm. One was a kindergarten ELD classroom that included five English-proficient students. At this particular school site, a mainstream kindergarten teacher was reassigned to another grade level due to low enrollment, one month into the school year. Her English-proficient students were dispersed among the other classrooms, which included one mainstream and three ELD classrooms. The ELD teacher remarked that when the English-proficient students first joined the class, the ELs were aware of the difference in language abilities. She described the students' reaction stating, 'the [ELLs] said, "Those are the English kids, what are they doing here?" They could tell the difference, one month into kindergarten' (EB3, 8 April 2010).[17] This teacher went on to explain how she had to facilitate students being comfortable to work together but that it was worth it since she preferred to have the English-speaking students in the class. As she described it, 'this way, I am not the only language model, they have students sitting with them, working with them, that speak English' (EB3, 8 April 2010). She valued the presence of the proficient speakers as model peers for her language learners.

The second exception was a 7th grade ELD classroom wherein the EL students left for 45 minutes of math instruction each day. In this instance, while the ELD students received math instruction from a math teacher (as opposed to their ELD teacher, which was the case in the other two middle school ELD classrooms observed), the students remained with their EL peers and were not integrated with mainstream students during their math instruction.

With the exception of the one group of students who left their ELD classroom for math instruction, all other 7th and 8th grade ELs remained in their ELD classrooms for all content area instruction. ELD teachers described how mainstream 7th and 8th graders rotated classrooms and teachers daily for different periods of content instruction, but not the EL students. One teacher noted this was especially troublesome for ELs when they transferred to the high school, into settings in which they would be expected to understand and be comfortable with changing classrooms and teachers for multiple periods across the school day (CA3, 18 March 2010). In the middle school examples, placement in four-hour ELD classrooms excluded ELs from the typical middle school practice of changing teachers and classrooms throughout the school day, an essential socializing activity in middle school and for transitioning to high school.

Even when EL students had the opportunity to break away from their ELD classroom grouping, opportunities for interaction with their English-proficient peers (such as before/after school) were rarely actualized. For example, during lunch, the one time of the day most ELs and English-speakers of the same grade level are accessible to each other, students had assigned seats in the lunchroom according to their classroom teacher, meaning that ELs sat with the other students from their ELD classrooms. Teachers noted that students tended to 'stick with other ELs, maybe not from our class, but others that speak their language. You know, they'll find their cousin, or a sibling and hang out with them during recess' (CA3, 22 March 2010). One ELD coach described the separation between the ELLs and the mainstream students as something the staff at her school tried to discourage, but felt it was challenging because of the way the state mandated that students be separated for four hours of language instruction. Describing her frustration, she noted, 'They are always separated; they don't get a chance to interact. This makes it harder and harder. Students get used to being with other ELLs and the mainstream kids know nothing about the ELLs, it's hard' (CA5, 2 March 2010). While the goal of Arizona's four-hour SEI model is for ELs to acquire English, its segregation requirement impedes opportunities for interaction between ELs and English-proficient peers – an integral aspect of second language acquisition.

Content of classrooms

Policies related to the content of ELD classrooms highlight that instruction within ELD classrooms must emphasize ELD, as opposed to instruction of the content areas. ELD implementation guidance only provides teachers opportunities to integrate additional academic content (such as math, science or social studies) into classroom instruction when it aligns with the English language goals of the classroom. Furthermore, the state emphasizes that all materials used in the ELD classroom must be in English and appropriate for students' level of English language proficiency.

Among the classrooms we visited, at the elementary level, there was a generous amount of materials that could facilitate students' learning of the English language. Although they were not always observed in use, books such as *Success in Language, Moving into English, ESL Survival Kit* and *High Point's Success in Language and Literature* were commonly present in both elementary and middle school classrooms. Specifically with regard to materials for the instruction of ELD content, all of the eight elementary classrooms observed had materials and resources in English for promoting ELD. Unfortunately, however, the integration of content instruction was rarely observed as part of the ELD classroom curriculum and instruction, even though the policy states that an ELD class may use content to promote English acquisition (ADE, 2008[18]).

In both interviews and observations, findings illustrate that ELD teachers lacked access to materials that support the teaching of subject matter content. This lack of content material, coupled with the rule that all instruction materials must be in English, resulted in minimal opportunities for exposure to grade-appropriate content area instruction in the ELD classroom. The few instances in which ELD teachers were observed attempting to integrate content area instruction involved teachers' locating or creating their own resources for content instruction. For example, in one observation at the elementary level, a teacher attempted a science lesson without science textbooks or other reading materials, and had only one set of manipulatives (CA2, March 2010). The result was a decontextualized science experience, wherein students were left to watch and listen as opposed to having access to the necessary recourse to conduct the science experiment themselves. While mainstream students at the same grade level were learning how to make hypotheses and predictions through hands-on experiences with science experiments and appropriate materials, the ELs' learning focused on listening and the observing and labeling of objects.

The one content area outside of ELD that each elementary teacher reported responsibility for teaching was math. The lack of appropriate material for content instruction dramatically affected ELD teachers' abilities to teach math. One ELD teacher was provided with no consumables (workbooks or materials for students to write in) for her students outside of those related to ELD. This posed a particular challenge for math homework, with the teacher remarking, 'How am I supposed to send homework home – I can't create worksheets every day' (CA1, 3 March 2010). The expectation at her school was that all students complete reading and math homework each night, but ELD teachers were left to create their own math homework materials while mainstream students worked out of grade-appropriate, school-provided math homework sources and texts. The four-hour model places a greater emphasis on ways to develop and promote English language acquisition than on seamlessly weaving grade-level appropriate content into the curriculum. Given this approach to preference for English instruction, it is not surprising that in the classrooms we observed we noticed a general dearth of developmentally appropriate math, science and social studies materials. The emphasis on English during ELD instruction, combined with the lack of appropriate content materials available to ELD teachers, equates to disparaging opportunities for academic growth for ELs placed in ELD settings as compared with their English-speaking peers.

Promotion of students

As discussed previously, there are very few explicit policies addressing grade promotion for students placed in ELD classrooms. What is known is that the state does not intend for ELs to remain in ELD classrooms for more than one year (e.g. A.R. S. §15-752, English language education). Further, the state claims that while in the ELD program, ELs will maintain an educational experience comparable to students in mainstream classrooms. While there is no apparent *rule* regarding grade promotion for ELs placed in ELD classrooms, districts did not deny students grade promotion because of language proficiency in the elementary districts we observed. All the elementary level teachers we interviewed reported that language ability did not hinder ELs from moving on to subsequent grade levels. In this regard, we concluded that in grades K-8, placement in ELD classrooms did not impact ELs' progress in terms of grade promotion. Regardless of time spent in the ELD classroom, however, the teachers we interviewed and observed agreed that grade promotion for ELs creates a 'false positive' for understanding ELs' ability to achieve and maintain success in mainstream grade-level classrooms.

Findings from interviews, observations and policy analysis of the four-hour SEI model demonstrate that the content in ELD classrooms is very different from that in mainstream classrooms. With the pressure to learn English at an accelerated pace and the emphasis on ELD, ELs have restricted exposure to grade-level content area instruction. As one ELD teacher summarized, 'Mainstream teachers follow the grade-level standards and curriculum, we don't' (CA1, 19 March 2010). This lack of attention to grade-level standards within ELD classrooms creates a false positive for success as students exit the language program and enter mainstream classrooms. Some might assume that because ELs have passed the AZELLA and are placed in mainstream classrooms, they are ready to engage in grade-appropriate learning experiences. Unfortunately, because ELs receive limited, if any, exposure to grade-level content instruction there is no system of accountability to ensure readiness for grade-level content area knowledge, despite having achieved English proficiency.

Although the state expectation is that ELs will pass as proficient on the AZELLA and be placed in mainstream classrooms after one year of ELD, even one year of restricted exposure to grade-appropriate content area instruction results in ELs who are underprepared in the content areas as compared with English-proficient, grade-level peers. Teachers also reported that, despite the SEI model goals, the majority of ELs take more than a year to reach proficiency in English. For every year these students spend in an ELD classroom, where instructional time is hyper-focused on language learning, they fall further behind their grade-level peers in content area academic knowledge and abilities. Therefore, even though schools are not retaining ELs, teachers stated that students often experience a false positive in terms of grade-level success as schools promote ELs from grade to grade without exposure to grade-level content. Teachers cautioned that, because of this limited or non-existent exposure to content, ELs struggle once they are exited into mainstream, content-based classrooms.

Also disconcerting with regard to false grade promotion, teachers described cases of students returning to ELD classrooms after exiting. Many former ELs who have been exited from ELD test back in at the end of their first year in mainstream classrooms because of a drop in English proficiency scores on the AZELLA. While the state is promoting the success of the four-hour ELD approach and the rise in English-proficient students, up to 30% in 2009/2010 from 22% in 2007/2008 as reported by the ADE (M. Johnston, personal communication, 15 November 2011), teachers in this study cautioned consideration for what is happening to students' language and content abilities once they exit from ELD and are placed in mainstream classrooms. The potential for repeated transitioning between ELD and mainstream classrooms further complicates and compromises ELs' exposure to grade-level content.

Case II: High school districts' findings as related to policy

Three high school districts participated in this study, representing both rural and urban districts. There were 10 teachers involved at the secondary level. All of the classrooms observed had grade-band classrooms, 9 through 12. In other words, EL students were grouped across grade levels (i.e. 9th–12th grade students were found in every ELD classroom). In some schools, there were mixed proficiency levels within each grade-banded ELD classroom.

Student grouping

High school ELs get four distinct hours (four periods) of ELD, unlike elementary age students who may spend their entire day in an ELD classroom. As per SEI policy, at the secondary level it is not required that the four hours are consecutive. However, in the classrooms we observed, they were. The requirement that ELs spend four periods of their six-period school day in ELD classes resulted in ELs having limited access to courses required for graduation and left them separated from English-speaking peers for the majority of each day.

ELs' school schedules are dominated, as well as dictated, by the four-hour block. Typically, high school ELs had six classes a day, four of which were for the ELD classes. For the remaining two periods, ELs were placed in different courses, usually two core content classes (e.g. math and science), but were often also in 'AIMS Reading' or 'AIMS Writing' (A, March 2010). If a content course had reached maximum enrollment capacity, ELs were placed in electives. At times, the ability to attend a course outside of the ELD classroom was the only means by which high school ELs were able to interact with mainstream teachers and non-EL peers. Unfortunately, some ELs moved from course to course as one large group, therefore staying in EL groups throughout the entire day.

Scheduling and designated student grouping (as required by the SEI model) are not the only reasons high school students are segregated from their English-speaking peers. While in the ELD classrooms, ELs were *physically* isolated from mainstream classrooms. We saw this primarily in two of the three districts where we conducted observations. In one district, the ELD classroom was in a separate building and located with the career and technical development classes. The teacher there repeatedly mentioned the fact that they were 'surrounded by special classes' and that they all feel 'totally segregated out here … they kind of have me off … there aren't many people over in my wing' (BA1, 22 March 2010). Another district not only had the ELD rooms in completely different buildings from the rest of the mainstream curriculum classrooms, including even the other English classrooms,[19] but the rooms reserved for the ELs were interspersed with the children classified as severely emotionally disturbed, the life-skills special education students and the Special Education department offices. In these two districts, ELs were not exposed to other mainstream teachers or students for most of the day, and the classrooms were set apart and distinct from much of the school. Therefore, ELs would associate and socialize with themselves between classes as they had no one else with whom to talk.

Content of classrooms

Instruction in high school ELD classrooms focused solely on the English skills of reading, writing, grammar, vocabulary and oral language. As per the four-hour model design, the areas of English were separated across the four hours of ELD, which some teachers found problematic. One veteran teacher commented on the difficulty of teaching English in such a discrete manner by saying, 'I have no idea how to keep them separate. I just include them all together. It's more natural that way' (AA1, 10 March 2010). Another concern was that the materials for ELs were not age, grade or standard appropriate for teaching English content to high school students. Whereas students would read elementary-level and early childhood books like *Lillian the Rat, I Love You Stinkyface, Clifford's First Autumn* and *I Am Not Sleepy and I Will Not Go to Bed*, non-EL students were receiving English reading lessons on youth and adult books, such as *A Raisin in the Sun*, works of Shakespeare and *Catcher in the Rye*. There were no supporting materials for the ELD teachers to use, with some classrooms lacking textbooks. This meant that not only were ELs limited in their support for learning English, but they also were prohibited from access to age- and grade-appropriate content and curriculum standards. Core content outside of ELD (such as math, science or social studies) was rarely used, or was used artificially, to help teach the English language, even though this is suggested by the ADE.[20] We only observed one teacher attempting to tie science content into the ELD lessons by talking about frogs and earthquakes (DD1, March 2010). These lessons, however, were superficial and not comparable to the exposure a non-EL student would receive in a mainstream science classroom.

Per Arizona's SEI policy, the emphasis is that English is the language of instruction for all ELD classrooms in order to teach English content. This does not mean, as is often perceived, that students cannot use their native languages. As stated previously, 'teachers may use a minimal amount of the child's native language when necessary' as long as the instruction is delivered in English (A.R.S. §15-751, Definitions, 5). In the districts observed, the schools followed the mythical English-only mandate in the strictest sense, at the ELs' cost. Classrooms contained posters where the first rule was often 'English only!' and supplemental reading materials were in English and never in other languages. In one high school ELD classroom, out of five rules, 'Speak English' was listed first, before 'Show Respect' (AA2, March 2010).

Some teachers were skilled at accepting a student's response in their native language. In cases we observed where teachers accepted responses in students' native languages, the teachers would hear the child's native language response, give the word in their native language to support understanding, and then scaffold the student into the lesson through English. For example, one student asked (in Spanish) what *forward* meant in a reading passage, and the teacher responded back to the student by repeating the word in Spanish before modeling the definition to the class in English and writing the definition on the board (DC, March 2010). Although some teachers allowed the integration of native languages to facilitate learning, there were other teachers observed who were opposed to any use of ELs' native languages. Even when these teachers understood their student's native language, they refused its use in the classroom (A & B, 2010). As one teacher commented, 'I understand Spanish, about 90% of what they say but I REFUSE to speak to them in anything but English' (emphasis as noted, BA1, 22 March 2010).

In two districts, teachers' faulty interpretation of SEI policy regarding the language of content instruction for ELD classrooms resulted in extreme language restrictionism. These teachers believed that the instruction is required to be only in English, even though the law states that a minimal amount of native language may be used (see, for example, A.R.S. §15-751, Definitions, 5). This interpretation of the law played out in teachers awarding ELs for reporting on one another when a language other than English was heard or used in the classroom. One teacher recalled 'a game where they'd get in teams and report on each other if they heard any Spanish', claiming that the students loved doing this (AA2, 3 March 2010). In another district, students were *language police*, patrolling for unwanted use of the native language. There, the teacher used play money to entice her students to report one another for non-English language usage. Students were able to collect fake dollar bills to get prizes from the classroom store. These EL students would inform the teacher if a peer used the native language during individual work time. During one observation, one EL student shouted out 'Guys, English!', and when another EL turned in her friends for using the native language during their group work, the teacher handed her classroom dollars while thanking the student for 'encouraging everyone to practice English' (BA1, 24 March 2010). If this teacher heard any native language use, she would take away students' classroom money as punishment for native language use.

Policing language was not limited to ELs in ELD classes. Anyone who entered the ELD room was subject to reprimand if they used a language other than English. For example, during one observation, a student bringing a pass from the office for one of the EL students walked in during the middle of the lesson. The teacher asked if the EL student needed to go at that present moment, and the student with the pass responded '*Si*'. Immediately, the teacher said 'English in here!' and the student answered 'Oh. (…) Yes' (AA2, 3 March 2010). With a required focus on ELD content, emphasized by teachers' interpretation of *how* this English content must be delivered (i.e. 'English-only!'), combined with the policy stipulations regarding ELs' grouping in ELD classrooms, the separation of ELs from the mainstream school, children and teachers is complete.

Graduation

High school ELs in Arizona might experience the most detrimental effects of the SEI model with regard to promotion/graduation. They are faced with the real possibility that they will not graduate as a result of their placement in the SEI model. This reality, in turn, affects not only aspirations they might have for higher education, but their overall future. Teachers and administrators expressed concern regarding the four-hour block scheduling and course requirement conflicts. One administrator noted that 'the SEI Model is abusive to kids. It isolates and segregates them from the public and denies them credits' (DA3, 5 March 2010).

It was evident from discussions with staff at the high school level that ELs are not exiting out of the ELD program in one year. One teacher blamed the students, saying 'they don't get that they miss out on credits and won't graduate on time if they're in here too long' (BA1, 22 March 2010). Others recognized that the SEI *model* was setting ELs up for failure. One EL chair commented that ELs were not exiting in one year and that 'the time frame depends on students…we have some students who have never been to school with limited education versus some students who have some English' (DA4, 5 March 2010). This EL Department Chair recognized that the design of the SEI model does not account for student differences in the process of language acquisition. One concerned principal reported that it was taking three years for students to exit the program, which was setting up juniors and seniors to be even further behind their non-EL peers (DD3, 2 April 2010) not just in content learning, but in course completion. What's more, it was reported in a few districts that when students are reclassified (RC), they may not get the continued language support they need, and thus do poorly academically. It was discovered that a number of RC students fail many of their courses when they exit the SEI model. Even if RC students receive support after exiting the program, RC students' academic success is hindered in comparison to their native-English-proficient peers because of the lack of content-based contextual exposure in the SEI model. These examples of under-preparation and lack of support invariably contribute to a long-term and more likely sustained achievement gap between EL and non-EL students.

Analysis of school EL curriculum, books and information collected from school personnel indicated that ELs receive one English credit and three elective credits per year for *all four hours* of ELD. While mainstream students typically earn four content area credits and two elective credits per year, the four-hour ELD model limits ELs' opportunity to earn content credits. This means that some ELs may only receive two or three content credits *every year they are in the SEI model,* and all ELs are hindered at meeting yearly requirements for graduation in a typical four-year timeframe.

A principal discussed the challenges faced by RC students after they enter the mainstream because they take almost all content area classes and very few (if any) electives to make up for missing out on content courses while enrolled in the SEI model. As a result, exited RC students' schedules are top heavy with academic content (DD3, April 2010) and inequitably rigorous. Students who are unable to enroll in the required content courses during the typical school year or day are sometimes allowed the chance to take the course at an alternative time. Principals and teachers in all three districts explained that in order for many ELs to catch-up they must enroll in summer school or after-school programs. Essentially, therefore, ELs or RC students are in some ways penalized for forced participation in the mandated SEI model; in all three high school districts, funding cuts meant that these alternative options were not even available. Overall, many high school ELs and RC students are precluded from graduating in a timely fashion and may take five or more years to graduate, if at all.

Connecting the Two: A Discussion of Findings

Across districts, schools, and elementary and secondary classrooms included in the study, the themes that emerged were salient. As a result of the imposition of the SEI model, ELs in Arizona's schools are not allowed the opportunity to fully participate within a school community. They are limited in access to content and curriculum compared to that of their mainstream, English-speaking peers. ELs are precluded from achieving high quality education, therefore falling further behind non-EL students in relation to success in mainstream classrooms, grade promotion and graduation. Since the implementation of the SEI model, ELs in Arizona have been isolated, segregated and hindered in their learning and the implications are grandiose.

While some ELs might have the benefit of hearing native English speakers in school, we identified evidence that most are consistently limited in their exposure to this type of input due to restrictions stemming from their ELD classroom schedule. As Cosentino de Cohen *et al.* (2005: 16) comment, 'the segregation of LEP students results in their isolation from the educational mainstream and the attendant loss of the benefits of interacting with English-speaking classmates: and a loss for English dominant students'. The exclusion of ELs from native-English-speaking peers is detrimental not just to the ELL student, but also to their English-speaking counterparts. Furthermore, Gifford and Valdés (2006) state that:

> the hypersegregation of (students), and particularly Spanish-speaking ELLs, suggests that little or no attention has been given to the consequences of linguistic isolation for a population whose future depends on the acquisition of English. Unfortunately, segregation of ELLs … has profound consequences for their acquisition of English. For ELLs, interaction with ordinary English-speaking peers is essential to their English language development and consequently to their acquisition of academic English. (Gifford & Valdés, 2006: 146–147)

The student grouping requirement as per Arizona's SEI policy segregates the children in Arizona's schools on the basis of their ELP levels. It creates an isolation that is both physical and social, which impedes ELs' access to full participation in the larger school community and continues to stigmatize language minority students. Observations showed that the SEI program's separation of ELs for a large portion, if not all, of the school day creates 'ESL Ghettos', which are fallacious learning environments where ELs will continue to fall further behind and languish in school (Gándara & Orfield, 2012; Gifford & Valdés, 2006; Valdés, 2001; Valenzuela, 2005).

It is important to highlight that many Arizona teachers are doing the best they can, given the circumstances under which they are required to teach. With limited materials and resources with which to instruct, and the strict interpretation of the policy by many who think that content is detached from ELD classrooms and that a student's native language is not allowed, ELs are not receiving an equal education compared to their mainstream peers. Findings showed that some teachers tried to incorporate content in ELD classes to better support ELs' transition when they exit the program. However, in-depth content instruction comparable to mainstream settings was practically impossible for a variety of reasons. With strict English-only ideology firmly in place in most ELD settings and embedded in the SEI model, the overt devaluation of students' native languages may have significant implications for a student's identity construction (cf. Norton, 2000).

Research suggests that a separation of academic content from language does not facilitate language acquisition; in fact, it can be harmful to the overall educational success of an EL student. As Krashen *et al.* (2007) advise:

> the primary purpose of schooling for all children, including ELLs, is the development of academic subject matter knowledge. A curriculum which separates subject matter instruction from language teaching in an effort to focus on the latter will not only risk creating significant educational deficits in learners, but will also fail to provide meaningful contexts for language acquisition in school. (Krashen *et al.*, 2007: 8)

ELs are precluded from access to the content they need to consistently maintain academic achievement parallel to that of their English-proficient peers. The heavy focus on English-only instruction is detrimental not only to students' language acquisition, but their overall ability to effectively meet school requirements for promotion and graduation. While we do not argue with grade promotion for ELs who have been placed in ELD classrooms, promotion exclusive of a solid foundation in grade-level content is, at the very least, disadvantageous to the EL students. Not only have the ELs in ELD classrooms missed out on core content, but they then often struggle to keep up and navigate the mainstream classrooms into which they are immersed after exiting the program. The reclassification of students based on AZELLA scores is a false positive for predicting their academic achievement in mainstream classrooms.

There is a concern regarding dropout rates for ELs (cf. Rumberger, 2004; Rumberger & Rodríguez, 2011). Due to the combination of graduation course requirements, lack of access to core academic content, and lengthy involvement in the SEI model, the pathway to school success for ELs in Arizona is severely hampered at best, and arguably inequitable. Research on dropout rates for ELs in Arizona's SEI model are not currently available. However, educators and policymakers can gain information based on the impact of similar language policies in other states. In Massachusetts, for example, between 2004 and 2006 the drop-out rate was the largest for ELs in SEI programs (Uriarte *et al.*, 2010). This was especially the case for EL high school students, as opposed to their non-EL counterparts in the general education curriculum. It is true that Massachusetts does not have the same type of SEI program as does Arizona; however, Arizona's policy is *more* restrictive. The implication here is that, when facing additional obstacles to graduate while under Arizona's highly restrictive language policy, EL students might simply drop out of school.

The SEI model in Arizona is unique because it requires ELs' enrollment in a language program which involves English-only instruction for four hours a day. The key issue at stake given Arizona's SEI model is not whether ELs should receive English language instruction. Rather, it is whether Arizona's current four-hour SEI model is a sound approach for meeting the needs of ELs (linguistic, academic and social). Four hours of discrete English instruction is the main cause of problems for ELs in Arizona schools. The mandate that ELs are segregated from English-proficient peers fosters a separation of students and restricts ELs' access to native English speakers and the mainstream school community. The emphasis on ELD content and English-only materials excludes students from access to grade-appropriate content and standards, and equitable curricula. These factors result in the realization of students' hindered ability to meet promotion and graduation requirements. The recent years of statewide SEI instruction in Arizona is the culmination of a decade of policy and over two decades of legal debate and, as a result, we suggest that an entire generation of ELs has been 'left behind'.

Notes

(1) See http://www.azleg.gov/legtext/47leg/2r/bills/hb2064c.pdf.

(2) 'Arizona law requires a minimum of four hours per day of English language development during the first year a pupil is classified as an ELL' (A.R.S. §15.756.01).

(3) '"Sheltered English immersion" or "structured English immersion" means an English language acquisition process for young children in which nearly all classroom instruction is in English but with the curriculum and presentation designed for children who are learning the language. ... Although teachers may use a minimal amount of the child's native language when necessary, no subject matter shall be taught in any language other than English, and children in this program learn to read and write solely in English' (A.R.S. §15-751, Definitions, 5).

(4) See, for example, A.R.S. §15, Article 3.1 for the full listing of statutes, at http://www.azleg.gov/ArizonaRevisedStatutes.asp?Title = 15.

(5) AZELLA stands for Arizona English Language Learner Assessment, is given to all ELs yearly, and is the gatekeeper for an ELL's entry and exit into the SEI model. The test has since been found to be invalid by the Department of Justice (DOJ) and Arizona is currently negotiating with the DOJ about the future of its testing.

(6) 'Arizona law requires English language learners to be grouped together in a structured English immersion setting' (A.R.S. §15-751, Definitions, 5).

(7) If a school has fewer than 20 designated ELs, they may put those EL students on individualized language learner plans (ILLPs).

(8) 'ELD means English language development, the teaching of English language skills to students who are in the process of learning English. It is distinguished from other types of instruction, e.g. math, science, or social science, in that the content of ELD emphasizes the English language itself' (ADE, 2008: 1).

(9) 'Arizona law requires materials and subject matter instruction to be in English' (A.R.S. §15-751, Definitions, 5; A.R.S. §15-752).

(10) 'Books and instructional materials are in English and all reading, writing, and subject matter are taught in English' (A.R.S. §15-751, Definitions, 5).

(11) 'The curriculum of all English language learner programs shall incorporate the Academic Standards adopted by the Board and shall be comparable in amount, scope and quality to that provided to English language proficient students' (S.B.R., R7-2-306, F.3).

(12) This was defined by the ADE as 'the specific teaching/learning objectives derived from the Arizona K–12 English Language Learner Proficiency Standards approved by the Arizona State Board of Education (SBE), January 26, 2004, and refined as needed to remain synchronized with the Arizona K–12 Academic English Language Arts Standards' (ADE, 2008: 1–2). Specifically, DSI 'is a sequential series of English language skills that provide a guide to teaching the grammatical foundations necessary for students ... and provides the critical grammatical foundation for achieving proficiency in listening, speaking, and writing' (ADE, n.d.: 1). Since 2010, however, while the DSI has not been abandoned, it has been incorporated into the ELP standards. Now, the ELP standards include a reading domain, a writing domain, a listening/speaking domain, and a language strand which consists of the DSI and vocabulary.

(13) 'The goal set forth in Arizona law is for ELLs to become fluent English proficient in a year' (A.R.S. §15-752. English language education).

(14) In some instances, ELs who were getting traditional ESL pull-out services while they were in the mainstream found themselves immersed in the four-hour model upon implementation of SEI in 2008.

(15) 'The LEA shall monitor exited students based on the criteria provided in this Section during each of the two years after being reclassified as FEP to determine whether these students are performing satisfactorily in achieving the Arizona Academic

Standards adopted by the Board…Students who are not making satisfactory progress shall, with parent consent, be provided compensatory instruction or shall be re-enrolled in an ELL program' (S.B.R. R7-2-306).

(16) Compensatory education is defined as 'instruction given in addition to regular classroom instruction, such as individual or small group instruction, extended day classes, summer school or intersession school' (S.B.R., R7-2-306 A.4).

(17) In order to preserve anonymity, all districts were coded alphabetically (A through E). To maintain clarity, another alphabet letter was added to the code to specify school sites. Teachers were then coded by number within the schools at which they taught, adding this number to the alphabetical codes. For example, one district had three schools and four teachers. Therefore, if researchers deemed that a specific quotation was necessary from a teacher, this was coded as District C, School A, Teacher 1 (CA1). A further illustration of coding methods is purposefully withheld in order to maintain anonymity of all participants.

(18) Since 2006, ADE has constantly altered the way in which they produce and present policy for consumption. What results is policy that is continuously changing or, in some cases, disappearing. This is highly problematic for educators (and researchers). For example, we the authors had citations for where information was presented by the ADE that are later than what might be evidenced here. Since the writing of this piece, some older sources have been reinstated and newer sources have been replaced or are simply missing.

(19) This was a concern since it was noted that the ELD classes were considered to be a part of the English Department. See the further discussion on graduation/content.

(20) Again, as per the ADE training presentation PowerPoints, 'ELD is not a math, science or social studies lesson. Content from academic subjects are the vehicles to help achieve the goal of developing English language' (cf. ADE, 2007).

References

ADE (2007) *Nuts & Bolts – Round 1. Training* [PowerPoint presentation, slides 78–79]. See http://www.azed.gov/english-language-learners/sei/.

ADE (2008) *Structured English Immersion Models of the Arizona English Language Learners Task Force*. Phoenix, AZ: Arizona Department of Education. See https://www.azed.gov/wp-content/uploads/PDF/SEIModels05-14-08.pdf.

ADE (2011) Parental notification: In English. See https://www.azed.gov/wp-content/uploads/PDF/ParentalNotification.pdf.

ADE (n.d.) *Discrete Skills Inventory (DSI)*. Phoenix, AZ: Arizona Department of Education. See https://www.azed.gov/wp-content/uploads/PDF/DSIAllLevels.pdf.

A.R.S. (2000) Arizona Revised Statutes. Article 3.1 English Language Education for the Children in Public Schools. See http://www.azleg.state.az.us/ArizonaRevisedStatutes.asp?Title = 15.

August, D. and Hakuta, K. (eds) (1997) *Improving Schooling for Language-minority Children: A Research Agenda*. Washington, DC: National Academy Press.

August, D., Goldenberg, C. and Rueda, R. (2010) Restrictive state language policies: Are they scientifically based? In P. Gándara and M. Hopkins (eds) *Forbidden Languages: English Learners and Restrictive Language Policies* (pp. 139–158). New York: Teachers College.

Combs, M.C. (2012) Everything on its head: How Arizona's structured English immersion policy re-invents theory and practice. In M.B. Arias and C. Faltis (eds) *Implementing Educational Language Policy in Arizona: Legal, Historical, and Current Practices in SEI* (pp. 59–85). Bristol: Multilingual Matters.

Cosentino de Cohen, C., Deterding, N. and Clewell, B.C. (2005) *Who's Left Behind? Immigrant Children in High and Low LEP Schools*. Washington, DC: Urban Institute. See http://www.urban.org/UploadedPDF/411231_whos_left_behind.pdf (accessed 20 March 2010).

de Jong, E.J., Arias, M.B. and Sánchez, M.T. (2010) Undermining teacher competencies: Another look at the impact of restrictive language policies. In P. Gándara and M. Hopkins (eds) *Forbidden Language: English Learners and Restrictive Language Policies* (pp. 118–136). New York: Teachers College Press.

Erickson, F. (1986) Qualitative methods in research on teaching. In M.C. Wittrock (ed.) *Handbook of Research on Teaching* (3rd edn) (pp. 119–161). New York: Macmillan.

Faltis, C. and Arias, B. (2007) English language learners task force: A response to the proposed structured English immersion models. Submitted to the ELL Task Force Hearings, Phoenix, AZ, 2 August.

Flores v. Arizona (2009) No. 07-15603, No. 07-15605, 1014, United States Court of Appeals for the Ninth Circuit, 577 F.3d 1014; 2009 U.S. App. LEXIS 18092.

Florez, I.R. (2012) Examining the validity of the Arizona English language learners assessment cut scores. *Language Policy* 11 (1), 33–45.

Gándara, P. and Orfield, G. (2012) Segregating Arizona's English learners: A return to the 'Mexican room'. *Teachers College Record* 114 (9), 1–27.

Gifford, B.R. and Valdés, G. (2006) The linguistic isolation of Hispanic students in California's public schools: The challenge of reintegration. *Yearbook of the National Society for the Study of Education* 105 (2), 125–154.

Hakuta, K., Butler, Y.G. and Witt, D. (2000) How long does it take English learners to attain proficiency? Policy Report No. 2000-1. Santa Barbara, CA: University of California Linguistic Minority Research Institute.

HB (2006) 2064, 57th Leg., 2nd Spec. Sess. (Ariz. 2006).

Hogan, T. (2008) Flores v. State of Arizona. In J.M. González (ed.) *Encyclopedia of Bilingual Education*. Thousand Oaks, CA: SAGE Publications. See http://www.sage-ereference.com/bilingual/Article_n122.html.

Krashen, S., Rolstad, K. and MacSwan, J. (2007) Review of 'research summary and bibliography for structured English immersion programs' of the Arizona English language learners task force. Arizona State University, Tempe, AZ. See http://www.asu.edu/educ/sceed/azell/review.doc.

Lillie, K.E., Markos, A., Estrella, A., Nguyen, T., Peer, K., Perez, K., Trifiro, A., Arias, M.B. and Wiley, T.G. (2010) *Policy in Practice: The Implementation of Structured English Immersion in Arizona*. Los Angeles, CA: Civil Rights Project, University of California.

Lillie, K.E., Markos, A., Arias, M.B. and Wiley, T.G. (2012) Separate and not equal: The implementation of structured English immersion in Arizona's classrooms. *Teachers College Record* 114 (9), 1–33.

Mahoney, K., Thompson, M. and MacSwan, J. (2004) *The Condition of English Language Learners in Arizona: 2004*. Tempe, AZ: Education Policy Studies Laboratory, Arizona State University. See http://epsl.asu.edu/aepi/EPSL-0405-106-AEPI.pdf.

Mahoney, K., MacSwan, J., Haladyna, T. and García, D. (2010) Castañeda's third prong: Evaluating the achievement of Arizona's English learners under restrictive language policy. In P. Gándara and M. Hopkins (eds) *Forbidden Languages: English Learners and Restrictive Language Policies* (pp. 50–64). New York: Teachers College.

Miles, M.B. and Huberman, A.M. (1994) *Qualitative Data Analysis*, 2nd edn. Thousand Oaks, CA: SAGE Publications.

Mora, J.K. (2000) Staying the course in times of change: Preparing teachers for language minority education. *Journal of Teacher Education* 51 (5), 345–357.

Murri, N., Markos, A. and Estrella, A. (2012) Implementing structured English immersion in teacher preparation in Arizona. In M.B. Arias and C. Faltis (eds) *Implementing Educational Language Policy in Arizona: An Examination of Legal, Historical and Current Practices in SEI* (pp. 142–163). Bristol: Multilingual Matters.

Norton, B. (2000) *Identity and Language Learning: Gender, Ethnicity, and Educational Change.* Harlow: Pearson Education.

Ramirez, J.D., Yuen, S.D., Ramey, D.R. and Pasta, D.J. (1991) *Longitudinal Study of Structured English Immersion Strategy, Early-exit and Late-exit Transitional Bilingual Education Programs for Language-minority Children.* Final report, Vols 1 & 2. San Mateo, CA: Aguirre International. See http://www.eric.ed.gov/PDFS/ED330216.pdf.

Rolstad, K., Mahoney, K.S. and Glass, G.V. (2005) The big picture: A meta-analysis of program effectiveness research on English language learners. *Educational Policy* 19 (4), 572–594.

Rumberger, R.W. (2004) Why students drop out of school. In G. Orfield (ed.) *Dropouts in America* (pp. 131–155). Cambridge, MA: Harvard Education Press.

Rumberger, R.W. and Rodríguez, G.M. (2011) Chicano dropouts. In R.R. Valencia (ed.) *Chicano School Failure and Success: Past, Present, and Future* (3rd edn) (pp. 76–98). New York: Routledge.

TESOL (2006) Testimony to the House Committee on Education and the Workforce: 'No Child Left Behind': Ensuring high academic achievement for limited English proficient students and students with disabilities, July. Teachers to Speakers of Other Languages, Inc. See http://www.tesol.org/docs/pdf/6678.PDF.

Uriarte, M., Tung, R., Lavan, N. and Diez, V. (2010) Impact of restrictive language policies on engagement and academic achievement of English learners in Boston public schools. In P. Gándara and M. Hopkins (eds) *Forbidden Languages: English Learners and Restrictive Language Policies* (pp. 65–85). New York: Teachers College.

Valdés, G. (2001) *Learning and Not Learning English: Latino Students in American Schools.* New York: Teachers College Press.

Valenzuela, A. (2005) *Leaving Children Behind: How Texas Style Accountability Fails Latino Youth.* Albany, NY: State University of New York Press.

Wiley, T.G. (2007) Accessing language rights in education: A brief history of the U.S. context. In O. García and C. Baker (eds) *Bilingual Education: An Introductory Reader* (pp. 89–107). Clevedon: Multilingual Matters.

Wright, W.E. (2005) English language learners left behind in Arizona: The nullification of accommodations in the intersection of federal and state policies. *Bilingual Research Journal* 29 (1), pp. 1–29.

Wright, W.E. (2010) *Foundations for Teaching English Language Learners: Research, Theory, Policy, and Practice.* Philadelphia, PA: Caslon Publishing.

8 Conclusion: The Consequences of Nullification

Terrence G. Wiley

This volume documents how popular slogans and ideologies have been allowed to trump research and professional judgment regarding what constitutes best practices for the education of language minority students. All of the contributors, except one contributing public advocacy lawyer, who has steadfastly stayed with *Flores* for two decades in its various iterations since 1992, have been directly engaged in documenting educational policies and practices in Arizona since the passage of Proposition 203 (Arizona Voter Initiative, 2000). Collectively, their body of research and policy analysis constitutes an in-depth case study of the ongoing needs of language minority students in the post-Unz era. Through the successful nullification of accommodation-oriented policies of the past (Wright, Chapter 3), advocates of English-only policies no longer have the option of blaming 'bilingual education' for the perennial achievement gap that persists, particularly among lower income students from language minority homes (Crawford, 1992, 2000). Without bilingual education as the scapegoat, the spotlight now shines on the failed promises of 'English for the Children' and other slogans that have substituted for sensible policy based on research and sound educational practices.

The Burden of Proof for SEI as Remedy

Under the federal *No Child Left Behind* Act (NCLB, 2001), states have had considerable discretion regarding how the law could be implemented. The previous Title VII funded efforts to provide accommodations for language minority children were allowed to sunset under NCLB. Nevertheless, bilingual education could still be chosen as a programmatic option to address the needs of language minority students under their new 'English learner' (EL) label (Wiley & Wright, 2004). States such as Arizona, California and Massachusetts have been allowed to offer alternative remedies in making accommodations for language minority students. With bilingual education restricted as an option in Arizona, so-called 'structured English immersion'

(SEI) became the only option. Thus, with SEI as the only sanctioned model in Arizona, in an effort to understand its genesis, implementation and efficacy, we can identity a number of research questions that have been answered in this collection. These are:

- Why and how was SEI championed as a remedy for language minority students?
- To what extent is SEI identifiable and supportable as a model in the scholarly literature?
- Is SEI based on sound theoretical principles and adequately developed as a program model?
- How well have teachers been able to understand SEI as a model for instruction?
- What are the pre-service and in-service professional requirements related to SEI for teachers?
- What constitutes in-service training for the SEI model?
- What is the content and depth of training required for an SEI Endorsement in Arizona?
- How well do school administrators responsible for the implementation of the new SEI model understand and endorse it?
- What does the four-hour block pull-out model of SEI look like in practice?
- Is SEI effective in (a) developing students' understanding of English for academic purposes, and (b) does it enable them to keep pace with their language majority peers in academic progress?
- Is the SEI model effective from the perception of the students themselves?
- What is the experience of students in the program?

Collectively, the authors have addressed these questions, and their findings provide cause for alarm. Lillie and Moore (Chapter 1), for example, have detailed the rise of popularly supported political activism in Arizona and elsewhere, where slogans and accusations have substituted for sound evidence. Beginning with California's Prop. 227 in 1998, the assault on bilingual education was widely held to be the root cause for the failure of language minority children. This characterization presented a distorted view of the reality of educational practice. Transitional bilingual programs (TBE), designed to transition non-English speaking children to English-mediated instruction, were falsely represented as 'Spanish-only' programs. While only a fraction of language minority children eligible for Title VII programs were actually enrolled in them, the underachievement of minority children was widely believed to result from bilingual programs, rather than from state-run educational systems. Through polemical attacks in popular media, bilingual education became the scapegoat for the 'achievement gap', while English-only instruction was touted as the panacea. As Lillie and Moore chronicle, a majority of voters accepted this line of reasoning in California, Arizona and Massachusetts. They also demonstrate how Canadian research on French immersion programs, which was designed for middle-class Anglo students, became touted as the model for largely Spanish-speaking language minority students in the United States. The social class and language status contextualization issues of the original Canadian research, and its appropriateness for lower income Spanish-speaking students, were generally ignored by those who championed the efficacy of the so-called SEI model.

As Hogan (Chapter 2) has noted, there is much that has changed since the Flores family filed its original lawsuit in 1992 against the Arizona Department of Education (ADE) for failing to take proactive measures in educating their daughter, Miriam.

Remarkably, little has changed in the nearly four decades after the landmark *Lau v. Nichols* (1974), given that we are continuing to witness the widespread endorsement of educational policies, such as pull-out SEI, which have proven to be detrimental to language minority children. Particularly remarkable is that nearly a century after ideologues of the WWI era sought to stifle the use of children's mother tongues in US classrooms, during a period of war and xenophobia (Donahue, 1995; Tamura, 1993; Tatalovich, 1995; Wiley, 1998, 2004), a country that often prides itself on being a 'nation of immigrants' has witnessed the resurgence of hackney English-only Americanization practices. Some of these involve the same potentially discriminatory practices that helped lead to the Civil Rights Movement and the call for bilingual educational accommodations (Blanton, 2007; Lyons, 1995; San Miguel, 2004).

Equally remarkable is the long saga of the *Flores* cases within the contemporary political and judicial environment, and that it would take the courts over two decades to resolve a basic issue of social justice involving equitable funding for the education of language minority children. As Hogan notes, the United States Supreme Court in the split 5–4 decision (*Horne v. Flores*, 2009), criticized the lower court for assuming that there might be a relationship between funding, equity and opportunity. The court thus held the state to a lower bar, while assuming that Arizona's implementation of Prop. 203 and SEI constituted an adequate change in circumstances. In fact, the new SEI policy is a change in circumstances that has weakened the quality of academic preparation for language minority students.

Interestingly, given the narrowness of the high court's focus, it failed to note other changes in circumstances that have been occurring over the past two decades – and especially over the past 10 years, in Arizona: where undocumented adults have been barred from opportunities to learn English, seek employment or receive health care; where Arizona's legislature and ADE have sought to ban ethnic studies; where those undocumented young people who have lived most of their lives in the US, are now denied access to state-supported higher education, health care or even the right to a driver's license. Somehow, these changes in circumstance are not seen as relevant to the narrowly defined issues in the *Flores* case. And yet somehow these types of issues were clearer when the landmark *Brown* decision was made in 1954. They were also clearer to legal scholars such as Leibowitz in the 1970s when he noted that if one found a form of discrimination occurring in the educational domain, there was frequently a pattern of restrictive or discriminatory behavior occurring across a wider field, which led him to conclude that the intent of any particular policy is always very clear to the groups affected by it (Leibowitz, 1971, 1974).

Through careful policy analysis, Wright (Chapter 3) has detailed how political spectacle dominated the passage of Prop. 203 in Arizona. Wright's analysis explicates what O'Connor and Netting (2010) following Guba (1984) referred to as *policy-in-intention*, the analysis of which helps us to understand the motivations behind the original formulation of a policy. Wright next demonstrates how most of the pre-Prop. 203 accommodation policies were systematically undermined, nullified, and replaced by poorly implemented policies and mediocre practices. These resulted more from ideology than research. Wright's next phase of analysis focuses on what O'Connor and Netting (2010) and Guba (1984) would call *policy-in-implementation*, wherein Prop. 203's implementation emphasized restrictions on the use of native language as a tool of instruction, and offered no coherent model for the development of the language students need to master academic content. If we were to draw a medical analogy, imagine the reaction of medical doctors if the states were to dictate a limited list of treatments that they would be allowed to administer, and all other known treatments would be banned. Educational administrators and teachers in Arizona are thusly now restricted from exercising their professional judgment or drawing on their professional training, even though some may have had more professional preparation than those who have formulated the new restrictive policies and practices.

In a further explication of *policy-in-implementation*, Moore (Chapter 4), analyzed the implementation of Prop. 203 by the ADE as it mandated that all certified educational personnel in the state complete SEI training by 31 August 2006/2009. Her findings indicate how SEI training policy, limited in its breadth and depth of content, functioned as a vehicle for promoting English-only ideology under ADE's prescriptive oversight. She also notes that ADE's hastily mandated teacher training did not allow professional development providers in various contexts sufficient time to adequately implement appropriate training. She found that they were not being prepared to exercise independent professional judgment of the SEI training curriculum and mandated practices. She also noted how ADE used surveys to monitor how the courses were being taught and how students in the courses were encouraged to inform on their mentors if they were perceived as being too 'political', thus creating an environment of intimidation.

In Chapter 5, Markos and Arias provide a comprehensive review of litera-ture regarding what teachers need to know in order to provide appropriate support for students learning English and using English to learn academic content. They conducted a detailed comparative analysis of the new SEI Endorsement mandated by the ADE and compared it to foundational curri-cula required in comprehensive teacher preparation programs. Despite the fact that the SEI Endorsement can be obtained after only 90 hours of profes-sional development, the state deemed it to be comparable to both the ESL and Bilingual Education Endorsements, which require either substantially more rigorous university coursework and/or a master's degree in education. Thus, the newly mandated curricula were substantially less rigorous, resulting in more underprepared teachers and a lower bar of professional expectations by the state.

Again, as Markos and Arias demonstrated, there has long been a substan-tial body of literature drawn from teacher education, applied linguistics and educational language policy analysis that can be drawn on when developing educational policies and practices, which ADE continues to ignore. Prior to the passage of California's Prop. 227 in 1998, and years before the ADE for-mulated its SEI four-hour block pull-out, Colin Baker's (1996) authoritative foundational text provided a taxonomy for classifying 'weak' and 'strong' program types for language minority students. This text was widely used in teacher preparation programs in California and Arizona at the time the new restrictive policies were imposed. Using Table 8.1 from that text, if we were to locate Arizona's current SEI program, it would fall under the 'submersion' label. The four-hour block pull-out model would fall under 'withdrawal' ESL, or among the 'weak' models of instruction. In hindsight, it is curious that the considerable body of literature available was not considered by ADE in formulating its educational policies, and would not be used to better inform the new SEI Endorsements devised by the state.

Returning again to a focus on *policy-in-implementation*, Grijalva and Jimenez-Silva (Chapter 6), present findings of interviews conducted with eight school principals at the time that the SEI pull-out, four-hour model of English language development (ELD) was being implemented. Using the Stages of Concern (SoC) protocol, they identified a number of concerns that responsible administrators voiced regarding the new model. These included: a fear that students would be segregated without access to other fluent English students; students would not have sufficient access to the core aca-demic curriculum, and would, thus, not be able to keep pace academically; there would be insufficient funding and support from the state; and that the top-down imposition of the model and its requirements would limit the abil-ity to exercise professional judgment and expertise.

The final chapter by Lillie and Markos, building on Lillie *et al.* (2010, 2012) presents two case studies regarding how the four-hour ELD pull-out model of SEI was experienced by teachers and students in classrooms. This

Table 8.1 Weak educational program options for language minorities

Type of program	Typical child in program	Language of the classroom	Societal and educational aims	Language and/or literacy aim
Submersion (aka structured English immersion)	Language minority	Imposes majority language	Assimilation	Monolingualism in English
Submersion (with withdrawal ESL)	Language minority	Imposes majority language	Assimilation	Monolingualism in English
Segregationist	Language minority	Minority language (forced, no choice)	Apartheid	Monolingualism
Transitional	Language minority	Moves from minority to majority language	Assimilation	Relative monolingualism in English
Majority language plus foreign language	Language majority	Majority language with L2/FL lessons	Limited enrichment	Limited bilingualism
Separatist	Language minority	Minority language (out of choice)	Detachment/ autonomy	Limited bilingualism

Source: Adapted from Baker (1996: 172). See pp. 172–197 for elaboration.
Notes: L2, second language; L1, first language; FL, foreign language.

chapter demonstrates what O'Connor and Netting (2010) and Guba (1984) would call *policy-in-experience*. Teachers may be analyzed in either the role of an imposed policy, or in the role of practitioner-implementer of policy. Lillie and Markos detail how teachers are trapped by the constraints of the imposed policy, while also being estranged from the experiences of their students, who are the ultimate recipients/experiencers of the policy (cf. O'Connor & Netting, 2010).

Lillie and Markos' data were drawn from interviews with teachers and direct classroom observations. Their findings indicate that the concerns predicted by school administrators in Grijalva and Jimenez-Silva's study were well founded. As Lillie and Markos concluded, the new four-hour model of

ELD in SEI isolated language minority students from their peers and provided them with a watered-down curriculum. Ultimately, findings demonstrate the segregation of language minority students and limited access to core academic content.

The Consequences of Nullification and the Burden of Mutual Support

Through the restriction of parental choice in determining program models and goals for children, both language minority and majority students lose opportunities for enhanced education. As Table 8.2 illustrates, there are stronger program models available, such as immersion, which allows for use of the mother tongue (as Markos and Arias noted), as well as heritage language maintenance programs. Moreover, there are also models, such as 'two-way' or 'dual-language' education, that are appropriate where both language minority and majority children can enhance their linguistic resources.

Table 8.2 Strong educational program options for both language minority and majority children

Type of program	Typical child in program	Language of the classroom	Societal and educational aims	Language and/ or literacy aim
Immersion	Language majority	Bilingualism with initial emphasis on L2	Pluralism and enrichment	Bilingualism and biliteracy
Maintenance/ heritage language	Language minority	Bilingualism with emphasis on L1	Maintenance/ pluralism and enrichment	Bilingualism and biliteracy
Two-way/dual language	Mixed language minority and majority	Minority and majority languages	Maintenance/ pluralism and enrichment	Bilingualism and biliteracy
Mainstream bilingual	Language majority	Two majority languages	Maintenance/ pluralism and enrichment	Bilingualism and biliteracy

Source: Adapted from Baker (1996: 172). See pp. 172–197 for elaboration.
Notes: L2, second language; L1, first language; FL, foreign language.

There are also mainstream bilingual education program models for language majority children that can help to expand the multilingual resources of the society as a whole. Two-way programs have been particularly popular, as both majority and minority parents have had the opportunity for parental choice of program. Again, under Prop. 203, as Wright noted (Chapter 3), language minority parental choice has been severely restricted. Thus, from the standpoint of parental rights, we may well ask why some parents should have more rights for educational choice than others.

From a societal point of view, even more is at stake in denying appropriate educational accommodations and support for language minority children. Hayes-Bautista *et al.* (1990), for example, over two decades ago, speculated on what kind of a country the United States could expect to be if the educational needs of a rapidly increasing native Spanish language speaking Latino school-age population were not met. They concluded that without an adequate education, the earning power of this population would be limited as would their ability be to pay taxes to support the pensions and health care needs of an aging Anglo population. They concluded that both populations were mutually dependent and carried the burden of mutual support. They suggested that the aging Anglo majority population would need to help support the education of the younger growing Latino population if that population were to help meet the needs of the aging Anglo population in the future.

The future has arrived! It is a pity that educational policies for language minority students have regressed, when better options are understood by educational professionals and available.

References

Arizona Voter Initiative (2000) Proposition 203, *English for the Children.*

Baker, C. (1996) *Foundations of Bilingual Education and Bilingualism* (2nd edn). Clevedon: Multilingual Matters.

Blanton, C.K. (2007) *The Strange Career of Bilingual Education in Texas, 1836–1981.* College Station, TX: Texas A & M University Press.

Crawford, J. (1992) *Hold Your Tongue: Bilingualism and the Politics of English Only.* Boston, MA: Addison-Wesley.

Crawford, J. (2000) *At War with Diversity: U.S. Language Policy in an Age of Anxiety.* Clevedon: Multilingual Matters.

Donahue, T.S. (1995) American language policy and compensatory opinion. In J.W. Tollefson (ed.) *Power and Inequality in Language Education* (pp. 112–141). Cambridge: Cambridge University Press.

Hayes-Bautista, D., Schink, W. and Chapa, J. (1990) *The Burden of Support: Young Latinos in an Aging Society.* Stanford, CA: Stanford University Press.

Horne v. Flores (2009) 557 U.S. 433, 129 Sup. Ct. 2579, 174 Lawyer's edn 2nd 406.

Guba, E.G. (1984) The effect of definitions of 'policy' on the nature and outcomes of policy analysis. *Educational Leadership* 42 (2), 63–70.

Lau v. Nichols (1974) 414 U.S. 563.

Leibowitz, A.H. (1971) *Educational Policy and Political Acceptance: The Imposition of English as the Language of Instruction in American Schools.* Eric Document Reproduction Service No. 047321. Washington, DC: Center for Applied Linguistics.

Leibowitz, A.H. (1974) Language as a means of social control: The United States experience. Paper presented at the VIII World Congress of Sociology, August, University of Toronto.

Lillie, K.E., Markos, A., Estrella, A., Nguyen, T., Trifiro, A., Arias, M.B. and Wiley, T.G. (2010) *Policy in Practice: The Implementation of Structured English Immersion in Arizona.* Los Angeles, CA: Civil Rights Project, University of California. See http://civilrightsproject.ucla.edu/research/k-12-education/language-minority-students/policy-in-practice- the-implementation-ofstructured-english-immersion-in-arizona/lillie-policy-practice-sei-2010.pdf. Accessed March 22, 2014.

Lillie, K.E., Markos, A., Arias, M.B. and Wiley, T.G. (2012) Separate and not equal: The implementation of SEI in Arizona classrooms. *Teachers College Record* 114 (9), 1–33.

Lyons, J. (1995) The past and future directions of federal bilingual education policy. In O. García and C. Baker (eds) *Policy and Practice in Bilingual Education: Expanding the Foundations* (pp. 1–15). Clevedon: Multilingual Matters.

NCLB (2001) *No Child Left Behind* Act. Pub. L. No. 107–110.

O'Connor, M.K. and Netting, F.E. (2010) *Analyzing Social Policy: Multiple Perspectives for Critically Understanding and Evaluating Policy.* Hoboken, NJ: John Wiley.

San Miguel, G. (2004) *Contested Policy: The Rise and Fall of Federal Bilingual Education in the United States.* Denton, TX: University of North Texas Press.

Tamura, E.H. (1993) The English-only effort, the anti-Japanese campaign, and language acquisition in the education of Japanese Americans in Hawaii, 1915–1940. *History of Education Quarterly* 33 (1), 37–58.

Tatalovich, R. (1995) *Nativism Reborn? The Official English Language Movement and the American States.* Lexington, KY: University of Kentucky Press.

Wiley, T.G. (1998) The imposition of World War I era English-only policies and the fate of German in North America. In T. Ricento and B. Burnaby (eds) *Language and Politics in the United States and Canada* (pp. 211–241). Mahwah, NJ: Lawrence Erlbaum.

Wiley, T.G. (2004) Language policy and English-only. In E. Finegan and J.R. Rickford (eds) *Language in the USA: Perspectives for the Twenty-first Century* (pp. 319–338). Cambridge: Cambridge University Press.

Wiley, T.G. and Wright, W. (2004) Against the undertow: Language-minority education and politics in the age of accountability. *Educational Policy* 18 (1), 142–168.

Index